The Maya of Morganton

LEON FINK

with research assistance from Alvis E. Dunn

The Maya of Morganton

WORK AND COMMUNITY IN THE NUEVO NEW SOUTH

The University of North Carolina Press   Chapel Hill and London

© 2003 The University of North Carolina Press

All rights reserved

Manufactured in the United States of America

Set in Carter & Cone Galliard

by Tseng Information Systems, Inc.

The paper in this book meets the guidelines
for permanence and durability of the Committee
on Production Guidelines for Book Longevity
of the Council on Library Resources.

Library of Congress Cataloging-in-Publication Data

Fink, Leon, 1948–

The Maya of Morganton : work and community in the
nuevo new south / Leon Fink.

p. cm.

Includes bibliographical references and index.

ISBN 0-8078-2774-6 (cloth : alk. paper)

ISBN 0-8078-5447-6 (pbk. : alk. paper)

1. Poultry plants—North Carolina—Morganton—
Employees.   2. Labor disputes—North Carolina—
Morganton.   3. Poultry plants—Employees—Labor
unions—North Carolina—Morganton.   4. Alien labor,
Guatemalan—North Carolina—Morganton.

5. Mayas—North Carolina—Morganton.   I. Title.

HD8039.P842 U55   2003

331.6′27281075685—dc21

2002013899

cloth 07 06 05 04 03 5 4 3 2 1

paper 07 06 05 04 03 5 4 3 2

To Sharon Mújica, Alma Yolanda Guerrero Miller, Alejandra

Garcia Quintanilla, Michael Pratt, Violeta and Flor de Leon,

Miguel Bautista, Eduardo Elias Cortez, and the Proyecto

Lingüístico Quetzalteco for helping me open a door

to the Spanish-speaking world

Contents

Illustrations

Acknowledgments

This project drew support from numerous quarters. My entry to the people and events unfolding in Morganton was facilitated from the beginning by the cooperation of attorney Phyllis Palmieri and Rev. Kenneth J. Whittington. Father Whittington's St. Charles Borromeo Catholic Church became my main base of interviewing—and refreshment—across several years of research.

To make the connection to the Case Farms workers, I needed not only to strengthen my fledgling Spanish—which serendipitously I had been casually augmenting over the previous few years—but also to travel to Guatemala to learn more about the lives of the emigrants. My most important early "acquisition" was Alvis E. Dunn for his stellar research assistance. Alvis, whose own academic specialty is colonial Guatemalan history, effectively served as my cultural interpreter across four summer stints of joint research and travel in the villages of Huehuetenango as well as helping me ease my way into Spanish-language interviews in Morganton. For my travels to Guatemala, I benefited from several generous conduits at the University of North Carolina at Chapel Hill (UNC–Chapel Hill): a Department of Education Title VI Faculty Research Award from the University Center for International Studies, a faculty research stipend from the Institute for Research in Social Science, a summer research award from the Institute of Latin American Studies, and a small grant from the University Research Council. My entrée to Guatemala was considerably enriched by study at the Proyecto Lingüístico Quetzalteco, a wonderful language school and social center in Quetzaltenango. In 1998–99 a Charles Warren Center for Studies in American History fellowship at Harvard University provided valuable writing time, as did a research and study leave proffered by department chair Peter Coclanis at UNC–Chapel Hill. A UNC–Chapel Hill freshman seminar course on Mayan history, History 06J "Five Hundred Years without Solitude," also helped me refine my ideas. As I gathered my research materials, the staff and resources at UNC's Davis Library once again continued its standing as my favorite place on campus. Once I moved to Chicago (fall 2000), the Newberry Library proved the perfect place to finish my writing.

Besides Alvis—who was completing his doctorate when I first connected with him—I benefited from student research assistance both in North Carolina (Gregory Kaliss, David Sartorius, Anna Fink) and in Guatemala (Amy Morris, Anna Fink). For summary transcriptions of my interviews, I am indebted to the Robert Conrad Fund of the Southern Oral History Program at UNC–Chapel Hill, directed by Jacquelyn Hall. I had the benefit of excellent transcriber-interpreters in Kristofer Ray, Mariola Espinosa, Elizabeth Pauk, and Anna Fink.

Along the path of this work, I have turned to several others—that is, besides the one hundred–odd enumerated interviewees and many published authorities cited in the book—for crucial bits of information and insight. On North Carolina and "southern" matters, I especially thank Michael Okun, John Inscoe, Gary Mormino, and Peter Coclanis. On Guatemalan, Latin American, and immigration issues, I am particularly indebted to the intellectual generosity of Paul Hans Kobrak, James Loucky, Marion Traub-Werner, Bruce Calder, Gilbert M. Joseph, Mae Ngai, Christopher Boyer, June Erlick, and Dorrie Budet. As a ready reference on contemporary labor issues, I also thank Nelson Lichtenstein.

As the manuscript gradually took shape, I received encouragement and helpful criticism from audiences and panels at meetings of the Organization of American Historians, Oral History Association, Missouri Valley History Conference, North American Labor History Conference, Newberry Library Labor History Seminar, and Chicago Historical Society Urban History Seminar. Both Margaret Rose and Miriam Cohen offered useful comments at an early conference presentation. At a more pointed and exacting level, a few friends and colleagues labored over all or parts of the manuscript: for this, I owe John French, Bruce Calder, and Julie Greene big-time. In addition, Rosa Tock checked the manuscript for Guatemalan misspellings, and Ray Brod created a rough draft of the map. In preparing the final draft for publication—whether checking the consistency of references or weeding out double negatives and other infelicitous expressions— I enjoyed invaluable editorial assistance from Stevie Champion. I also pay tribute to Paula Wald and David Perry for their encouragement and editorial support.

I always have been lucky to count on Susan Levine as first and last reader on my manuscripts. This time, she also put up most graciously with my frequent journeys to western North Carolina and beyond. As suggested more than once above, the family contribution was augmented by our daughter Anna's linguistic skills and general knowledge of the world of immigrant workers, for which I am both proud and grateful. Even as the efforts of all those listed above have improved the manuscript enormously, the blame for errors that remain is mine alone.

Abbreviations

ACTWU   Amalgamated Clothing and Textile Workers Union
AFL-CIO   American Federation of Labor–Congress of Industrial Organizations
CEH   Historical Clarification Commission
CFCTF   Case Farms Contract Task Force
EGP   Guerrilla Army of the Poor
ESL   English as a Second Language
FMCN   Martí National Liberation Front
FRG   Frente Republicano Guatemalteco
FUNCEDE   Fundación Centroamericana de Desarrollo
IIRIRA   Illegal Immigration Reform and Immigrant Responsibility Act
INS   Immigration and Naturalization Service
IRCA   Immigration Reform and Control Act
IUF   International Union of Food, Agricultural, Hotel, Restaurant, Catering, Tobacco, and Allied Workers Associations
KFC   Kentucky Fried Chicken
LIUNA   Laborers International Union of North America
NICWJ   National Interfaith Committee for Worker Justice
NLRB   National Labor Relations Board
OSHA   Occupational Safety and Health Administration
PAC   Civil Self-Defense Patrol
PAN   National Advance Party
REMHI   Recuperation of Historical Memory (Catholic Church of Guatemala)
RUIDA   La Raza Unida Indigena de America
SEIU   Service Employees International Union
UFCW   United Food and Commercial Workers
UNC–Chapel Hill   University of North Carolina at Chapel Hill
UNITE   Union of Needletrades, Industrial, and Textile Employees
US/GLEP   U.S./Guatemala Labor Education Project

The Maya of Morganton

Introduction

It was sometime in early spring 1997 when I first heard about a labor conflict in Morganton, North Carolina, a usually quiet industrial center of sixteen thousand people perched at the edge of the Great Smoky Mountains. I would soon learn that this was no isolated incident or temporary labor relations breakdown that I had stumbled upon but a decade-long war of position between determined and well-organized workers on the one hand and a classically recalcitrant employer on the other. It began with an overnight walkout in 1991, erupting into a mass work stoppage and multiple arrests in May 1993 and climaxing in a four-day strike and successful union election campaign in 1995. Confronting the company with a weeklong walkout and hunger strike in 1996 and subsequently standing firm for six years in the face of the company's absolute refusal to sign a collective bargaining contract, the workers at Case Farms poultry plant etched a profile of uncommon (if still frustrated) courage in demanding a voice and degree of respect at the workplace.

From the start of my inquiries, news from the Case Farms battle posed a threefold fascination for a North American labor historian living (until the fall of 2000) three hours from Morganton by car in the university town of Chapel Hill. First, the events in Morganton were remarkable enough in themselves. For over twenty years I had watched "organized labor" virtually disappear off the map in North Carolina, losing battle after battle in campaigns among textile, furniture, and meat-processing workers. Indeed, when I had arrived in Chapel Hill in 1977 as the university's first designated "labor historian," one joke went that "only a Fink" could get such a job at a southern school. I laughed but did think twice when I discovered that my closest labor history colleague was Gary Fink at Georgia State University! Throughout my tenure at UNC, the state was locked in a seesaw battle with its South Carolina neighbor for the dubious honor of being the least unionized state in the country, a country that as a whole was experiencing a severe slippage of union representation in the private-sector workforce. What is more, the food-processing industry—especially meat products, of which poultry was a part—had earned a reputation as the most determined of union foes. In meatpacking, for example, where a set of "new-breed" packers based on corporate mergers and buyouts set the pace, both unionization and wages had fallen by half in the 1980s alone.[1]

But there were two additional reasons to be intrigued by the Morganton story. The five-hundred-person Case Farms plant, estimated in 1995 as 80 percent Spanish-speaking—of whom 80 to 90 percent were Guatemalan and the rest Mexican—highlighted a demographic transformation of the U.S. labor force, nowhere more startling than in what one commentator has called the "*nuevo* New South" and, within the region, nowhere more so than in North Carolina, where the growth of the Hispanic population reached a whopping 394 percent in the decade 1990–2000.[2] Even more remarkably, the fact that the "Guatemalans" were nearly all Highland Maya—people who trace their bloodline and their languages back to the ancient "corn people"—suggested a most dramatic confrontation between what Joseph Schumpeter called the "creative destruction" of market capitalism and the social organization of one of the hemisphere's oldest cultures. How was it, then, that in a state with not a single organized chicken-processing factory, a group of Central American refugees bucked the tide of history? Who were these people, where did they come from, and why did they act the way they did? Were they crazy and disoriented or did they know something about social struggles of which others were ignorant? In thinking about the uphill task that the immigrant poultry workers had assumed, I could not help but remember the comment reportedly uttered by slave rebel Nat Turner before his execution: "Was not Christ crucified?"

These are the issues I have sought to address in the following pages. In doing so, I have inevitably encountered other questions that have drawn my attention. Apart from the labor struggle itself, the perception and reception of the modern-day Maya in North Carolina became a crucial part of my story. How did an established community of whites and blacks react to the new émigrés? Who were the workers' local allies? And how did the union that came to represent them—the Laborers International Union of North America (LIUNA)—fit the Morganton revolt into its own organizational strategies? A final arena of concern focuses on the nature of cultural adjustment among the new migrant workers. With what capacity and vision but also at what cost did the Guatemalan Maya transplant them-

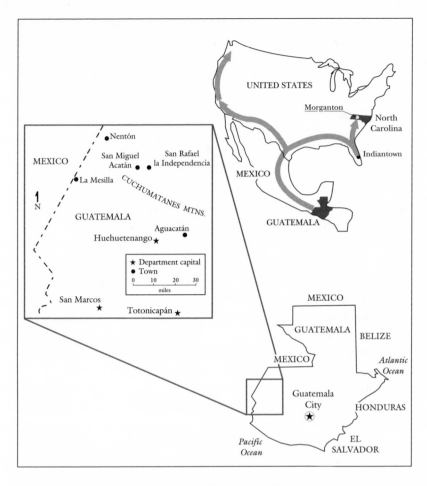

Guatemalan migration to Morganton, North Carolina

selves to a new North American setting? How did the act of migration and, for some, permanent immigration affect their community's welfare, both in the United States and "back home" in Guatemala?

The story of the Maya in Morganton effectively joins one of the newest buzzwords of social science, "globalization," with one of the oldest, "community." Juxtaposing the two concepts, in fact, permits us to cover a great deal of interpretive ground. The entry of Guatemalan war refugees and later those we might well consider "economic refugees" into the poultry plants of North Carolina reflects the increasing fluidity of both world investments and labor markets. In ways that recall the experience of their nineteenth-century immigrant predecessors, the émigré Mayan workers "use" community at once to defend themselves against employer exploitation and to advance the interests of family and friends across international borders. These new immigrant carriers of a rural, communal culture may indeed offer instructive lessons to a more metropolitan labor movement in the United States. Even as contemporary sociologists inveigh against the decline of a broad-based "civic culture" in today's consumer society, more and more of the hard work of the country is actually in the hands of people with a quite sturdy family and community structure—if little else. The combination of group ties and the necessity of relying on those ties in an alien environment creates an opening for worker mobilization. This is not to deny the obstacles that confront today's bottom-rung labor force. Both modern-day power and money are stacked against them as never before. Nor is it to suggest that members of the Mayan diaspora are not themselves undergoing profound cultural displacement and acting in ways different from their revered ancestors. All of the above are true. The very richness of the mix, however, creates one of the more dramatic trials of the human spirit provoked by the faceless forces of globalization. This book is one testimony to those trials.

Mixing narrative with commentary, each chapter of the book is organized around a specific theme of its own. Chapter 1 ("The Way It Is in Morganton") prepares us for the arrival of the Maya by concentrating on the previously settled population—whites, blacks, and Hmong refugees—of the town. In the midst of fears and some resentment of the newcomers' demands on local services, a "progressive," church-based group of professionals offered a crucial welcome. Chapter 2 ("Flight of the Happy Farmers") focuses on the initial Guatemalan migrants—Q'anjob'al-speaking Maya from the mountain villages of the northwestern province of Huehuetenango—framing the first worker protest at the poultry plant against a longer background of Guatemalan civil war, terror, and escape. Even as a climate of coercion in Guatemala and the bias of U.S. immigration policy shrouded effective identification of the immigrants' past political experience, a hint of transnational peasant wisdom in dealing with authority emerged among the raw factory recruits. Chapter 3 ("How the Dead Helped to Organize the Living") looks behind the pivotal strike of 1995 to the wellsprings of solidarity among the single largest group of Case Farms workers—Awakatekos and Chalchitekos from the commercial agricultural valley of Aguacatán. An exploration of selective, family-level migration strategies reveals both the source of communal solidarity across borders and new grounds for divisions among a conflict-ridden people.

Chapter 4 ("No One Leader") examines the process of local union build-ing with emphasis on the fragility of leadership. The alliance between a Salvadoran woman union organizer with young male workers from both Guatemala and Mexico survived continuous challenges from without and within. Chapter 5 ("The Workers Are Ready") sets the Morganton union struggle within a context of national labor and political forces attempting to jump-start a larger workers' movement for social justice. In particular, the Laborers union, fresh from federal indictment for corruption, tried to save its soul as well as its economic welfare by backing an exotic underdog.

By way of conclusion, the book takes two different analytic approaches. Chapter 6 ("Changing Places") steps back from the workplace to inquire into the individual struggles of adaptation and identity among the global laborers and their families. Three different patterns of migration—birds of passage, assimilation, and transnational citizenship—it is argued, mix un-easily within the contemporary global marketplace. Chapter 7 ("Sticking Together") connects the Morganton union story at once to prior immi-grant history and to contemporary struggles for solidarity at both ends of the global migrant stream. Remarkably, and perhaps counterintuitively, we watch as migrant Mayan workers in the United States grope for a broader solidarity, while potentially fratricidal conflicts over "identity politics" and interethnic rivalries threaten their home communities.

Here, then, is the common thread of *The Maya of Morganton: Work and Community in the Nuevo New South*. To understand the motives and behav-ior of Third World workers—either on their home turf or as immigrant recruits to more developed metropoles—we need to fit them into a global political economy of competitive markets, changing technology, and a managerial logic of labor control. Yet, we must also recognize them as agents who continue to draw on local wisdom in advancing the interests of family, friendships, and community even in a faraway land.

Finally, I would like to add a brief word on the oral history sources for this work. Unlike studies in sociology, anthropology, or other social sci-ences, this book, as the reader will immediately notice, identifies its subjects by their real names. This is, in part, a disciplinary distinction. "History" generally takes the individual as its primary unit of analysis and insists that individuals, in their very peculiarity, "count." It is all the more important, then, that those who—like immigrant poultry workers—have heretofore been left out of public awareness as well as the scholarly record should make their properly identified mark.

Yet, I am not ignorant of the special risks involved in writing about today's new immigrant workforce. No doubt, Case Farms—like virtually every other low-wage manufacturing firm across the country—employs a significant number of illegal (i.e., undocumented or improperly documented) workers. But when I raised the issue of confidentiality with workers themselves, they regularly waved it off. Many with whom I talked arrived in the United States early enough to apply for naturalization. In a few instances, they told me that they had given me their "Case Farms" name, not their given name, and I investigated no further.[3] Moreover, the overwhelming majority of those consulted for the book no longer work at Case Farms and in some cases are no longer in the country. I received explicit permission to quote all those cited in the text. For anyone who hesitated, I offered the option of anonymity or off-the-record comments. As it happened, the only respondents who took up either of these options were former company executives or their legal counsel.

1

The Way It Is in Morganton

Like many aspiring southern towns, Morganton, North Carolina, offers a contradictory impression to the inquiring outsider. In one reflection, it turns the face of tradition and familiarity toward an otherwise anomic and ever-changing world. In the early 1970s, for example, a refugee from New England arrived in North Carolina with her law school–teaching husband and soon set to writing about "a town with a heart, a people who reflect an inner happiness." "An unparalleled shift in population is under way in America," declared Marion Lieberman in a regular column, "Morganton on My Mind," published in the local weekly *News-Herald*. Like herself, she believed, "many are coming back to—or discovering for the first time—the serenity and comfort of a small town."[1] And, no doubt, to an erstwhile city dweller, there is a distinct folksiness to social relations in Morganton. It is still a place where, during the summer's heat, one can find a few older white folk gathered under a shade tree with fans, happy to treat a visitor to a lemonade and an unhurried discussion of events hither and yon. There is talk of a friend working in the nearby village, Glen Alpine, they call "Glenpin"; of the dangers of air-conditioning as a cause of pneumonia and an irritant to "arthuritis"; of the recent Fourth of July celebrated with "a big kadoo uptown"; and of a new local professional "rasslin'" hall featuring "a bunch of boys from Burke County." The down-home hospitality of the community extends to its religious institutions: on the outskirts of town, for instance, local Methodists invite passersby to join "the perfect church for those who aren't."

Yet, it is not so much old country charm but modern, urban innovation that one senses in the gleaming steeples and glistening mansions of Union Street, which initially bisects the town east and west and ultimately leads past shopping malls and a municipal greenway. With good reason, Morganton prefers to see itself as a dynamic, progressive community that has repeatedly embraced economic and social changes invading what was once an agricultural village nestled in the Catawba River Valley at the base of the Blue Ridge Mountains. Named after Revolutionary War hero Daniel Morgan, who led a combination of regular troops and local militia to a stunning victory at the Battle of Cowpens, the town, the oldest settlement in the western part of the state, was commissioned in 1784 as the seat of Burke County. In the course of its history, Morganton was a stopping-off point for legendary frontiersmen Daniel Boone and Davy Crockett as well as the birthplace of its most famous latter-day representative, Watergate inquisitor Senator Sam J. Ervin Jr. Economically, the area initially served as both a transportation and a commercial gateway connecting the plantation South to new western markets. That slaves should compose more than a quarter of the Burke County population in 1860 testified to the wealth and influence of a coterie of leading local families.[2] By the late nineteenth century, agriculture was joined by industry, as the lumbering trade, furniture factories, and to a lesser extent textile mills increasingly absorbed the local labor force. Drexel Furniture, for example, destined to become a state and national industry leader, got its start in Morganton in 1903.

The biggest spur to economic development, however, did not arrive until after World War II with the construction in 1960–61 of an Interstate 40 link across Burke County. A local Chamber of Commerce report boasted in 1964 that "since 1960, twelve new industries located in Morganton or within its environs." Included among the new, humming enterprises of that decade were several furniture firms, a shoe company, a fish hatchery, a knitting mill, a machine tool operation, and Breeden's Poultry and Egg, Inc., which later became Case Farms. Altogether, local industry boomed in the postwar period; as late as 1995 about 47 percent of the Burke County labor force was engaged in manufacturing. Aside from industry, the local economy depended on government workers (more than in any other city outside the state capital in Raleigh) centered in the psychiatric Broughton Hospital, established in 1882 as the Western North Carolina Insane Asylum; the Western Carolina Center, which has served since 1963 as a research and diagnostic center for the severely mentally disabled; the state school for the deaf, established in 1894; Western Piedmont Community College, established in 1968; and the Western Correctional Center, a model state prison that promised "private rooms for each inmate (or resident)" when it opened in 1972.[3]

Although in the Civil War Morganton had paid dearly for its adherence to the Lost Cause—the town was ransacked by Union general George

Downtown Morganton, looking down Union Street.
Photo courtesy of Pam Walker.

Stoneman's raiders in 1865—local leaders (including several descendants of the older slaveholding elite) proved more nimble in dealing with latter-day race relations. Thanks to the uncommonly large local public sector, African Americans in Morganton gained access to steadier and higher-paying jobs than were commonly available elsewhere. Prior planning by local church and political leaders—including Senator Ervin's daughter-in-law, Elizabeth Ervin, who served on the school board—ensured that integration of the local high school proceeded without incident in the mid-1960s, years ahead of most of its North Carolina neighbors.[4] Rev. W. Flemon McIntosh Jr., a popular black schoolteacher and football coach who helped smooth the town's desegregation effort, proudly called Morganton a "conservative-progressive community . . . we make each step safe and sound, in the best interest of everybody."[5] Yet, the very economic and educational opportunities that opened to local African Americans in the 1960s also led many of them to go elsewhere: by 1990 blacks represented less than 7 percent of the local population.[6] "I lost two of my own children to that," sighed McIntosh with a smile.[7]

Socially, the town and its environs have played host to a variety of newcomers over the years. While remaining, like its western North Carolina neighbors, largely a demographic offspring of early British Protestants and

Scotch-Irish pioneers, the area has, in fact, absorbed three rather uncommon immigrant colonies in the past century. At the turn of the twentieth century several hundred French-speaking Waldensians—a Calvinist sect that had undergone numerous repressions and dislocations—made their way to Burke County, thickly settling in a community they named Valdese (famous for furniture, hosiery, textiles, and bakery products). Then, beginning in the late 1970s, some five hundred Laotian Hmong families—refugees from the Vietnam War who had originally been airlifted to Minneapolis, Minnesota—also resettled in Morganton, with help from area churches and federal monies.[8] The latest immigrant wave, which started almost unnoticed in the late 1980s but has grown irrepressibly since, speaks with a Spanish accent. At once a reflection of a larger Latino, especially Mexican, migration affecting the entire United States (and nowhere more dramatically than among the formerly ethnically insular southeastern states), Morganton's newest immigrants present the distinctive profile of being majority indigenous Maya from Guatemala. Though spanning the globe in their diversity, the area's three twentieth-century immigrant groups—counting the Waldensians, the Hmong/Laotians, and, most recently, the Guatemalans—share at least two qualities in common. They are all people of the mountains, and they each have experienced a past of group persecution.

In short, Morganton has just cause to think of itself as a southern town, but with a difference. John Vail, who ran the area legal services office (1988–97), provided one useful snapshot of the town in the years immediately prior to the Guatemalan arrival. A New Jersey native, Vail selected Morganton as a desirable family location for its "higher demographics"—there was more money and education in Morganton, and the politics there struck him as more enlightened than in most places in the region, a claim symbolized by unwavering local support for a democratic city council and regular reelection since 1985 of a Jewish mayor, Mel Cohen.

To be sure, Morganton also fit expected southern political-economic proprieties: old wealth centered in real estate interests and powerful law firms exercised disproportionate weight in public affairs. Labor unions, a political anathema across North Carolina and long beaten down in the town's furniture-making sector, survived in only one workplace, a small firm making carbon fiber products.[9] Indeed, as one local schoolteacher, who would himself soon try to help organize the new immigrant workers, put it, general reaction to the word "union" in North Carolina was "worse than 'AIDS,' worse than 'cancer.'"[10] Given the state's dominant political culture, it is perhaps not surprising that a young Sam Ervin served as commander of a National Guard unit called in to quell the Gastonia textile workers' strike of 1929. As Jean C. Ervin, the ninety-two-year-old sister of the town's most distinguished native son, recalled, "[Sam] was hit by a rock [thrown] by one of the strikers, good thing he was wearing a helmet!"[11]

In such a modestly sized but upwardly aspiring community, the local poultry plant was, as John Vail remembered it, the town's "dirty little secret." To be sure, Breeden's Poultry company had begun innocuously enough. Tom Breeden, a local barber, had, with the help of his wife, started up a little weekend poultry business in the mid-1950s. As one recent study of the poultry labor force indicates, "Raising chickens for eggs and meat had been, for decades, a supplementary household or domestic producer operation, fueled mainly by women and child family labor, whose symbols had been Mother Hen and the farm wife's 'egg money.'"[12] Before long, Breeden had extended his local poultry and egg hobby into a thriving, full-time "New York dress business"—"they'd dress the birds—leave the feet and everything but take the feathers off, ice them down and put them into barrels, then haul them to New York and sell them." In these early years of the industry, according to Charles Ramsey, who had learned the poultry dressing business while a student at Berea College and went to work for Breeden in 1962, the work was "hand done—[we] killed by hand, picked them on old drumpickers where you'd hold them by the feet. Over the years we made equipment in our own shop, [including one machine] where you use your foot with a spring to cut their feet off. We managed to make stuff to peel the gizzards, things to harvest the oil glands. . . . I can remember when you could run eighty birds a minute, it would take about eighty people to run those eighty birds." The 1960s and 1970s, said Ramsey, who was Breeden's plant manager from 1975 on, saw a tide of inventions applied to the production process. "When I left [in 1995] they were running 120 birds with about forty people, so you can see how far the plant has come in forty years, there's equipment to do every job now." In short, what began as a marginal operation had grown over a few decades into a substantial business enterprise. As if to complete its arrival on the area's stage, a Breeden daughter married an Erwin, one of the oldest and most successful families in the Catawba Valley. Yet, the material success of the poultry plant could not efface its unfavorable local reputation. Not only did the plant emit a noxious stench, but also the labor force regularly absorbed and regurgitated local employees of last resort, allegedly including Broughton Hospital patients and alcoholics.

Breeden's problems with labor recruitment were part and parcel of the peculiar dynamism of this post–World War II industry. Prior to that time, as Herbert Hoover's "a chicken in every pot" campaign promise suggested, chickens generally needed extended stewing. But postwar entrepreneurs like Arthur W. Perdue combined new processing techniques, name-brand recognition, and integrated control of egg growers, farmers, feed producers, and processors under one corporate roof to virtually revolutionize what became known, by the early 1960s, as the "broiler" industry. In subsequent years, the marketing of fast-food chicken—spearheaded by the pre-eminence of Kentucky Fried Chicken (KFC) in the 1960s and accelerated by McDonald's introduction of Chicken McNuggets in the 1980s—and rising health concerns about red meat created an explosive demand for chicken products that continues to the present day. Two facts summarize the recent trends: in 1992 U.S. consumption of chicken surpassed the consumption of beef, and whereas as late as 1980 most chicken was sold whole, by 2000 nearly 90 percent of the chicken sold in the United States had been cut into pieces.[13]

Market success, however, has bred a demand for labor not easily satisfied through conventional sources. For one, a search for a uniform-sized chicken—required for both assembly-line (or, rather, disassembly-line) production processes and fast-food automatic frying vats—has placed a continuing premium on locating processing plants near rural growing areas. Second, since a consolidation move in the 1980s (eight large processors now control two-thirds of the U.S. market), production has concentrated in the South, where mild weather and low land and labor costs maximize managerial initiative. Moreover, as big and small producers alike fight it out for market control, a still-competitive industry has succeeded in keeping a tight lid on wage costs. Since the early 1970s the poultry wage, the lowest in the entire food industry, has languished at roughly 60 percent that of the U.S. manufacturing average. Through a combination of regional incentives, by the end of the 1990s approximately half of all poultry processing had concentrated in four low-wage, anti-union states: Alabama, Arkansas, Georgia, and North Carolina.[14]

From the beginning of the industry's development in the 1950s and 1960s, low land and labor costs favored location in southern states, and that trend continues. Once the surplus labor of depressed, southern farming areas was tapped out in the 1980s, however—against the backdrop of a generally booming Sunbelt economy (offering other, usually more pleasant as

The Way It Is in Morganton

well as more remunerative options to the traditional factory labor force)—
poultry employers proved both desperate (and adventuresome) in seeking
a new low-wage recruitment base. The answer came swiftly. Latino workers
represented less than 10 percent of the overall poultry labor force in 1988,
but by 1993 this aggregate figure had jumped to 25 percent. In Morganton,
and in other poultry centers like the tristate Delaware-Maryland-Virginia
peninsula (home to Perdue Farms), the demographic change would be even
more dramatic.[15]

Almost from the beginning of the Breeden plant's expansion came a search
for new labor. The late sixties witnessed the entry of African American
workers into a formerly all-white labor force; by the mid-1980s nearly a
quarter of the workforce was black. "There was feelings there," remembered
Ramsey, "but we didn't have a lot of troubles." The trouble was more in
keeping the plant running. "Burke County has all kinds of furniture industry," explained Ramsey,

> they've got all kinds of [textile] mills. So they got very competitive for the help,
> and locally you wouldn't have enough people in Burke County to fill the jobs.
> I've gone in on days where you needed to be running two quad lines of birds,
> and you wouldn't have enough to run but maybe a line and a half because you
> couldn't get the people to handle it. So then we started running buses; we used
> to bus people from down in Lincolnton [fifty miles away] and different places
> like that. As a matter of fact, we had people living as far away as Cleveland
> County, and they'd take the bus home in the afternoon.

Too many were also taking the bus elsewhere. For many workers, Ramsey
said, poultry work proved to be an entry-level job, equipping new recruits with an industrial work ethic that they could use to their own advantage. Poultry workers "could bring their lunch in the morning, and if they
wanted to go somewhere else they could find a job, take their lunch with
them and be at work somewhere else the next day."

Katherine Harbison, just seventeen years old when she first took a job
"pulling craws" (extracting the windpipe from the chicken neck) at Breed-
en's after she and a few other African American friends dropped out of high
school in the late 1970s, indirectly confirmed Ramsey's complaint that local
workers did possess some minimal choice over their work assignments. Re-
senting the extended workdays that the company had adopted in the face
of a shrinking labor pool, Harbison recalled, "me and these other couple of

girls got together at lunchtime and we decided we was going to punch out at 4 [P.M.] because we know they couldn't fire us, we [had] made our eight hours."[16] Despite threats of dismissal, Harbison continued at Breeden's for several years, regularly refusing overtime assignments, as part of an unskilled, low-wage workforce that was not easily replaceable.

Tom Breeden, in Ramsey's charitable terms, was a "people person." Tightfisted when it came to wages and benefits, he nevertheless, according to Ramsey, personally cared about his employees and even set up a modest profit-sharing plan. Whatever Breeden's employment strategy, however, he could not stem the tide leaving his factory. As Ramsey observed, "he saw the crunch coming. That's probably why he sold the place."[17]

In 1988 Tom Shelton, fired from the presidency of Perdue Farms after a falling-out with owner Frank Perdue, added Breeden's Poultry to an earlier acquisition of the independent Case Farms company in the Amish district of Winesburg, Ohio (where it produced its "Amish Country Pride" brand label). Shelton's own background was in the agricultural side of the business (i.e., raising the birds), and from the beginning he approached the challenge of an efficient processing factory strictly as a technical issue. Shelton, remembered Ramsey, was a "numbers person." Denny Hughes, a turkey farmer from Indiana who had left Perdue to oversee the chicken-growing and sales operations at Case Farms (1988–91), described the struggle to increase both the poundage and the number of birds killed per week: "We had labor [scarcity] problems galore then. We didn't have the labor force to kill the birds. So we might plan, let's say we were gonna need half-million birds [per week], well the labor was so bad here in this area that maybe you've got 200,000, now I'm exaggerating [but] you had customers out here and you couldn't fill the orders."

By the mid-1990s the Maryland-based Case Foods Company (which marketed the Case Farms brand) in Salisbury was struggling to expand its market niche. Despite the presence of several huge players like Tyson Foods, Con-Agra, Gold Kist, and Perdue Farms, poultry processing remained an extremely competitive, if organizationally intricate, business. The same "vertically integrated" corporate processors owned the chickens and the feed (which were commonly leased to small contract growers), the slaughterhouses, and the freezing and packaging plants and control the distribution networks and exports.[18] Ranked thirty-second among the top fifty poultry-processing firms in 1995, Case Foods—employing 1,125 workers at two hatcheries, one feed mill, and two processing plants—had expanded its average weekly output of ready-to-cook chicken by nearly 40 percent

The Way It Is in Morganton

Case Farms poultry plant, 1996.
Photo by Chuck Liddy, *Raleigh News and Observer*.

since 1990.[19] With profit for chicken averaging 2.5 to 3.5 cents per pound, economic success required a constant meshing of all aspects of the production process, from the hatcheries to packaging and marketing. Given the competitive pressure, the bottom line depended, for the most part, on the speed and volume of the plant and how well the workers adjusted to both.[20]

Work in a poultry plant, under the best of conditions, presented a demanding and unpleasant routine. The processing plants were organized so that birds enter one end of the plant and trucks carrying packaged and priced products depart from the other end. At Case Farms in the 1990s, an up-to-date process started at the second-floor "live-dock" area, where a forklift raised the bird cages from trucks onto a conveyer belt. In the initial receiving, or "live bird" area, workers in a dimly lit room (an assumedly calming influence on the animals) pulled live, scratching birds from crates and hung them on hooks by their feet. The automated line next brought its occupants to the "kill room," where a cordon of electric shocks stunned the birds before a row of razor blades (the Hispanic workers called this the "guillotine") delivered the final coup de grâce and the belt moved, transporting the carcasses through scalders and feather-plucking machines. Following subsequent processing areas—evisceration, U.S. Department of

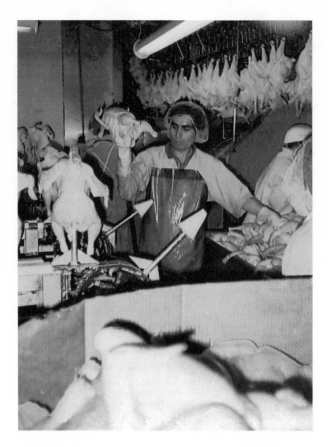

Inside Case Farms: "whole-bird" processing operation.
Photo courtesy of Luís Alberto "Beto" Gonzalez.

Agriculture inspection, and chilling—the birds were "re-hung" and sent downstairs. On the bottom floor the birds entered the two most labor-intensive sections of the plant—grading (or "whole-bird") and trimming and processing (or "cut up"). Whereas the whole birds that passed an eye inspection test were sent straight to packaging, the majority of specimens underwent further processing. At Case Farms, the workers in this area were spaced closely along four assembly lines with approximately fifty people per line: "They put [the birds] on the line, then they have a man who cuts their legs off before another man makes the incision on the shoulders, cuts the wings. Then they have saws on each line, where they cut the wings into different parts. They sell the tips and everything; the only things they don't sell are the insides, except for the liver. Everything else is processed for the

The Way It Is in Morganton

market."[21] Generally speaking, as one advanced through the production process the work environment became progressively cooler (temperatures varied from 120 degrees near the scalders to below freezing in the packaging area), slippery with chicken fat, and wet from the constant hosing down—an environment requiring rubber boots, gloves, layers of clothing, and aprons.[22]

As to why an older workforce of local whites, blacks, and even Hmong refugees provided an insufficient recruitment base for the local poultry plant, Denny Hughes explained: "It was just poor working conditions. It's not even the pay, to my understanding there's not that much difference between the pay in it and one of the [local] furniture factories. Would you rather go into a place that's clean and dry or wet and bloody and cool all day long?"[23] In addition to the basic physical environment, poultry plants were notorious for unreported accident claims as well as the third highest reported rate of carpal tunnel syndrome among U.S. industries. The U.S. Department of Labor reported that one of every six poultry workers suffered a work-related injury or illness every year.[24] Perhaps former worker Katherine Harbison put it most eloquently: "There ain't no best job in there. All of 'em's bad. It'll mess your hands . . . it'll just mess your whole body up."[25] The wife of a local furniture factory manager related that her family's African American maid of many years once decided to leave domestic service for a "regular" job at the chicken plant: "She only lasted a week before coming back."[26] Given the combined circumstances of a booming economy and harsh, unappealing work, it was becoming impossible to attract local people into the poultry plant.

Then, in the spring of 1989, Norman Beecher, whom Shelton had brought in as Case Farms's new human resources manager, received a tip through industry circles and a church group about a new source of labor. "I called a good friend of mine in a Mississippi poultry operation," Beecher said, "and asked him what he was doing to get people. And he put me on to the Guatemalans." From his employer-friend Beecher learned of a Catholic church in West Palm Beach, Florida, that was helping Guatemalan refugees working in the citrus belt around Indiantown, Florida. With no citrus to harvest in May, Beecher found an eager set of recruits. After attending Mass, he set himself up in the church office interviewing parishioners; with the help of a Catholic charities worker who both translated and facilitated work permits, he quickly signed up ten men who agreed to drive up to Morganton in a pickup truck the next weekend. "Those ten went to work and were doing so good," Beecher remembered, "that supervisors started coming to me saying, 'Hey, I need ten more.'" Three weeks later Beecher returned to a packed Florida recruiting office. "One fellow had a van. He said he'd bring twenty of them."[27]

Once Beecher succeeded in attracting an initial core of Guatemalans, he could pretty much let nature take its course. Recruitment was largely self-generating, as word quickly spread through family and friendship networks of a new jobs magnet to the distant north. With a likely subsidy from both the potential recruit and the company, a Guatemalan with a van in Morganton might make a handsome profit by a periodic run to Indiantown. A trace of the new labor force showed up in the 1990 federal census. Among a mere 58 "Hispanics" in Morganton—and 344 in Burke County as a whole—enumerated separately as Mexicans (22), Puerto Ricans (5), and Cubans (4), were 23 people—131 in the county—listed simply as "Other."[28] The undesignated Hispanics were almost certainly Guatemalans. More than most locals realized at the time, the "other" had indeed arrived in Morganton.

Within management, there was instant satisfaction with the experiment. For one, the addition of these precious new hands required only the most minimal additional investment. Case Farms secured initial lodging for the new workers in a trailer park and an old hotel revamped into apartments. To get people to work, the company organized a van pool and distributed bicycles. In the first years of immigrant recruitment the only other reported social intervention by the company was to facilitate a private postal service for workers to send money home to their families. Such minimal initiatives produced a giant return. "They showed up every day," Hughes remembered. "Of course somebody had to go get 'em, but they showed up everyday. There was some humor, most of 'em . . . they're a little on the short side, you had to give 'em a job that they could reach [but] I think they were always satisfied with them, and I think they still are today, as far as I know. Dependable workers."[29]

For a brief time, the Guatemalans actually possessed a special employment advantage under U.S. immigration and refugee law, even over other Latin American recruits who had already made a significant impact on chicken plants in Georgia and Arkansas. Beginning in fall 1986, the Immigration Reform and Control Act (IRCA) affected would-be immigrants in important ways. On the one hand, IRCA implemented a generous legalization program for some two million undocumented individuals who had arrived prior to 1982; on the other hand, it beefed up border surveillance and established tough new sanctions for employers who hired more recent, illegal aliens. While throwing a new obstacle in the way of undocumented

Mexicans and others, the new rules left a slight window ajar for Guatemalans and other émigrés from war-torn Central America in the form of appeals for asylum under the Refugee Act of 1980. To be sure, the initial opening was not very inviting; for example, less than 1 percent of Guatemalans who filed for asylum between June 1983 and September 1986 were granted protection. Throughout the 1980s, in fact, American refugee policy toward Latin America marched to the drum of U.S. State Department policy, which favored the entry of exiles only from "hostile" (read Communist Cuba and Sandinista Nicaragua) countries.[30] The situation changed markedly for the better when the Immigration and Naturalization Service (INS) entered into a settlement agreement with advocates for both Salvadoran and Guatemalan asylum applicants in *ABC v. Thornburgh* in 1991. The INS now guaranteed due process under more lenient guidelines (i.e., "without consideration of nationality") for future claimants and agreed to readjudicate the claims of every Salvadoran and Guatemalan class member who had previously been denied relief. In the wake of *ABC*, a tide of Guatemalan asylum applications poured in; given the huge backlog of such applications, applicants (and their employers) could count not only on an initial, temporary work permit but also on regular annual renewals pending a distant asylum hearing.[31]

This "good" immigration news for the Guatemalans lasted for approximately seven years. On March 17, 1997, in a period of growing anti-immigrant fears in the United States and the signing of peace accords in Guatemala and El Salvador (thus removing the formal pretext for asylum in the first place), the INS indicated to asylum applicants that reconsideration of their cases would soon begin. At the same time, tightened controls centered in the Illegal Immigration Reform and Immigrant Responsibility Act (IIRIRA) took effect on April 1, 1997. "IraIra," as it is called by immigration attorneys, not only expedited the removal of "inadmissible aliens" (including those who arrived with false documents or no documents), it substantially toughened the sanctions on those who had overstayed their lawful residency in the United States. Whereas previously those with seven years of U.S. residency, a record of "good moral character," and a likelihood of "extreme hardship" if sent back might count on "suspension of deportation" should they be caught without valid papers, IraIra insisted on a demonstration of "exceptional and extremely unusual hardship" to already legal close kin and (in a clause that all but knocked out all the Guatemalan émigrés) increased the number of years of physical presence required to ten for any claim for what was now called "cancellation of removal."[32] Although passage of the Nicaraguan Adjustment and Central American Relief Act of 1997 (NACARA) sought to take some of the sting out of IraIra and provided some hope for the early Guatemalan arrivals (i.e., those with a seven-year residency) that they might continue to press suspension of deportation claims, the days of asylum applications and legal work permits were now long gone.[33] The brief period from the late 1980s through the mid-1990s—the very years of employment change at Case Farms—constituted the golden years of opportunity for the U.S.-bound Guatemalan emigrant.[34]

Aside from the sudden availability of Guatemalan labor, personnel manager Beecher recalled another selection factor. "I didn't want [Mexicans]. I got nothing against Hispanics, because these people [the Guatemalans] speak quite fluent Spanish, but Mexicans will go back home at Christmastime. You're going to lose them six weeks. And in the poultry business, you can't afford that. You just can't do it. But Guatemalans can't go back home. They're here as political refugees. If they go back home, they get shot. So they stayed on with us, and we went from running 50 percent production and in six weeks, I had it fully staffed and running at 100 percent production." Case Farms owner Tom Shelton, though seldom on the scene in Morganton, directly approved the immigrant-hiring process. When production improved, said Beecher, "he was tickled to death."[35]

"It kind of snuck up on us," noted Bill Poteat, editor of the *Morganton News-Herald* (1980–99), about the Hispanic presence in Morganton. Poteat remembered a Saturday morning jog in 1996 with a former resident who was visiting home for the first time in ten years:

> We crossed the park and of the 402 people in the park, 400 of them were Hispanics and two of them were us, then we came uptown and of the people on the streets, 80 to 85 percent of them were Hispanic, and he's like, "Hey, Bill, what's goin' on here, what's this?" and I said, "Well, this is the way it is." It reminded me of the old analogy of "you drop a frog into a pot of boiling water and he'll jump out, but if you slowly increase the temperature he won't know the difference." I guess he was like the frog who hadn't been here and wondering what in the world is going on and I'm the frog who's been here and it's like, "Hey, I guess it's happened." To a visitor it's kind of a shock.

Poteat also explained the delayed reaction to the Central Americans as a product of their demography. In contrast to the Hmong refugee families who were resettled with the help of local church agencies in the late 1970s and early 1980s and immediately entered the schools, churches, and various workplaces, the Guatemalans initially were overwhelmingly single men. They "worked at Case Farms, went home to their trailers, and that's it." Although the journalist Poteat was well aware that the early pattern had undergone change, he observed that a lot of people still viewed the Hispanics as a "temporary thing." Many in town, he suggested, dreamed that "one day they'll wake up and they'll [the Hispanics] be gone. . . . I think they're mistaken on that."[36]

Other observers shared Poteat's sense of the mystifying effect of the new immigrants on the local populace. "Most of the town," noted Maureen Dougher, a Catholic Church worker who spent several years in Bolivia before returning to Morganton in 1985, "still have no idea what has happened here." On local streets, she said, the Guatemalans were still regularly confused with the Hmong, and most people were unaware that the Mayan immigrants had spread out from Case Farms into all manner of area workplaces.[37] Though townspeople for years could only speculate about the degree of the social transformation around them, the returns from the 2000 census finally put hard numbers behind their impressions. In one of the greatest immigrant surges in the country—and certainly the single most dramatic instance of the Latinization of the region—the Hispanic population grew 394 percent in North Carolina, compared to a national increase of 60 percent, across the decade of the 1990s.[38] Yet even the statewide rate of change paled with that of Burke County—a whopping 824 percent increase from 344 in 1990 to 3,180 reported Spanish-speaking residents in 2000![39] Among signs that North Carolina was laying out the welcome mat to new immigrant workers was the fact that it was one of only four states in the country to give out drivers' licenses without proof of legal residence.[40]

For most of Morganton's professional classes the new migrants represented only a shadowy if sometimes troublesome presence on the local radar screen. At the Byrd, Byrd, and Ervin law firm, for example, criminal defense lawyer Robert L. Ervin, Harvard-educated grandson of "Senator Sam" and son of a circuit court judge, enjoyed little contact with the Guatemalans apart from occasionally representing them in court. The communication problem with the "Hispanics," as he called them, was both linguistic and social. "There's a significant language barrier because there's not many people up here who are fluent in Spanish. And even those that are might know sort of a European Spanish as opposed to a Mexican or a Guatemalan Spanish. Plus, most of the Hispanics have worked, at least initially, in unskilled kinds of industries and tend to live in groups either out somewhere in the county or in clusters within the city limits of Morganton." Aside from the conflicts at Case Farms (for which he did some non-labor-related legal work), Ervin identified "some very practical problems" imposed by the new immigration. "The court system really hasn't been prepared to deal with them. You have nobody in the courthouse, initially, who was prepared to cope with speaking Spanish. So it suddenly created a demand for interpreters. It did the same thing to the area hospital. It has created a significant problem for the school system. My own sense is that it is a real strain on the teachers."[41]

Opinion within the local schools appeared to substantiate Erwin's concerns. Joel Hastings, director of ESL (English as a Second Language) programs in the county schools, pointed in 1997 to the particular challenge of educating the district's 150 Mayan-speaking children. "Everything we're seeing [with them] is [that it is] just taking four years or longer to speak the English language and six years or more for [full] comprehension. . . . We had a child this past year that was eleven years old that came straight from the jungles of Guatemala, had never been in school, spoke Q'anjob'al not Spanish. How do you take a child that's been in the jungles practically all their lives and sit them in a classroom with other kids who all speak English and make the necessary accommodations for them to be successful?"[42] One silver lining from the inevitable gap that opened up between the Guatemalans and other school-age children was the general lack of discipline problems among the new students. "When you look at one hundred fifty kids dispersed among 13,000 students, typically the students are so involved in learning English, in being accepted, that there's other priorities [for them] instead of disciplinary issues."[43]

Reelected to the town's chief political office since 1985, Mel Cohen was known as a "very progressive" mayor who in the past had actively encouraged development of a local community relations commission. Yet Cohen, like other town leaders, had little direct contact with the Guatemalan workers. Though he acknowledged that they had some community spokespeople, "I can't tell you their names right off; their names are hard for me to pronounce as well as to spell." His reticence in dealing with the Guatemalans was enhanced by a basic ambivalence about their presence in the community. The new migration, he judged, "had had possibly more of a negative impact than a positive impact" on the town, a problem Cohen readily divided into five components:

One, their ability to understand the language; two, their ability to adhere to our quality of life; three, sending most of their money back to Guatemala and not spending it locally; four, their lack of respect for community property; and five, their ability to live in an environment, or habitat, less than standard. . . . [Because of] their ability to do that, landlords tend to neglect [the property] whereas ten years ago, we wouldn't have had that problem. A substandard housing problem would have been taken care of because people wouldn't live in it; now landlords have people that will live in substandard housing unless we get it reported, which we generally don't, by them. . . . They have wonderful work habits, they're hard-working people, but we have these problems.

Under quality-of-life issues, the mayor cited littering as perhaps the most annoying habit of the new residents: "They have no regard for keeping where they live clean. When they leave a facility, a public facility like a playground, they leave trash, probably because they did that back in Guatemala." Despite such misgivings, the mayor felt that the town was doing what it could to welcome its newest citizens. Cohen took pride in adding the Spanish-language Univision to the city's cable contract and was urging city agencies to translate government signs into Spanish as well, though he acknowledged that the Guatemalans posed a particular problem in this regard because many communicated in indigenous tongues, identified by the mayor as "so many different dialects of the Spanish language."[44]

Among official Morganton, the police encountered the Maya in the most extreme and occasionally hostile situations; yet, curiously, the small police force under Chief Robbie Williams appeared to possess a more sympathetic understanding of the immigrant workers than did many of their professional counterparts. Like every other agency in town, offered Ray Barlowe, a major on the force with nearly thirty years' experience in local criminal investigation and departmental management, the police faced a "tremendous" problem of communication with the Guatemalans. "It's amazing that, as Americans, we all expect everyone to learn our language overnight, and it's probably the most complex language in the world." Routine problems afflicting the Guatemalan community included robbery ("where elements of the African American community have found out that Guatemalans do not trust banks and tend to carry large amounts of cash on hand at home"), drunk driving, and occasional personal fights and prostitution arrests. On top of such routine challenges, noted Barlowe, "there's also an inherent problem with the Guatemalan people trusting anyone in uniform. Coming from their home culture, they were faced with two types of [cops]: those that were corrupt and looking for money, or someone who was going to put them in the army." Slowly, and only after some serious blunders, Barlowe believed, the police established better relations with the people who came to work at Case Farms. As an example of the local learning curve, Barlowe cited the department's unhappy experience with its first Spanish-language translator in breaking up a fight between two local Guatemalan workers: "When the two men [initially] refused to cooperate, the translator took [one of the men] into a separate room without the police. In a few minutes the man was happily recounting the details of the story. . . . The investigator asked the translator what he had told the man that made him open up and tell his story. The translator replied: 'I told him that you were going to have him executed if he didn't tell the truth.' Well, immediately we no longer used that translator."[45]

When it came to the tensions at Case Farms, the Morganton police sought to "let labor and management resolve their own disputes" but to make sure "things don't get out of hand." In coming to terms with local labor problems, Major Barlowe walked a fine line between his own views and the duties of a public servant:

> There are a number of people that view the Guatemalans as coming into this area and taking away jobs from [local] people, [but] unemployment [figures] show that that's not the case. I think that the industries where the Guatemalans are working are industries that traditionally have had problems retaining employees; it's minimum-wage work that is hard work in assembly-line situations. It's not work that you're going to be gratified doing. It's not work that you can really say that you're going to make a career out of. The Guatemalan work ethic itself is one that I think was easy to take advantage of, that's what maybe these [labor relations] disputes rose out of, was the issue of where does labor's rights need to take into account pay and working conditions. . . . I've heard a lot of people say, "Well, Case Farms brought these people in, they ought to have to provide them educational expenses, they ought to have to do these things for them. Case Farms are people that are making a profit off of their work."[46]

For the people of Morganton, the arrival of the Guatemalans and other Hispanics was an unplanned, largely unwanted event whose consequences had nevertheless to be faced. Early local hostility, for example, was signaled in the rejection of an application for a Hispanic grocery at the site of an old laundry in a residential neighborhood. With backing from worried neighbors, the Board of Adjustment turned down the request on grounds that the store "would change the character of the surrounding area."[47] It was not difficult for the visiting oral historian to hear similar opinions on the streets of Morganton. The landlady of one (white) Case Farms worker de-

The Way It Is in Morganton

clared that the "Hispanics" had "ruined" Morganton: "They've taken the jobs and houses of the Americans." Not surprisingly, a statewide survey in 1996 registered widespread disquiet with the rapid growth of the Hispanic population: about 40 percent of respondents called the trend "bad" and two-thirds "wouldn't like it if Hispanics moved into their neighborhoods."[48] The only organized anti-immigration protest reported in Morganton was sponsored in November 1999 by the North Carolina Council of Conservative Citizens and supported by a local organizer of the Reform Party. Attracting about thirty people, only half of whom were residents of Burke County, a council leader explained: "We are losing the culture war in this country. Why do we have to obey the law to a T and they don't have to obey nothing?"[49] Discountenancing both major parties for genuflecting to Hispanic voters, a letter to the editor in the *News-Herald* in early October 2000 insisted that "only Pat Buchanan" would "put a stop to illegal immigration and greatly reduce legal immigration to the United States."[50]

The Guatemalan migrants were not the first group in Morganton to bear the burden of "getting something for nothing." Hmong refugees who had arrived a decade earlier often experienced the same hostility and ignorance from the local community. "They felt we came to steal their jobs," said Seng Lee, an electrical engineer, whose family constituted the first Hmong arrival in Morganton. As Seng and his wife Xai recalled, they had had to confront whites who claimed that they did not pay taxes, as well as blacks who resented Asians for their economic success. "They feel like the more of us that come over here, they don't have any space. I understand how they feel, too. I usually tell them, 'It's not like I wanted to [come here], it's just something we had to do.'" Although they knew little about the new Central American immigrants in town, the Lees immediately sympathized with the struggle their neighbors would face in maintaining their group identity and self-respect. Seng's own children (now in elementary school), for example, often identified indiscriminately with the growing local immigrant pool: "I guess they look at [people's] hair. Anytime they see someone with black hair, they don't know if it's Hmong or Hispanic or Chinese. They say 'Hey, Dad, a Hmong guy came by looking for you.' . . . But when they're with Americans they know who they are, they know they aren't American. They know that. . . . Everytime they see our kids, they [the townspeople] just call them Chinese. So sometimes they come back and say 'I'm Chinese.' No, I say, you're not Chinese, you're a Hmong."[51]

For the Maya, as for the Hmong before them, indifference and mild suspicion, rather than angry resentment, constituted the dominant reaction of the established citizenry to the immigrants' arrival in Morganton. Unmediated by a public relief effort, the Guatemalans, even more than the Hmong, were more often victims of neglect than of active hostility. Given their language, their places of work, their physical presence on the outskirts or in the shadows of the town's daily life, the Guatemalan workers—though less so their children—lived in a world apart. It took nearly a decade, for example, before any Mayan/Hispanic presence showed up at the annual Historic Morganton Festival, a September celebration of local arts and crafts sponsored by downtown merchants. There were, in short, few locals who welcomed the immigrants with open arms.

Yet, the exceptions mattered. A small band of citizens, whether from professional training, moral conviction, or ethnic affinity, helped to mediate the migrants' passage. The latter group is exemplified by Daniel Gutiérrez. Gutiérrez, an English teacher in Mexico City who came to Morganton on a work permit to teach Spanish in 1990, experienced the Guatemalan arrival at several levels. As early as 1993, he and other elementary school foreign-language teachers were transferred into ESL classrooms to meet the needs of a new school-age population. But even earlier, his first contact with the Guatemalans occurred in home visits as a teacher. "When I got inside there was no furniture, no bedding, no table . . . we began serving them in getting furniture, health care, transportation, basic issues that at that point we didn't realize were a big deal." Quickly, Gutiérrez and other local Latinos—including the Cuban Rodríguez family and the Rojas from Puerto Rico—reached out and got "more and more involved" with the new workers. Often sought for translation (a role that would later lead him into the center of the Case Farms disputes), as well as other personal advice by the migrants, the bilingual Gutiérrez emerged as an unofficial representative of the Spanish-speaking community, a person local Anglos trusted to deliver donated clothes and furniture to the most needy cases. Gutiérrez, himself a lay evangelical minister, watched the First Assembly, the town's first Spanish-speaking church, grow from twenty-five members in 1991 to two hundred members within five years.[52]

Besides the few resident Hispanics, there were other local citizens with the interest and initiative to respond to a new community need. Veterinary surgeon Don Hemstreet and his wife Joy, for instance, became close friends with a Guatemalan family after their own daughter, Molly, volunteered in an ESL class. Others acted from more formal positions. As early as 1992, national Red Cross agencies hired former ESL teacher Gisela Bourg-

Williams to direct Project Amigo, an outreach program to provide the new Guatemalan community with health care and other survival skills. Basically, Bourg-Williams sought to give new, young families survival skills in making the cultural transition. "I tried to get them to understand health care issues, like shots and going to the doctor. . . . In their old community, everybody watched one another's children. If they were left alone, grandmother would sit there and watch ten or fifteen kids run around without any problem of dangerous things. Here, we had to teach them that you can't leave your children alone in your home; you need to put your children in a car seat if you're going to drive; you need insurance if you're going to drive; drinking and driving is illegal; abusing your wife is illegal."[53]

As an outgrowth of the Red Cross project (and with money from the state's Smart Start fund for preschool children), social worker John Wanless was hired in 1994 to help enroll Hispanic children in the community's Head Start programs. Wanless publicly expressed optimism about the town's new Guatemalan arrivals. "These people are very resourceful or they wouldn't be here," he told a local reporter.[54] Privately, he was more apprehensive. His own wife, an educated Mexican-born woman accustomed to the multicultural society of Houston, Texas, had initially been shocked by the ignorance and prejudice she had encountered as a Hispanic on the streets and in the stores of Morganton. The Guatemalans, he felt, started from a far more endangered position. Politically repressed and kept uneducated by their government, the Maya, in Wanless's view, were a hard-working people, inclined to obey orders from employers or other authorities. "In a lot of ways," he thought, "[the Maya] are just like children, and I think that's why Case Farms decided they wanted a lot of Guatemalans—they felt like they would obey."[55]

Because of the already-sensitive nature of their work in Morganton— Burke County commissioners chose not to spend tax money on "foreigners" when the Project Amigo grant ran out—social workers like Bourg-Williams and Wanless steered clear of direct involvement in the growing tensions at the Case Farms plant. Still, they could not help but sympathize with the workers' grievances. Bourg-Williams remembered getting a telephone call from a managerial employee at the chicken plant:

He says, "You know, I don't understand the hygiene of these Guatemalan people. They urinate on the walls." . . . Well, we came to find out that what had happened was that they couldn't have breaks when they needed to go to the bathroom. They couldn't hold it so they did their thing on the wall. . . . I went in there [to the plant] a couple of times, and I was disgusted. . . . I think folk like myself and other folks who are working with the Spanish-speaking population feel like they shouldn't be treated that way; that it's not fair and not right. Whether unions can help them or not, . . . they shouldn't be treated like slaves.[56]

In the same way that Bourg-Williams and Wanless offered social services, Catawba Valley Legal Services contacted the immigrants at specific points of need. From the beginning of the decade, its director John Vail and attorney Phyllis Palmieri represented individual Guatemalans in matters of substandard housing and illegal evictions, unemployment compensation, welfare benefits, and immigrant asylum issues. Their connections to the new immigrants were facilitated by paralegal Edna Barbarough, one of the few Anglos in town fluent in Spanish.[57]

Undoubtedly, the central institution for Guatemalan socialization in Morganton was St. Charles Borromeo Catholic Church. It was there that they found one of their most effective advocates in Rev. Kenneth L. Whittington. Coming from a predominantly Catholic country, it is likely that the migrants did not realize how lucky they were to arrive in a small North Carolina town with an established Catholic Church. After all, following closely behind South Carolina and Tennessee, North Carolina has the lowest percentage (3.2 percent in 1999) of Catholics in the United States. In the Charlotte diocese to which Morganton belongs, there were in 1999 a total of 119,000 Catholics in a population of nearly four million.[58] Born to a Protestant family in northern Virginia and trained in music in Germany, St. Charles's pastor, "Father Ken" (as he was affectionately known), had entered the Catholic Church after extended soul-searching as a young adult capped by a job in Greensboro, North Carolina, as a church musician. From the beginning, what struck him as distinctive about the Catholic Church was the "mix" of people there: "This spoke very loud and clear to me." Soon, Whittington had converted and begun training for the priesthood. First serving as assistant priest at the cathedral in Charlotte, he was assigned to Morganton as pastor in 1992. Long cloaked in the formal dignity of Father John Toller, who had been transferred to another parish, St. Charles Church first struck him as "very clean" and "locked." He soon noticed the presence at Mass of several "Hispanics" who "didn't seem to know what was going on. . . . They intrigued me, and though I spoke no Spanish at all, I had to do something special to reach them." During his

Father Ken Whittington on Pentecost Sunday, 1995,
with Ana Sebastién José.

second summer in Morganton, he learned the Spanish Mass from a visiting
Mexican seminarian and began regularly holding dual Sunday services. By
mid-decade about two hundred to three hundred Guatemalans attended
St. Charles, representing a good third of the entire parish.

Initially, Father Ken and his church associates found it hard to keep the
new parishioners' names straight. With Spanish family names that sound
like first names to North American ears and the frequent repetition of
the same names (especially among the Q'anjob'al, whom we will meet in
Chapter 2), Mayan emigrants like Andrés Tomás, Tomás Andrés, Manuel
de Manuel, and Diego de Diego no doubt produced confusion. Maureen

Dougher, the Spanish-speaking lay activist who had helped assimilate the new arrivals at St. Charles, observed that even many Guatemalans did not know each others' names. Her point, on its face implausible if not downright patronizing, may in fact have been valid in two senses. First, among themselves, the Guatemalans regularly used their own Mayan names and language. Second, an outside interviewer would eventually come up against the question, "Do you want my 'Case Farms name' [used to enter the country and the company and pass immigration] or my 'real name'?"[59]

It was not just the newcomers' exoticism or even their interest in the church that impressed Whittington. "They were a very warm people, a gentle people," a factor that stood in eerie counterpoint to "the intense violence many had experienced in their lives. . . . So we began to share on that level. I think as a community, many began to feel at home here in the church, and they began to use it very, very much. There's [now] hardly a day goes by that we don't have something going on that they themselves engineer."[60] With characteristic wit, the priest compared the parish's two major immigrant groups: "The Hmong come to church only when it is useful to them, [whereas] the Guatemalans are there when the door opens. The Hmong are very organized, but it takes six meetings [for them] to do anything and at the sixth meeting, they are likely to say that the time to act was at an earlier meeting. By contrast, the Guatemalans can't organize a meeting or make a plan, but they all show up to do the job."[61]

Under Father Ken's guidance, St. Charles became the single most important point of contact in town between established residents and the new Mayan arrivals. It was no accident, as we shall see later, that initial Case Farms worker protests and later union meetings were regularly convened at the Catholic church. Over time, such connections, though still strained by linguistic and sociological distance, melted earlier suspicions between old and new parishioners. Denny Hughes, then working in sales at Case Farms, was a case in point:

My first thought . . . I regretted seeing them [the Guatemalans], they came into our [Catholic] church, they crowded us up in church. [Then] I kind of got my eyes opened. We had a work session here at the church, and me and my kids had taken it as our responsibility to make the grass grow green, and we were up here and we had Mass first, and while we were having Mass there wasn't a Guatemalan in there but we started to hear noises out there around the church and we come out and there must have been fifty of them. They didn't have the real nice electric hedge trimmers, like I'd brought with me to use, [but] they stayed [all day] with us, and that changed my attitude on these people.[62]

For Hughes, as for many town residents who got to know them, there was a special quality—something at once good and innocent yet also vulnerable—about the Guatemalan Maya that set them apart from the modern world. Father Ken spoke of their peculiar "communal spirit": "It's wonderful but I also think it's something that will bring them into conflict with our society, because it's so different from our own individualistic approach to things. I think it's about their Mayan religious heritage which is deeper and more integrated into their lives than is their Catholicism. . . . The way they pray, the way they can suffer loss and still go on, the way they can endure pain—all point toward their Mayan faith."[63] Father Ken liked to tell the story of the Guatemalan church janitor who several years before had planted corn all around the church that grew to be fifteen feet tall. "There was something magical about that corn when it started to grow and the people's attraction to it. You could see them going and touching it. I can't articulate it." Gisela Bourg-Williams stressed similar virtues. The Guatemalans, she insisted, were "a unique and wonderful people with a lot to teach us." As evidence, she cited her contacts with Mayan women, who in many ways offered an appealing alternative to consumer culture—a native tradition of arts and crafts, a "Mother Nature upbringing," including carrying a baby on their back, and a general "learning of how to survive with the least amount of things; they're happier than we are with us being so materialistic." For many of their Anglo friends in town, the uniqueness of the Mayan way of life assumed almost mystical significance. As Don Hemstreet put it: "You understand corn, you start to understand the Guatemalan people, because they are people of the corn. Truly they are people of the corn."[64]

To their North American admirers, the indigenous sojourners from Guatemala forced a critical reckoning with "Western" secularism and materialism. It is a sentiment classically evoked by Venezuelan anthropologist Elizabeth Burgos-Debray, who recorded and edited Mayan Nobel Peace Prize–winner Rigoberta Menchú's now-famous testimonial, *I, Rigoberta Menchú: An Indian Woman in Guatemala* (1984): "As we listen to her voice," writes Burgos-Debray, "we have to look deep into our own souls for it awakens feelings and sensations which we, caught up as we are in an inhuman and artificial world, thought were lost for ever."[65]

The spiritualism attributed to the Maya was no doubt enhanced by their distinctive language and dress which served to separate them from Western norms. In point of fact, a center of Bible belief like North Carolina contained no shortage of spiritual sojourners. It happens that the most otherworldly commentary I encountered in many visits to Morganton included this refrain: "In the beginning the earth was triangular, and I've got a triangle on my arm that was put there with 144 stitches. . . . The two triangles in the Star of David represent a triangular earth spinning and becoming round. It's a star of prophecy. . . . God wants us to forgive and be merciful and to have heaven on earth. He can even give us angels to serve us where we don't have to work."[66] This testimonial was delivered not by a Mayan shaman, but by a Texas-born Pentecostal, a former Mr. Omelet worker on temporary disability. In the case of the professional anthropologist as well as the ordinary citizen, it is perhaps easier to be inspired to transcendence by the exotic stranger than by one's everyday neighbors.

On balance, it is fair to say, the arriving Guatemala Maya presented a puzzle and a challenge to the established citizenry of Morganton even as this North Carolina town equally presented its own mysteries to the new arrivals. For the citizens of Morganton, the Maya meant different things. For employers, immigrant workers represented a golden resource that could recharge regional industries with needed skills at an attractive price. For local officials, the new immigration was principally a policy problem—akin to dealing with a water shortage or failing schools. For most local citizens, the new arrivals triggered not so much hostility as discomfort—the very existence of these "birds of passage" may have suggested that we are all less the shapers of our world than the victims of forces beyond our control. For some bystanders (fortunately not many), the problem was, and remains, more severe—a horde of aliens would ravage the landscape, threatening the very foundation of the community, and deprive others of their chance for the good life. Finally, there were those citizens who saw in the immigrants an opportunity less for economic gain than for spiritual-cultural renewal. Like the progressive reformers who once inhabited Chicago's Hull House—people like Jane Addams, John Dewey, and Alice Hamilton—Morganton's progressives responded with a sense of moral duty (and perhaps even noblesse oblige) to the material needs of the newcomers while hoping that the newcomers would, in turn, make their host society a more democratic as well as a more cosmopolitan place.[67]

All towns like to see themselves as someplace special, and Morganton was no exception. A local historian insisted in 1996 that Morganton was "a southern town that is different from every other town in the state and

The Way It Is in Morganton

probably different from every town in every other state as well."[68] Yet, in its rich and inevitably differentiated way of receiving a group of poor but energetic strangers, Morganton gave voice to one of the most common if not quintessential themes of U.S. history. In this small southern town, the questions of who is an American, who will do the work, and under what conditions echoed with renewed insistence.

2

Flight of the Happy Farmers

As early as September 1991, barely two years after the entry of the first Guatemalans into the local labor force, a conflict erupted at Case Farms. When, with no prior notice, the company reduced the length of a skeletal nighttime shift in which many of the new hires were bunched, some twenty Guatemalan workers simply walked off the job. Charged with cleaning machines awash in blood, grease, and chicken parts, the night workers had struggled to complete their jobs within a long shift stretching from 8:00 P.M. to 7:00 A.M. the next morning. By delaying the evening start-up time to 9:30 P.M., the company suddenly imposed a speedup and effectively cut the workers' pay. Under the circumstances, the unhappy workers not only departed the plant but also prepared to return to the Florida communities from which they had originally embarked for Morganton. Some had already left town before an anxious management sought to resolve the dispute.

In retrospect, the walkout of 1991 marked the beginning of a new wave of Guatemalan worker protest at Case Farms. Yet, if it is generically linked to larger events that would follow, it is also separated from subsequent developments by the demographic peculiarity of the participants. These first protesters bore the characteristic mark of a tight-knit group of war refugees who barely spoke Spanish, let alone English. Rosa Benfield, a nurse from Guatemala City who had followed her U.S.-born husband back to North Carolina after his stint as a marine guard at the U.S. embassy, was one of the first contacted through friends at the St. Charles Catholic Church to help resolve the conflict. "Americans are used to paying [somebody] a wage and the worker working no matter what," she explained. But the Guatemalan Indians "were different," Benfield remembered. "It was not just money that was important to them. They just walked out if they didn't like the working conditions."[1] To Benfield and two local Legal Service representatives, attorney Phyllis Palmieri and Spanish-speaking paralegal Edna Barbarough, it became apparent that the "striking" workers—for they called their walk-out a *huelga* (strike)—constituted a self-defined communal bloc that de-ferred to one "elder," Francisco José, better known among the workers as "Don Pancho."[2] Benfield entered Don Pancho's apartment and tried to engage the women of the family. They would not speak and, indeed, de-ferred on all questions (perhaps because they did not speak Spanish) to Don Pancho himself—"He was the patriarch."[3]

Making sense of the first immigrant protest at Case Farms requires some knowledge of the immigrants themselves. At a general level, with only a handful of exceptions, the Guatemalans in Morganton were people of Mayan descent who claimed as their home the modest-sized *pueblos* (towns) or tiny *aldeas* (hamlets) that dot the sides of the imposing peaks of the Cuchumatanes mountain range in the nation's northwestern *departamento* (province) of Huehuetenango. Although the indigenous peoples of Guate-mala number twenty-one distinct language groups in all (and six in Hue-huetenango alone), the Morganton arrivals derived from a few, select threads of this larger tapestry of Highland Maya society. The first to come —including Don Pancho and all his night shift workmates—were Q'an-job'al speakers from the remote (even by Guatemalan standards) area sur-rounding the neighboring towns of San Miguel Acatán (population 19,000 in 1994) and San Rafael la Independencia (population 10,000), an area situ-ated well over a mile high on a rocky plateau.[4] Positioned as they were in one of the most-difficult-to-cultivate ecosystems in the world, these people grew the "holy trinity" of corn, beans, and squash for subsistence; they also raised some livestock—mainly sheep for wool—and wheat for market. Many Q'anjob'al were virtually monolingual, speaking only a few words of Spanish in conjunction with their own language. As if to minimize out-side linguistic demands required of them, the Q'anjob'al tended to com-bine a few Spanish first names in their naming practices. For an outsider, it was confusing but not uncommon to meet a Tomás Andrés and an Andrés Tomás from the same village; indeed, a Mexican in Morganton insisted that he had met a San Migueleño named Andrés Andrés.[5]

Since the original Spanish conquest of the sixteenth century, the re-gion has experienced a curious mixture of administrative subjugation by a Spanish and later Ladino (all those with a Hispanicized cultural iden-tity) minority with a large measure of cultural autonomy for the indige-nous majority.[6] Initially cushioned by geography from direct control by the central state, the highland peasantry of Guatemala, both Indian and

Ladino, faced an uphill struggle to maintain their way of life once coffee cultivation was introduced into the region in the nineteenth century—suffering theft of ancestral lands, forced relocation and labor drafts, and debt bondage.[7] Living in a beautiful country with rich natural resources, Central America's largest Indian population tasted a rural poverty—statistically second-worst to Haiti in the hemisphere—that contrasted sharply with the wealth of plantation owners and commercial grandees residing in Guatemala City and in the regional capital of Quetzaltenango. Despite selective displays of manipulation and repression by government authorities, social order in the Cuchumatanes was long maintained through a de facto accommodation by the Ladino elite to the socioreligious authority of local Indian leaders.[8]

The tenuous tranquility of the highlands was shattered in the 1970s by the spread of a guerrilla revolt begun in 1960 against the military dictatorship in power since the U.S.-inspired coup of 1954. For thirty-six years —with particular intensity in the highlands from 1978 to 1983 but raging continuously in different areas of the country until the signing of the peace accords in December 1996—the armed left and the various military-dominated governments in Guatemala squared off in a Cold War–stoked conflict that represented the hemisphere's longest-running guerrilla war.[9] With the rise to power of General Romeo Lucas García in 1978 and continuing through the regime of General Efraín Ríos Montt (1982–83), the war reached its violent crescendo in the departments of El Quiché and Huehuetenango as the government engaged in massive counterinsurgency campaigns aimed at eradicating a popular base for the Guerrilla Army of the Poor (EGP), one of three insurgent forces operating in the country. Overall, according to a subsequent U.N.-sanctioned historical truth commission, the war claimed an estimated 200,000 casualties in dead and disappeared, while some six hundred indigenous communities were all but wiped off the map in government-sponsored attacks.[10] Moreover, according to official estimates, "one million Indians (one Maya in four) fled or were displaced from their homes between 1981 and 1985 as a result of counterinsurgency tactics."[11] Among these, many tens of thousands, including both ex-combatants and those caught in the cross fire, began to flee the region in the early 1980s, seeking refuge in Mexico and eventually the United States, Canada, and even Australia.[12]

A growing guerrilla presence in the area by the late 1970s brought a massive counter-response from the national armed forces. During the period 1978–80, the army tried to crush autonomous Catholic and other civic

Flight of the Happy Farmers

Village of Lajcholaj, Guatemala.

organizations considered to be allied with the guerrilla insurgency. In 1981 it began the "Tierra Arrasada," or scorched-earth policy, destroying entire towns in an attempt to dry up the base of guerrilla support. According to one study of the Q'anjob'al region, "the brother municipalities of San Miguel Acatán and San Rafael la Independencia were the hardest hit by the repression."[13] Amnesty International and other human rights reports are replete with accounts of massacres in the late 1970s and early 1980s, including at least seven incidents in San Miguel Acatán and two in San Rafael.[14] On August 19, 1981, for example, the army reportedly entered Suntelaj, an aldea of San Miguel Acatán, and killed fifteen people identified on a school fund-raising list after forcing them to dig their own graves; only months before, following the public appearance of guerrillas in Lajcholaj, an aldea of San Rafael, a large group of men were rounded up, locked in a house, and burned to death.[15]

The most painstaking and graphic documentation of atrocities committed during Guatemala's civil war surfaced in the 1999 report to the United Nations by the independent Historical Clarification Commission (CEH). Accusing the Guatemalan military of "acts of genocide"—supported directly and indirectly by the U.S. government—against the Maya, *Guatemala: Memory of Silence* documents 669 massacres, of which 88 occurred in the state of Huehuetenango. Although the report describes individual cases of guerrilla retribution against indigenous community leaders and their families who sided with the government, the agent of violence in 93 percent of the cases was the army or its often-coerced paramilitary ally, the Civil Self-Defense Patrols (PACs). Among the volumes of CEH evidence released to the public at this writing, one example from the bombardment and massacre in the aldea of Coya, San Miguel Acatán, in 1981, powerfully conveys both the initial process of politicization among the indigenous people and the chilling effect of the government counteroffensive on their communities:

At the beginning of the 1970s the five hundred indigenous Q'anjob'al families who made up the agricultural aldea of Coya founded a cooperative which bound together the majority of neighbors within the community. In the same period the Guerrilla Army of the Poor (EGP) began to operate in this zone. . . . An ex-guerrilla recounted that "when they [the guerrillas] asked us to organize ourselves with them, only a few people declined, for we were poor and everyone wanted to live better." . . . By the end of 1979, in addition to an Irregular Local Forces unit and a Local Clandestine Committee, the EGP had founded the Che Guevara Front which operated in the area.

In mid-1981 the Army began to patrol in the area. [At first a coordinated show of force by the people of several neighboring villages chased off the soldiers.] Then, on July 19, 1981 at 6 A.M. some three hundred soldiers arrived by different routes in Coya. They set off mortars and fired on the community, killing some twenty-five people. At first the community thought its own system of collective self-defense would force the soldiers to leave, but this time the system no longer worked. At 6:30 A.M. an army plane began to shell the village. Again and again it flew by and dropped bombs. The people ran and tried to hide.

After the aerial attack, the soldiers entered the village. The people they met outside their houses, they killed. They also entered various houses and killed between ten and twenty people; half were hacked with machetes and the others were shot. The executions were indiscriminate [including the machete death of a baby girl]. . . . The CEH estimates that some 45 people died in this attack. . . . The soldiers stayed for more than two months in Coya. During this time they violated various women and robbed people of food and objects of value.

On September 28, 1981, at one in the morning, the soldiers removed twenty-nine men from their houses. Their names appeared on a list of supposed guerrillas in the community. All were active members of the local cooperative. . . . They imprisoned the men in a house left vacant by a North American. The wives of the imprisoned men showed the soldiers the *cédulas* [government identity cards] of their husbands to prove that there had been a mistake in the list. From this action ten men were set free, because their names were not on the list. The women of the nineteen who remained in custody tried to bring food to their husbands but the soldiers prevented them, shouting out threats. For four days the men were tortured. "The soldiers tied them up and kicked them around as if the old men were footballs. At night they [the soldiers] took off their clothes and threw water at them. . . ."

On October 1, at five in the morning, the soldiers woke up the prisoners and took them barefoot, with feet and hands bound together, to a cave at the site of a former copper mine known as "El Rosario." There, at 7 A.M., they shot at them. Then they threw grenades into the cave to assure themselves that there were no survivors. From a distance the community heard the sound of the armaments.

In 1982, from the people who stayed in Coya, the Army organized a PAC. The military offensive provoked a change of attitude toward the guerrillas. The community began to reject them. A community neighbor commented: We saw that the guerrillas had deceived us with promises that they couldn't fulfill and owing to our organization, the Army now wanted to kill us. From that moment on, we no longer wanted to join the guerrillas.[16]

The actions in Coya were only one of several hundred incursions by the army that effectively smashed the guerrilla resistance through counterforce now widely condemned as atrocities, even genocide, against the Maya. After the signing of the Guatemalan peace accord in December 1996, there remained a struggle within the country to assign responsibility and accountability for such crimes, and to exact some form of restitution for the affected surviving communities.[17] At the time, however, the only recourse of the Q'anjob'al people was to move northward en masse.[18]

The outright terror of war combined with the simultaneous devastation of local economies to produce a flood tide of Guatemalan emigrants to the United States by the mid-1980s. Even as the fighting in the countryside of Huehuetenango gradually subsided (as the guerrillas, now devastated as a fighting force, took refuge in occasional hit-and-run actions), poverty and unemployment did not. By the 1990s, therefore, the earlier stream of "war refugees" gave way to a chain migration of "economic refugees" drawing on family and village ties. Both groups of migrants fled by foot, bus, and van rides across Mexico, crossed into Texas or Arizona, then generally headed west to pick crops in California or east to do the same in Florida. There, the village of Indiantown near West Palm Beach became a prime catch basin of Guatemalan settlement.[19] The new arrivals harvested tomatoes, cucumbers, oranges, and lemons, and worked in con-

struction or yard—especially golf club—maintenance (what our interviewees called "lan-scá-pe") until information of greater opportunity elsewhere
beckoned. It was just such a pledge of better pay, "inside" work, and more
familiar mountain surroundings that led many to Morganton and the Case
Farms poultry-processing plant. Once a "colony" of migrants found work
and homes, new arrivals, often with family connections to the settlers,
might be summoned directly from the homeland.

Generally speaking, the decade of the 1990s witnessed two stages of migrants entering Morganton. The early arrivals (roughly 1989–94), including many who had experienced the era of wartime intensity in the Cuchumatanes, made their way to North Carolina in a roundabout fashion, often
with a considerable layover in other locales as agricultural laborers. Second-
stage migrants (since 1995) were much more likely to travel directly from
Guatemala to Morganton, usually on a personal tip from a relative or
friend, with specific plans to begin work at Case Farms or with other area
employers.

Don Pancho and his Q'anjob'al compatriots were part of the first stage.
In search of work, Don Pancho first left Guatemala in 1976. He picked
cotton and harvested peaches and spinach in Arizona before migrating to
Florida in 1980 on the advice of a Mexican friend whom he met in the fields.
"There's everything there," he was told, "oranges, lemons, tomatoes, chiles,
everything." And initially, the long-distance economy worked pretty well
for him. Paid six dollars a box for oranges, he could earn sixty dollars a
day—not as much as the bigger and stronger Mexicans who might earn
eighty to ninety dollars but enough to live on and send money home to
his family. Then, in November 1981 he learned that, in response to guerrilla
activity in the local area, the army had moved in and initiated a wave of
killings, including the massacre in Lajcholaj. Don Pancho hurried home.
"I kept thinking there would be peace, but there was no peace." He was in
San Miguel when, one evening in March 1982, an army patrol rounded up a
local *alcalde* (mayor) and other officials in charge of the voting list, pushed
them face down into the Guatemalan flag, and beat them to death. Over a
period of few months several of Don Pancho's close friends were executed
by government forces—"I don't know if they were guerrillas, a few could
have been, others not." His own family, he first insisted, "wasn't involved."
"Maybe a few were," he allowed, "at night, who knows?"

Don Pancho and his family took refuge with his in-laws (his father-in-
law owned a hardware store in the district capital of Huehuetenango and
ran a bus service between "Huehue" and San Miguel/San Rafael); terri-

Flight of the Happy Farmers

Francisco "Pancho" José with wife María and son
Pascual in their Morganton living room.

fied, they determined to flee the country. The main border crossing from
Huehuetenango to Mexico is at La Mesilla on the Pan-American Highway which leads to Comitán, Mexico. As part of his travels, however, Don
Pancho mentioned a place called Nentón, which is not on the way to La
Mesilla and not on the way to anywhere unless one were going to cross
the border at a site other than a road (Don Pancho's daughter Anna still
remembers living in a cardboard box in the woods during the evacuation).
The family stayed in Comitán for three months, moved northward to Sina-
loa, picking tomatoes, then onto Ensenada in Baja California for two and
a half years. Late in 1984, after receiving money from a cousin in Colorado, family members paid a North American "Indian" *coyote* (smuggler)
fifty dollars and crossed into Arizona. In Alamosa, Colorado, Don Pancho
joined his extended family picking fruit and mushrooms. Again in search
of work, Don Pancho in 1988 returned to Florida, where a large community of Q'anjob'al had by now settled in Indiantown.[20] There, within the
year, a Guatemalan-born state labor inspector with some education told
Don Pancho of a poultry factory in Morganton to which other Migueleños
(inhabitants of San Miguel Acatán) had recently departed. Quickly, Don
Pancho signed up for one of the van rides (the basic conveyance for migrant
laborers) north; on arrival in Morganton, he was immediately hired into

the night shift, where most of the fourteen villagers who had preceded him were already hard at work. Soon, his wife María and their children traveled from Colorado to their new home.

Among a group of twenty Q'anjob'al friends who greeted Don Pancho on his arrival in Morganton was a young couple, Andrés and Juana Pascual, from Suntelaj near San Miguel Acatán. According to Andrés, his uncle was killed by the army in the period of the 1981 massacre, and he himself had been abducted, stripped, and questioned in the middle of the night by guerrillas. Fleeing his home, Andrés hid out in other pueblos before entering Mexico in 1983. For months he worked construction jobs while slipping back and forth across the border to see his family. The following year, he and Juana acted on a plan to leave Guatemala for good. Together with a friend, Andrés crossed into Comitán, Mexico, on foot and kept on walking. Fifteen days later he arrived at the Arizona border near Nogales. "There we contacted a Mexican [coyote] who knew how to cross. I have a friend in Florida who had a telephone, and I told him that I had come to the U.S. He said, 'Take a van of one of my friends and you can come to Florida.'" Andrés proceeded to Indiantown, where his wife joined him a year later. In the summer of 1989, a call from Juana's sister, Melchiora, already in Morganton, summoned them to North Carolina.[21]

The one Guatemalan who preceded the Q'anjob'al group to Morganton was Andrés Tomás Santiago, a Jakalteko-speaking Maya (i.e., from the neighboring Huehueteco town of Jacaltenango) also living in Indiantown. He had already traveled as far as Alabama looking for work but had not found any. On advice likely emanating from the Case Farms human resources (or personnel) manager, Norman Beecher, Andrés had heard that there was poultry work in North Carolina. He drove all the way from Florida with his wife and child and got directions to the factory at a gas station. He immediately obtained work and returned two weeks later to bring friends back—while also earning extra money—to North Carolina.[22]

Soon there was an almost constant van service ferrying Guatemalan workers to Morganton. Matías Tomás, one of Andrés's first recruits, recalled: "The company rented a government house [public housing] for us to live in. We bought bicycles and we all rode nineteen bikes to work. But the [manager] of the house knew that there were so many of us living there by all the bikes outside, and he kicked us out. Then the company rented us some trailers. There were ten trailers. We were there one year. Then we rented more government houses."[23]

For Matías Tomás, settlement in the United States had proved some-

Flight of the Happy Farmers

thing of a deliverance from the turmoil that had previously beset his path. Born in 1956, Matías had pretty much grown up on his own. His father had abandoned his mother before he was born. When Matías was only a year old, his mother went off with another man and left him in the care of his grandmother in the village of Concepción Huista (within the municipality of Jacaltenango), where the Q'anjob'al like Matías were a minority among Jakaltekos. Entering the fields at age eight, he had no schooling; at the time of his interview he still could neither read nor write more than his name. At age ten, he left home to work in coastal coffee *fincas* [plantations] in the department of Escuintla. On the coast he met his future wife, Petrona José, in 1979, and he often returned to visit her family in Lajcholaj, the small village near the town of San Rafael la Independencia. An enduring sense of social grievance among the indigenous peoples together with its uneasily negotiated terrain made the region a prime recruiting ground of the EGP at the end of the decade. Matías described the appeal that the guerrillas made to the villagers: "[They said] they would make a strike or something, then we were going to divide the money, divide the land, take the money of the rich . . . we were very poor, this was the counsel of the EGP. Those that . . . would accept them might have to go with them, to help them." Matías insisted that neither he nor his family displayed any interest in the guerrilla cause. Clearly, others did, however. Guatemalan historian Víctor Perera refers to "the guerrillas' success in recruiting hundreds of thousands of Mayan peasants to their cause." In any case, when the army mobilized for counterinsurgency under the regime of General Romeo Lucas in 1981, it spent little effort distinguishing between loyal and insurgent *naturales*. While Matías was away on the coast, his father-in-law was dragged from his house naked in the middle of the night and executed together with about fifty other villagers. As in the case of Don Pancho's family, Matías's commentary on the surrounding political conflicts was sometimes contradictory. On one occasion he admitted that "the war began to do damage to us, the guerrillas." On another he maintained that despite a strong guerrilla presence in the area, he had "no sympathy either with them [the guerrillas] or the *nacionales* [the army]. My father-in-law the same."[24]

Reeling from the constant threat of violence and loss around him, Matías recalled simply: "I didn't care to join. This was when I sought out the will of God and I came here. I hadn't planned to cross the border, but through the will of God I did and I came here [to Morganton]. To this day I am very grateful for what God has done for me in this great nation. [He has] given me work for food to eat and to send to my family in Guatemala." Matías traveled directly from Lajcholaj to Arizona in August 1987 and then quickly decamped to Florida. For a brief period his wife's sisters and mother joined him there, but then they returned to Guatemala. Matías expected to follow them, but after two years of work in construction, a cassette he received in the mail from a friend warned that the situation was still unstable and too dangerous for the local men to return. Instead, Matías in 1989 accepted the invitation of Andrés Tomás Santiago to travel to Morganton. Two years later, his wife Petrona joined him; their children remained in Lajcholaj to be raised by their grandmother.[25]

As it happened, another old Lajcholaj resident arrived in Morganton shortly after Matías. Efraín Sebastién Martín, like Matías, left Guatemala in 1987, "not for problems in my house, with my family, but because of the problems outside, the violence." Indicating the widespread dissemination of his Q'anjob'al kinsmen throughout the United States, Efraín traced his travels and search for work from Mexico to Florida and then to brief stints in New Jersey and Michigan before a telephone call from *un familiar* (a relative) in Barrías (a Huehuetenango town near the border of Mexico) informed him of a job opening at Case Farms.[26]

How do we move from the background of the Q'anjob'al refugees to their actions at Case Farms? Despite their motivation to find and hold a job, workers unused to the tight supervision and time management of a machine age historically have proven an obstreperous lot. Comparing the responses of the Lowell, Massachusetts, mill girls of the 1840s with Southern and Eastern European steelworkers of the Progressive Era, Herbert Gutman's famous essay of 1973, for example, analyzed "a recurrent tension . . . between native and immigrant men and women fresh to the factory and the demands imposed upon them by the regularities and disciplines of factory labor."[27] Indeed, this was true in Guatemala itself. When, in the late 1870s, a Spanish firm established a cotton textile mill in the K'iche'-Maya *municipio* (county) of Cantel, things did not go smoothly. Initially, not only did locals refuse to work there, but also threats to burn down the factory led to the deployment of the national army. Worker protests and strikes continued to hobble production until the 1930s, when management finally accommodated to village work habits and accepted union representation for the workers.[28]

With the Q'anjob'al, however, it was not just industrial "inexperience" but a specific past experience that conditioned their response to workplace conflict. To be sure, to the best of my knowledge, *not one* of the first-stage

Flight of the Happy Farmers

Q'anjob'al in Morganton had *ever* held a factory job prior to entering the poultry plant. In this sense, therefore, theirs might be seen as but another instance of the conflicts inevitably surrounding the raw inductees to urban-industrial capitalism. Yet, if removed from the formal world of factory discipline, the Highland Maya of Huehuetenango—including the Q'anjob'al exiles to North Carolina—had long known and adjusted to the factorylike command of coffee plantation bosses during seasonal labor shifts.[29] Moreover, the home region had its own history of labor protest, most notably in the miners' march from Ixtahuacán, Huehuetenango, to the nation's capital in 1978.[30] In short, acquaintance with boss control over working conditions as well as both the logic and the potential peril of workplace protest were likely well developed among the indigenous population.

Such a background imposes caution on any quick reading of the first Case Farms walkout. On the one hand, the Q'anjob'al workers demonstrated deference to a senior community leader, who appears to have felt personally insulted by the new work routine. On the other hand, Don Pancho's use of the term "huelga" to define the walkout is also a sign of a heightened political awareness that he was applying to his new American situation.[31] How much, if any, of the spirit of active, even armed, resistance in the Guatemalan Highlands had spilled over into factory protest in North Carolina? This is a tricky question, one that highlights some fascinating, if frustratingly contradictory, evidence.

In speaking of the political violence in the land where he grew up, Don Pancho himself became noticeably sad and uncomfortable. After listening to a description in an anthropology book of the massacre of indigenous people by government soldiers in Huehuetenango, his voice trailed off, saying "yes, yes, so it was." As for himself, he denied any allegiance or sympathy with the guerrillas or the army. "They were equal, both of them. They both shook us down, the guerrillas arrived and demanded food, the army arrived and demanded food. If not [i.e., if they did not get what they came for] they killed us. They both were our enemies."[32] Likewise, Don Pancho's ten children, the eldest of whom was barely ten when the family left Guatemala, inherited a story of double-sided danger. "I remember my great-grandmother," said his second-eldest child, Ana, "she stayed in the house and told my mother to go hide, because there were some guerrillas coming to the house. If mother didn't hide, they would rape her, because my father wasn't there. We were just little and my grandmother held us. The guerrillas didn't do nothing to us; they just looked at us with unhappy faces." The fourth child, Isabel, gave a characteristically different perspective: "[The army] had people gather, soldiers surrounded [them] in a big circle, where they all pushed children and mothers and fathers into the middle. Somehow my father had escaped with my mom, and they hid in a tunnel, that's how they escaped the soldiers."[33]

Efraín Martín was one of the Guatemalans who followed Don Pancho out of the plant in 1991 to protest the new night shift policy at Case Farms. Efraín never reentered the poultry factory but rather traveled first to Florida, then returned to Morganton months later to take a job in construction. "I don't know the exact reason for the protest," he says now, clearly distancing himself from a moment of social disorder. "They said there's a strike and I went out." Like Don Pancho, Efraín also distanced himself from the earlier social conflicts in his home country. He recalled the exact date in Lajcholaj when the army killed "forty-nine" persons, including "five or six familiares." According to Efraín, however, the massacre was not the fault of the local people, but of outsiders (i.e., guerrillas) who "came in, took over houses. . . . [They] said that there was no way out, there was no opportunity, they didn't like that one person should have [running] water in his house, they wanted everyone to share the poverty . . . *gracias a Dios* [thank God] I didn't join in that problem." Efraín believed that in general he had made a sharp, positive break from those troubled times. In Florida, he met his wife María, who had come from a nearby aldea in Guatemala, and together they raised five beautiful children. He worked hard, attended Mass in Morganton, and regularly sent money home to his mother, who, along with an older brother, represented his last links to Guatemala.[34]

The accounts of Don Pancho and Efraín Martín undoubtedly fit an important cross section of the indigenous experience during the worst of the war years in the early 1980s. It is an image of Mayan peoples as both political innocents and double victims—preyed upon by armed Marxist, mostly Ladino insurgents as well as by marauding and vengeful soldiers, again directed by a Ladino elite. The Q'anjob'al accounts match those that anthropologist David Stoll encountered during his fieldwork in the Ixil Triangle, east of Huehuetenango, a center of some of the worst violence in Guatemala's civil war. Resisting a model of indigenous "rebellion" or "resistance," Stoll emphasized that "what Ixils say in public and private" was filled "with refrains like 'we were deceived,' 'we're in between.'"[35] In more recent writings, Stoll extends his skepticism toward a more general denial of claims to popular support by Guatemala's erstwhile armed opposition.[36]

Exactly how to sort out post hoc oral testimony on such an issue is indeed an interpretive challenge. Given the "searing experience of the rebels' defeats, their inability to protect the population, and the terrible price that this failure entailed," eyewitnesses had every reason to place themselves outside the guerrilla's ranks.[37] When one adds to this a natural, probably healthy mistrust of outsiders with notebooks or tape recorders, the exact historical relationship of the indigenous villagers to the guerrilla movement is not susceptible to transparent conversation in Guatemala.

In the United States, as well, there are good reasons for Guatemalan exiles to play down political commitment and experience of any kind. Pronounced memories of Guatemala's war years, for one, are stamped for most with the imprimatur of America's complex and shifting immigration statutes. Although many of the early Mayan claimants, given the widespread repression in their homeland, made "extremely sound" cases for permanent asylum, a combination of slackening war at home and quickening outmigration raised problems under U.S. law.[38] As immigration lawyers soon discovered, many of the entrants, aided by either well-meaning or not-so-well-meaning amateur advocates seeking the protective cover of the *ABC* cases (see Chapter 1) had filed what some immigrant lawyers called "happy farmer" applications—simplistic, often spurious claims that they had been peacefully cultivating their fields until one day violent outsiders (usually guerrillas—a designation presumably more acceptable to officials in both the sender and new host country) had arrived, threatened to recruit them, and effectively evicted them from house and home.[39] As attorney Phyllis Palmieri recalled, such applications were commonly filled out by *notarios* (notaries public) in the Hispanic community "by the thousands at $300 to $400 a pop."[40] Unfortunately, some of the claims were made so haphazardly that they could not stand up to scrutiny; often the applicants were denied refugee status and cited for deportation.[41] By the mid-1980s, in short, the story of indigenous victimhood at the hands of the guerrillas, authentic as it may have been in many cases, was also stimulated and legitimized by a utilitarian imperative.

There is no simple way to decipher the impact of powerful forces of war, political mobilization, and exile on the memory and narrative of those who ultimately sought both work and refuge in Morganton. But clearly, not everyone reacted the same way to Guatemalan violence, whether in Guatemala or North Carolina. On this point the comparison between Don Pancho and Efraín Martín on the one hand and Matías Tomás on the other is illustrative.

Like many others of his *paisanos* (countrymen), Matías found solace in a new world of evangelical faith. Although raised in a Roman Catholic family, he harkened to the words of a Protestant missionary, Andrés Basilio, in San Rafael in 1986. "He told us that the people must stop killing one another, that we must have patience, that [through faith] we would survive all that happened. . . . I am grateful to the Lord that He has saved me from worldly things. I have learned not to fight with the rich man who has his land. You can't rob him and take his land away. I am poor, they are rich, God has a purpose for us all. He has said to us, you are going to stay this way, you are never going to have many things, but you are not going to suffer."[42]

As an evangelical Protestant, Matías Tomás reflected a significant trend in Guatemala. Though dating to the late nineteenth century, Pentecostal sects (manifest in speaking in tongues, faith healing, and prophecy) exploded in size after the social dislocations of the 1976 earthquake, giving Guatemala the most concentrated and fastest-growing Protestant presence in Latin America. By 1990 an estimated 35 percent of the population identified as Protestant.[43] The phenomenon also developed in close relation to the political turmoil in the country. Pentecostalism received a significant boost from the top during the brief but influential regime in 1982–83 of General Ríos Montt, who revealed on assuming power his own conversion to the California-based Church of the Word. As the Catholic Church became increasingly identified as the chief (and thus most dangerous) institutional voice of opposition to the army's spreading repression in the countryside, the evangelical Protestant churches beckoned as seemingly safe havens for those wishing to steer clear of the contest for worldly authority. In reaction to both the political violence in the country and the search for an alternative personal path of self-reform and self-improvement, Pentecostal congregations and the broader charismatic movement (which spanned both nominal Protestantism and Catholicism) registered huge gains among the Guatemalan people.[44]

Matías vividly remembered the early walkout of the Q'anjob'al workers in 1991, as he did the subsequent labor upheavals of 1993, 1995, and after, for among all the first-stage Guatemalan arrivals, only Matías had never left Case Farms. Nor had he ever participated in a strike or in the union organizing campaign. "Those that have entered the union, they are my friends. . . . They want me to go with the union but I don't go with them. . . . When I left Guatemala, I accepted the Lord Jesus Christ and I can't return to the past. If I joined in a strike against my boss or the rich and my friends, then I would be returning to the past. But now I am a Christian and I can't fight against another person. . . . In the Bible, although I don't read, I know

Flight of the Happy Farmers

it says you can't serve two masters [here, he quoted Paul and Matthew]." Acknowledging that others in his church had reached a different opinion about workplace issues, Matías turned the other cheek in secular disputes. "If my countrymen hate me or criticize me, I don't care. I say hello to them and I love them." Following the news of his homeland on Univision, Matías saw a larger divine logic at work in the universe. "Right now we are in the last days. There are many signals. There is no peace," he said, quoting Matthew 24 and Revelations and continuing to preach. For Matías, participation in the social conflicts of this world ended in 1986, if not in the massacre five years earlier. His resignation toward secular authority was just that. He offered no homage to those with wealth and power; rather, he simply chose not to contest them. Without apparent malice, Efraín Martin said of Matías's loyalty to Case Farms: "He always had contact with the boss which was all the better for him."[45]

If Matías's stance represented one kind of pragmatic calculus of power by the weak, his brother-in-law, Diego de Diego, went one step further in utterly condemning political protest, whether in Guatemala or at the North Carolina poultry plant. Diego, a native of Lajcholaj, was only five years old at the time of the local wartime massacre. Yet, contrary to official reports, he insistently identified the perpetrators as "the guerrillas." Moreover, once he had followed other family members to North Carolina and begun work at Case Farms in 1995, he determined to steer clear of all union organizing activity. According to Diego, local conflict reflected in workplace stoppages and subsequent union activities had nothing to do with the Guatemalans. "It was the Mexicans, 'puros Mexicanos,'" he insisted, "who stopped the lines at Case Farms; we Guatemalans wanted only to work."[46]

The reactions of Diego de Diego and Matías Tomás to political and industrial authority were starkly different from those of Don Pancho, Efraín Martín, and other fellow villagers who first walked out of Morganton's poultry factory. Even if the latter (as they claimed) avoided direct involvement in the political struggles of their homeland, they had nevertheless learned a certain realpolitik of their own. They recognized power and the abuse of power, as well as the opportunity for resistance when it presented itself. Theirs was an outlook trained not so much for mobilization as for calculation and survival. Moreover, they did not look to outside authority or power for their salvation and protection, but to themselves and their own tight community of family and friends. There is, for example, the report of Don Hemstreet, a local veterinarian and thirty-year resident of Morganton, who recalled with wonderment a late-night encounter with

Don Pancho, whom he knew through his wife's assistance to the Guatemalan community:

> It was one of those chilly mountain nights and as we cut through a back street, across a part of town that most considered to be a bit on the rough side, as we topped a hill, we saw Pancho. Now it was odd enough to see anybody walking around that time of night . . . but this was the strangest sight I ever did see. There he was, his five children filing along in a line in front of him. He was bringing up the rear, a long switch in his hand, herding them like an old banty hen. We stopped and asked him if anything was wrong. He answered in broken English, "Teaching how to walk." That was all and off they went. Pancho is tough.[47]

Perhaps the Q'anjob'al workers listened to Don Pancho simply because he was one of the older workers and his sense of grievance was automatically respected by the others. Another possible clue, however, was presented in the Q'anjob'al town of San Rafael la Independencia during the summer of 1997. There villagers readily admitted that "the people here joined the guerrillas, and afterwards came the army. . . . It was not good." María Rosa Jiménez, Don Pancho's sister-in-law, remembered when her aunt left for the United States after soldiers killed her uncle at Lajcholaj. Many were killed, she said, a few by the guerrillas, the others by the soldiers. Likening Don Pancho's position to that of her aunt, she described him as a guerrilla activist who had had to flee for his life. Don Pancho himself expressed puzzlement at such evidence. "The people who know me best," he insisted, "know that I was in Florida during the problem times." In Morganton, fellow San Migueleño Andrés Pascual (who asked Don Pancho to serve as godfather to his youngest child) offered a final coda to the discussion of the Q'anjob'al political past. On the one hand, Andrés allowed that the guerrillas were "very strong" in San Miguel; on the other hand, he maintained that none of his Q'anjob'al acquaintances in Morganton had ever been involved. Pressed further on whether Don Pancho or others might have had such experience in their younger years, Andrés replied, "Uh huh, sí, bueno, pues [well], you never knew about it when someone went into the mountains."[48]

The hesitations and contradictions reflected in the testimony of Don Pancho and his fellow villagers are typical of indigenous narratives about violence in Guatemala and other parts of Central America. Anthropologist Kay Warren, who studied the Mayan village of San Andrés Semetabaj across three decades of national upheaval, noted the particular ways that

Flight of the Happy Farmers

Inside Diego de Diego's two-room home in Lajcholaj.

Matías Tomás at home in Morganton beneath the Guatemalan national
symbol, the quetzal, and slogan, "the Country of Eternal Spring."

locals represented the terror they experienced: "Most described the situation as something rural communities were caught in but not of their own making. . . . The language was often veiled or oblique, often condensed into fragmentary observations with unspecified agents. The listener was expected to fill in the obvious: the Mayas were involved in the opposition and that the government was trying to eliminate the Maya leadership. Those unable to deal with strategic ambiguities were by definition strangers with whom it was not wise to share information."[49] Likewise, in his investigation of the memory of La Matanza, the 1932 massacre by government troops of some ten thousand peasants, mostly Indian, following a rural uprising in El Salvador, Jeffrey L. Gould found a marked discrepancy between the events as historians reconstruct them (where Indians played important roles in the peasant revolt) and the stories subsequently related to him by indigenous eyewitnesses (which identify only Ladinos and Communist outsiders as rebellious agents). Invoking the social-psychological power of shame, Gould concluded that "the fear of Ladino power has suppressed indigenous agency and fragmented collective memories of 1932."[50] Like Warren's and Gould's interlocutors, immigrant testimony in Morganton tended to occlude past historical agency in the face of the pragmatics of present-day survival. Yet, the same people's pattern of behavior told a different story.

On balance, the first, brief walkout of Guatemalans at Case Farms is emblematic of the larger mystery attending the plant's new immigrant workforce. How is it that a group of workers "on the run" from outside authority, people who claimed not only no political allegiance but also no awareness of the formal political conflicts going on around them, would have the temerity to stand up to their bosses on a specific grievance? Even accepting the testimony of the Q'anjob'al as being more historically "acted upon" than "acting up," it is obvious that as a group they set limits to what they were willing to endure in a specific situation. As such, their actions at Case Farms resembled millions of other informal work protests in the United States. It is true that the Q'anjob'al protest passed quickly into history. A group at St. Charles Church, on hearing of the dismissal of some of their new parishioners, first went to Father John Toller to ask him to intervene. When he proved unsympathetic, Legal Services sent a letter to the company accusing it of violating the "right to organize" provisions of the National Labor Relations Act. Company officials, probably more worried about losing a new labor force than the legal issues involved, took a conciliatory approach. Blaming the whole affair on miscommunication, they

Flight of the Happy Farmers

sought to reach the disgruntled workers, some of whom had already begun work at a turkey plant miles away or returned to Florida, and offered them their jobs back—on the old terms—with the promise that higher wages would be forthcoming, little by little.[51] According to Matías Tomás, "many said that the company gave them something for the time that they lost but others said that that was a lie." Although a few strikers returned immediately and others never did, Don Pancho and Andrés Pascual were among some eight to ten workers who drifted back to the plant nearly a month after the walkout. Like most of the early Q'anjob'al recruits, however, they stayed only until they found less arduous jobs in the area's furniture industry. Reflecting his own accommodation to the powers that be, Tomás said of those he still considered his friends, "They got angry [*se pusieron bravos*]; it was better that they not come back."[52]

Spontaneous in generation and inchoate in organization as it was, this first conflict with the new immigrant workers at Case Farms did not dissuade the company from implementing its new labor recruitment policy. Rather, like an old-fashioned schoolteacher, management applied a mixture of firmness and patience in hopes that its new charges would learn a timely lesson. As personnel manager Norman Beecher recalled telling the workers' Legal Services lawyer: "I want them, I don't have a problem, [tell them] to come back to work." Yet Beecher also sought to instill a respect for company authority. "They were the best cleaners I'd ever seen, but I didn't raise their pay . . . I just couldn't do that."[53] As a "people-oriented person" who had himself "come up the hard way," he wanted to give the new workers a chance to prove themselves. Still, there were limits. Reflecting the larger industry point of view, Beecher (who left Case Farms before the union fight erupted) proudly declared that he had never worked in a "union plant": "The personnel manager's job is ten times easier in a union plant than a non-union plant. There's nothing you can do without going through a steward. He's the one that controls the people. . . . Everything's controlled by the union—the benefits, any kind of policies that are drawn up. They do it all. . . . When you're unionized, you can't go out on the floor and deal with the people, you can't do it. That's bad. Then it's no longer human resources, it's union resources."[54]

3

How the Dead Helped to Organize the Living

"We didn't organize anybody," a LIUNA representative in the Morganton campaign of 1995 recalled. "There was union there before the union got there."[1] It was a long way, in terms of social movement building, from the quick walkout by some twenty Q'anjob'al at Case Farms in 1991 to the co-ordinated strike of a several-hundred-person workforce in May 1995. In the meantime, not only had the labor force become overwhelmingly Spanish-speaking and Guatemalan Maya, but also both in composition and attitude the Maya of Morganton themselves had changed. From an exotic fringe constituency within the town's laboring community, the new immigrants in less than a decade had advanced in numbers, confidence, and leadership. The community's self-assertion was on display in two new flash points of conflict at the poultry plant, sandwiched around an abortive attempt at a broader social movement.

The first eruption occurred in May 1993, when approximately one hundred workers stood up in the plant cafeteria and refused to work unless the company addressed a list of alleged abuses—including unpaid hours, the lack of bathroom breaks, poor working materials, and unauthorized company deductions for safety equipment like smocks and gloves, as well as inadequate pay. On this occasion, the plant managers summoned local police, and fifty-two workers were charged with trespassing. Of the arrested workers, all but a handful were Guatemalan. Following mediation by law-yers from the local Legal Services office and state labor officials, the workers agreed to go back to work and Case Farms dropped all legal charges. The 1993 incident "almost" drew the interest of organized labor. On a tip from attorney Phyllis Palmieri, a representative of the United Food and Com-mercial Workers (UFCW) visited Morganton to check out the situation but apparently found insufficient grounds to develop an organizing campaign.[2] Even as the workers returned to the processing lines, however, the sources of conflict went untreated. Shop floor resentments continued to smolder, giving rise to a more sustained strike two years later.

Meanwhile, the protest briefly took another form. Within a year of the May 1993 strike, some Case Farms workers had enrolled in an organization, La Raza Unida Indigena de America (Indigenous United Race of America), which called itself by its acronym RUIDA, a play on *ruido* (noise). Led by Mexican American *abogado* (unlicensed legal advocate) Richard Trejo, who had recently arrived in Morganton from the Southwest to live with his mother-in-law, Edna Barbarough (see Chapter 1), RUIDA quickly became a holy terror to the established allies of the Hispanics in town. Blaming other community leaders for "selling out" the workers in the May 1993 settlement—a charge exacerbated by the company's firing of ten workers for insubordination the following November—the tough-talking Trejo appealed to his base of a few dozen Mexican and Guatemalan workers as a kind of Lone Ranger of the immigrant poor, an *asesor de la gente* (advocate for the people), as one adherent put it.[3] RUIDA made headlines in July 1994, when it convinced Case Farms workers not to meet with a state Department of Labor investigator who was following up an unfair labor practice complaint based on the ten workers' dismissal. In the same period it convinced a Guatemalan team to withdraw from a citywide soccer tournament on grounds that it could not cooperate with tournament organizer John Wanless, and it blasted a local Human Relations Commission forum for its lack of Hispanic representation.[4]

Altogether, the 1993–95 interlude, as Phyllis Palmieri noted, was a "bad time." "There was poor communication with the Latino community. . . . There was discouragement on the union [UFCW]'s part." Worst of all, in her view, there was Richard Trejo, whom she speculated privately might have been a company agent: "To me he was like a provocateur from the 1960s— a leftist who does the job of the real source of oppression."[5] The "noise" RUIDA made locally did not last long. When the INS began in early 1995 to tighten up on asylum applications whose preparation Trejo had made his chief enterprise, he left town almost as mysteriously as he had arrived a little more than a year earlier.

The second workplace confrontation occurred in the spring of 1995. On Thursday, May 11, Guatemalan workers in the "live bird" area stopped work when a request for a bathroom break was allegedly denied. After briefly huddling together and refusing to resume their operations, they quickly designated three young male workers (later dubbed the "trés muchachos") to approach site manager Ken Wilson with their grievances regarding arbitrary supervisory control of bathroom breaks as well as increasingly stressful line speed, continuing deductions for work gloves, and chronically low pay. Instead of talking to the group of three, Wilson had them arrested for trespassing. After a weekend of uproar within the Guatemalan community, a plantwide shutdown ensued—announced at a Monday morning rally of approximately three hundred Guatemalans outside the plant gates—lasting four days. Though the protesters agreed to return to work following threats to replace them en masse, their strike produced the first tangible response from the company, including reinstatement of the three arrested workers, dismissal of one particularly obnoxious supervisor, and promised installation of new microwave ovens and drinking fountains in the plant.[6] Even more importantly for the long run, the revolt, in attracting the attention of the outside world, brought the Guatemalan workers into more sustained contact with the forces of American trade unionism.

Tellingly, however, it was not the fiercely independent and war-ravaged Q'anjob'al but the comparatively urbanized and politically quiescent people from the tiny *municipio* (county) of Aguacatán who were at the center of the extended buildup to unionization in Morganton. As Mexican-born Carlos Salido, who had joined his uncle at Case Farms just five days before the 1995 walkout, recalled with only slight exaggeration, "The only people that were in the strike were us [Mexicans]—and the people from Aguacatán."[7] Not only was the strike of 1995 an Aguacateco (as I call the town's residents) affair, but also the evidence suggests that a new Aguacateco-run leadership group had been established by the time of the 1993 in-plant disruption.[8] In part, this ethnic angle on the Morganton events may simply reflect a temporary numerical preponderance within a chain of ethnic succession into the town over time.[9] By the mid-1990s an estimated three hundred Aguacatecos—roughly twice the size of the Q'anjob'al contingent—had settled in Morganton.[10] Yet, the evidence suggests that the explanation goes beyond mere numbers. At the most general level, non-Mayan observers of the Guatemalan community in Morganton readily contrasted the relatively "urban" sophistication of the Aguacatecos to the "backwardness" of their more isolated rural cousins, the Q'anjob'al.[11] With only slight exaggeration, participants described the 1995 strike organizers as "strictly Aguacatecos."[12] What, then, were the sources of community mobilization and solidarity among the migrant workers from Aguacatán?

Like most towns in the department of Huehuetenango, Aguacatán is nestled between steep mountain ridges. Both its size (in 1994, with 33,000

How the Dead Helped to Organize the Living

residents, it was the fifth largest population center in the department) and its proximity to the departmental capital (according to Spanish practice, also named Huehuetenango) had made this verdant, well-irrigated valley a more bustling agricultural and commercial center than its more inaccessible Q'anjob'al neighbors.[13] The local *campesinos* (peasant farmers) had long been caught in a vise of forced day labor, working on the coffee plantations to supplement the meager plots that they could cultivate on their own. They were able, however, to take advantage of the absence of Vagrancy Laws (officially abolished by the progressive national government in 1944) to enter commercial agriculture—tomatoes, onions, and especially garlic were the favored crops—when a road to the valley was completed in the early 1950s. For the first time a small indigenous middle class appeared, and campesinos began to stay in the valley rather than engage in the seasonal migrations to the lowland coffee plantations. Significantly, too, schooling was extended to far more Aguacatecos than in more remote centers like San Miguel Acatán.[14] By the 1960s and 1970s Aguacatán was experiencing its greatest socioeconomic advances: not only were agricultural cooperatives reaching international markets with the local garlic crop, but also 1970 marked the election of the town's first indigenous mayor.[15]

These economic and political developments slowly eroded an earlier ethnic division within the town. The minority ethnic population included substantial numbers of K'iche' settlers (an estimated 33 percent of the population in 1993) who had moved in from the east along the highland slopes leading out of the valley, a tiny pocket of Mam-speaking émigrés (2 percent), and Ladinos (10 percent) who comprised both a landholding elite and a laboring class. The Awakateko-speaking majority, however, was itself internally divided. As a result of a late-nineteenth-century amalgamation of two valley settlements, the "Chalchitekos" (34 percent) lived on the eastern side of the village plaza and church courtyard, while to the west resided those who called themselves the "Awakatekos puros" (21 percent).[16] All but indistinguishable to the outsider, until the past few decades the two groups maintained separate *comités* (community governments), endogamous marriage patterns, some small differences in vocabulary, and different brocaded designs on the women's *huipiles* (traditional blouses), not to mention attitudes of mutual suspicion.[17]

Modernization in Aguacatán brought a general melting of older customs, hierarchies, and antagonisms that one anthropologist of the region summarized as "a revolt against the dead." Control of property in Aguacatán, as in other Mayan communities, descended from the father to sons via

Awakateka and Chalchiteka women in Aguacatán, Guatemala.
Note the distinct neckline designs of their huipiles.

an incremental division of land over time, or "installment inheritance."[18] But the cult of the fathers touched more than property ownership. "[Aguacatecos] believed that their parents and grandparents did not give up their authority and power when they died, but instead continued to take an active interest in the affairs of the living." The dead, by this reckoning, insisted on the practice of the *costumbres* (traditional customs and rituals) to honor their continuing presence; to this end, *shamanes* (native priests) were summoned to interpret messages from the dead about events and relationships in the living world.[19] Most important were the fiestas that lasted for several days and involved "parading the statues of saints through the pueblo in procession, getting drunk on hard liquor, listening to marimba band music and dancing"—as well as the serious business of communal meetings where local and interfamily grievances were aired and resolved.[20] Organization of the fiestas was carried out by the *cofradías* (ritual brotherhoods), presided over by an authoritative set of ruling elders. To be sure, this entire network of traditional Indian social organization had been long subordinated to Ladinos, who controlled the town's government.[21]

Amid other economic and political changes, this regime of folk Catholicism gave way to new religious divisions between the traditional religious system, missionary Catholicism, and evangelical Protestantism. The change

How the Dead Helped to Organize the Living

Courtyard of Aguacatán's Catholic church with traditional altar for
folk Catholic or costumbre prayers at right.

was heralded in a tide of Catholic and Protestant missionary activities in
the 1950s: even the death of a Maryknoll priest in a plane crash in the region
in 1955—interpreted by *costumbristas* (practitioners of Mayan folk Catholic
rituals) as an omen and punishment—did not reverse the growing foothold of the modern-day faiths. Among Catholics, the *catequistas* (catechists
allied with the priest and the official church) triumphed over traditionalists
in the 1960s, winning control of church property and the use of the local
saint's image in holiday parades. The conversion of Ti'x L'un, the son of
the ruling elder of the Aguacateco traditionalists, to Catholicism, symbolized an important turning point in the larger revolt against the dead.[22] That
Ti'x L'un's son, Gabriel Rodríguez Yol L'un (or "Padre Gabriel") would
enter the priesthood and subsequently serve as the town's *sacerdote* (priest)
sealed the cultural transformation. The result, by the late 1970s, was a community split less by ethnic or religious divides than by specific economic
conflicts as well as a growing Pan-Mayan resentment against centuries of
Ladino domination.[23] As in other indigenous communities, Indian self-
government, existing in uneasy relation to official politico-administrative
authority, increasingly took refuge in informal *comités cívicos* (community
committees) that addressed specific local needs.

Important if not impartial witnesses to the "modernization" of Aguacatán were Harry and Lucille McArthur—Canadian-born Protestant missionaries, Wycliffe Bible translators, and trained linguists—who lived in the valley from November 1952, three years before the first Catholic priest took up permanent residence, to 1981, when they were dispatched on a new mission to the Solomon Islands. The McArthurs arrived in Aguacatán a year after Mam-speaking Protestant missionaries failed to communicate with the Aguacatecos. Within six months of their arrival, the McArthurs—following a pattern already established for other Mayan languages and aided by 78 rpm records and little hand-wound record players—had begun transcribing the indigenous language into the Latin alphabet and Spanish spelling forms.[24]

At one and the same time, the McArthurs promoted literacy and a conversion process that depended, as they saw it, on rescuing the Aguacatecos from their fear of the dead. As Lucille observed: "They really were afraid of the dead spirits. All of their *costumbres* were to appease [the spirits], so they would be left alone. Harry went up to the graveyard one time with a witch doctor whose son had stolen from him. He went up to the graveyard to do *costumbre* on the grave of his mother and father, specifically to ask them not to get involved." Harry made use of his careful study of Mayan folklore as well as Christian doctrine in his approach to the local villagers:

> We used their own terminology—things like the word "stishwatz." "Stish" means "in exchange for." "Watz" is "face." To greet someone you would say "bombewatzer" or "how is your face?" But face doesn't really mean face, it means your whole being. It's a representation of your whole self. And so animals like these chickens who were killed and their blood caught and burned on an altar—this was in place of that person who it was being offered for. It was called "stishwatz." So we used that for terms of sacrifice in the Old Testament. And we said that Jesus Christ was God's son, a special person who was God sent to Earth. He was their "stishwatz"—he died and gave his blood for them. They picked that up very well.[25]

In both a spiritual and a secular sense, the McArthurs—like their Maryknoll–Catholic Action counterparts—played a significant role in the development of Aguacatán. Many future teachers and Mayan language promoters learned Spanish under the McArthurs' tutelage or with the aid of their Bible translation and accompanying primers. That over five thousand students were attending local primary schools and nearly five hundred were enrolled in secondary schools by the early 1990s owed something to the missionaries' literacy crusade. Nor could one doubt their religious influ-

How the Dead Helped to Organize the Living

ence. After a mere year and a half, the McArthurs had made about seventy converts; by the late 1970s evangelical Protestantism had enrolled nearly a quarter of the local populace, and by the mid-1990s approximately sixty chapels were scattered across the township.[26] Yet, with a hint of wit borne of a sharp anthropological eye, Harry McArthur hesitated to claim the entire evangelical flock as true Christians. "Their original belief system," he explained, "was based on materialism. All of their prayers were concerned with protecting their flocks, making corn grow, etc." To this end they engaged in an elaborate set of sacrifices, demanding of both time and resources. "Many of them," Harry suspected, "moved from one religion to another because it was much cheaper to be an Evangelical than to be an *Ajpon* [Awakateko word for costumbrista]. . . . It was also cheaper to be Catholic than to be *Ajpon*," he quickly added.[27]

If the combined forces of missionary religion and economic modernization initially dislodged Aguacatán's traditional ways, Guatemala's civil war and its aftermath of economic stagnation and out-migration further corroded older communal identities. Overall, according to a 1997 study during the war years, some 300 to 450 people were killed in the district (mostly by the army) and thousands fled, at least temporarily.[28] The fact that General Ríos Montt was a former resident of Aguacatán did not save it from the army's "scorched earth" policy against guerrilla infiltration in the early 1980s. Local schoolteacher Emiliano Rodríguez Castro recounted the worst of the wartime scenes in 1980–82:

> They [army soldiers] burned farms, corn, clothes, everything. The people filed down from the mountain villages—women, men, children, dogs, hens, all the animals, fleeing from there to here. I had an aunt, they massacred her whole family, that affected us psychologically. There was no peace. It was a difficult time for Aguacatán. It's difficult to see exactly who belonged to the guerrillas, for they didn't say. I have friends now who say, "I was a guerrilla, I was in the movement, and we did it because it was a cause, we had to do something." [About them] I cannot be sure. But, yes, certainly, there were *compañeros* who indeed were active.[29]

Yet the impact of the violence was uneven. Compared to its effect on the territory of other Highland Maya like the K'iche' and the Q'anjob'al, the war had a less devastating presence in Aguacatán. While Chalchiteko aldeas communities to the east end of the municipality (which were also physically contiguous to K'iche' territory) as well as several K'iche' mountain villages faced the wrath of government soldiers, both the town center and the entire western or Awakateko area largely escaped retribution.[30] Víctor Hernández, a resident of an Awakateka *cantón* (political district) near the town center, recalled a brother who had been working elsewhere in Huehuetenango but returned to his native Aguacatán in the mid-1980s because of the relative stability there. "In general," said one resident, "there was not that much contact with the army or the guerrillas. The town was a bridge to other towns, and the military and the guerrillas would pass through with not much contact."[31] Rather than cause a mass exodus, the strains of the wartime siege in the Aguacateco countryside accumulated more slowly.[32] For decades dating back more than a century, conflicting land claims and assertions of communal autonomy among valley villages had erupted into sometimes violent conflicts; now the cloak of national civil war only exacerbated these ancient feuds.[33] The fractious times likewise turned up the heat under a host of personal and business quarrels often fueled by a sense of *envídia* (envy) among neighbors.[34] As Padre Gabriel explained: "There were many difficulties with rents or with disputes. It was [sometimes] difficult to say whether conflict was between the army and true guerrillas or not. The context of the war allowed these things to happen. People would accuse others of being guerrillas or with the army and they were persecuted or killed. . . . When someone was killed or kidnapped, it could be said that they were a guerrilla, but perhaps it was over a dispute." In one of the worst reported incidents, a dam safeguarding the irrigation of precious garlic-producing fields was blown up by the estranged residents of a neighboring aldea.[35]

A combination of wartime conditions and personal conflicts accounted for Aguacatán's first political exile. Marcelino López Castro—the eldest of eight children in one of the town's most accomplished Awakateko families, head of the local garlic and onion cooperative, and nearly a candidate for mayor in 1980—was serving as appointed commander of the local PAC, the civilian self-defense patrol established by Ríos Montt for counterinsurgency duty in 1982. At least as Marcelino told it, the position was more political than military: he never engaged the "enemy" and remembered arresting only one aggressive drunk. Others suggested that the local patrol was sufficiently lax in internal discipline to allow guerrilla sympathizers to slip in and out of their regular patrol duty.[36] Yet, sometime in 1984 an army lieutenant had spied Marcelino drinking in a local cantina with a suspected guerrilla with whom he had been trading in the garlic business. In the middle of the night Marcelino and two friends were dragged to the mountains to be executed. Breaking out of a neck restraint and eluding

How the Dead Helped to Organize the Living

a hail of bullets, however, Marcelino escaped and was able to hide with relatives in the city of Huehuetenango and then seek refuge in the capital, where Amnesty International ultimately brokered a political asylum to Canada in 1986.[37]

Whatever their direct toll, the war years interrupted Aguacatán's earlier socioeconomic dynamism. For one thing, a struggling, ever-expanding rural population increasingly migrated to the town center.[38] In the meantime, no industry or manufacturing had surfaced in the district, and farmers complained of declining crop yields, which were variously blamed on lessening rainfall, deforestation and erosion, an infestation of worms, and a soil "burnt" by chemical fertilizers.[39] By 1994 only 24 percent of township households had electricity, and only 30 percent possessed indoor plumbing (50 percent lacked even outhouses, and only the town center had a sewage system). It was against the background of such economic stagnation and unmet social needs, rather than in a direct response to military action, that many Aguacateco men prepared to leave their homeland by the late 1980s. The importation of cheaper, foreign-grown garlic and onions—the former from China, the latter from Mexico—into the Guatemalan market in the 1990s only further eroded the traditional base of local agriculture.[40] In the case of the Aguacateco exodus, in short, these were not families on the run so much as men of diverse ages trying to support their families—including wives, children, and parents—from afar.[41]

How the pre-migration experience of the Aguacatecos may have contributed to their reactions once in Morganton requires a closer look at individual cases. Let us first meet several of those who became active in the labor protests. More than 60 percent of those arrested in the 1993 disturbance were in their twenties or younger, but among the more "senior" activists were Paulino López Castro, age forty-eight, and Francisco Fuentes, age thirty-five, both names that would be heard from again among the Aguacateco community in Morganton. Paulino López, a campesino with only two years of schooling, had fled Guatemala in 1987 shortly after his brother Marcelino's dramatic escape to Canada. Paulino's flight was not directly triggered by his brother's problems; rather more important was a sudden collapse in the garlic market. In addition to a disastrous investment in imported specimens from Chile and Taiwan and rising competition from Mexican and Brazilian imports, internal dissension crippled the cooperative's leadership in which Paulino had taken an active part. It took him eighteen days to reach Aguacateco friends in Oregon and Washington where for several months he picked fruit. Several years of agricultural labor followed, with Paulino seasonally cycling between the Northwest and the West Palm Beach, Florida, area, while also working in occasional forays to visit family back in Aguacatán. In early 1993 word of indoor work in a more temporate climate drew Paulino, like a cousin and a few other Florida friends before him, to Case Farms.[42]

Among the Aguacatecos Paulino López recognized on arrival were the brothers Francisco and Oscar Fuentes. A clever and energetic man, Francisco, the elder brother, probably had more to do with the rising concentration of Aguacatecos in Morganton by the mid-1990s than anyone else in town. From his arrival in 1992, Francisco, who seemed more confident than his confreres in Spanish and in generally handling social contacts with the outside world, was looked up to by other Guatemalan workers.[43] It was Francisco Fuentes, for example, who organized a regular van service back to Florida to haul *paisanos* (fellow countrymen) to Case Farms. In an informal arrangement with the company, Fuentes, by his own account, charged people $20 for the ride and a $30 "referral fee" for a job in the poultry plant; over the course of a few years, he took credit for transporting nearly three hundred workers to Morganton.[44] Others reported that he also received up to $50 per worker from the company for his services.[45] Once the newcomers arrived in town, it was Fuentes again who helped them locate in trailers that he had rented.

Such a "caretaker" role, however self-interested, induced Francisco Fuentes to take some responsibility for the treatment of "his people" in the plant. With their three *compañeros* sitting in jail following the initial confrontation with management in 1995, the brothers Fuentes organized the first community meeting outside Francisco's house on Sunday, May 14. According to witnesses, more than two hundred Aguacatecos showed up and vowed that no one would return to work on Monday. As one strike participant recounted, it was "Oscar Fuentes and his brother Francisco" who "called together the people—the Aguacatecos."[46] Oscar was most often cited as the "ideologue" and more powerful speaker, while Francisco exercised quiet but commanding authority within the community.

Morganton was not the first place where Francisco Fuentes had shown both bold community leadership and entrepreneurial ambitions. A lay Protestant pastor possessing confidence and unbridled self-expression, Francisco openly acknowledged his active, if temporary, involvement with the guerrilla movement back home, including friendship with two men who were later executed by the army. Pressed into service in 1976 by a

How the Dead Helped to Organize the Living

cousin who was already a guerrilla leader, Francisco, who used a pickup truck to deliver produce from the family plot in the Chalchiteko aldea of La Estancia to local markets, became a valuable "supply man" and "organizer" of new guerrilla outposts in distant villages. Yet, even amid the turmoil of armed struggle, Fuentes looked out carefully for his own survival. According to his testimony and that of his high-school-aged son, Max, Francisco maintained good relations with local men who had been recruited into the army and willingly complied when his truck was commissioned for army maneuvers. As Max related (in English), "My dad was a leader with the guerrillas and then he was a leader with the army also . . . but when the army found out he was goin' both ways, they decided to take him out." On a leak from an army friend, Francisco quickly left Aguacatán for a less-agitated climate in nearby Chiantla. Continually pressured to return to guerrilla action or face the consequences, Fuentes finally exited the country for the United States in 1987. The guerrillas, according to Max, had promised his father that "they were gonna win and once they did they were gonna get the president out and then the guerrilla leader was gonna, you know, buy him a house in the capital . . . [but] he knew they wasn't gonna win." Although he experienced unsettling moments at the U.S. border, where he was twice detained and once sent back to Mexico, Fuentes's future in the United States was "saved" by a Quaker human rights network that finally landed him work and lodging with a wealthy family in Visalia, California. From this contact, as well, Fuentes began to pick up some English-language skills that dramatically separated him from most of his kinsmen. Among the earliest Aguacatecos in Morganton, he was attracted by an alternative to the constant, often frustrating search for construction and agricultural labor jobs.[47] That the ex-guerrilla would emerge in Morganton as a modern-day mixture of *padrone* (Italian labor recruiting boss) and *cacique* (Latin American Indian boss) — alternately exploiting and defending his fellow immigrant workers — suggests the inadequacy of such time-honored dichotomies as "resistance" versus "accommodation" in making sense of individual responses to real-life settings.

The ideological roots of the Guatemalans' labor protests are hard to define. So far as Paulino López knew, for example, none of the activists had any prior political or labor experience. That they invoked the term "huelga" in 1993 and again in 1995, he attributed to a general awareness of strikes on coffee plantations and recurrent teachers' strikes, as well as the famous Guatemala City Coca Cola strikes that stretched across the decade of 1975–85.[48] Paulino spoke repeatedly of the strike as a matter of "reclaim-

Parents of Francisco and Oscar Fuentes by their *milpa* in Aguacatán.

ing our rights" and of the workers' appeal to "our human rights." When pressed to explain further, however, he mixed a "rights" discourse (which arguably had come to prominence in Guatemala only since the recent U.N.-sanctioned peace process) with reference to an older Guatemalan—and indeed larger Latin American—tradition of state-sanctioned patron-client relations.[49] "In the [coffee] plantations," recalled Paulino,

> the owners always tried to mistreat the workers, and thus the Aguacatecos learned to defend themselves by stopping work. . . . In the late 1960s and early 1970s . . . there was a government "labor inspector" to regulate such things. In the case of a work protest the people would call for the inspector, always he helped the workers. This tradition existed in Aguacatán, it is remembered in Morganton even after two decades of military regimes. Yes, the people always kept in their minds that they must activate their human rights, that's just what happened here in Morganton with Case Farms.[50]

As Paulino's testimony accurately described, Guatemala's labor courts, established by the revolutionary government of Juan José Arévalo in 1944 and continued in subsequent regimes, provided a means of appeal—despite many obstacles in practice—for poor campesinos to those with real power and authority.[51] The *lack* of such mediated redress in the United States and blatant *disrespect* for workers as human beings seems to have provided the

How the Dead Helped to Organize the Living

crucial opening for worker organization (and subsequent unionization) at Case Farms.

Abstract notions of justice and injustice, of course, did not determine who would stand up to authority in a showdown. Here, for example, the connection between Paulino López and his nephew José Samuel Solís López suggests the significance of distinctive family ties and influence within a larger field of social action. José Samuel, in fact, was just twenty-six years old when he followed his uncle from Guatemala to Morganton via Indiantown some months after the 1993 strike. An avid reader and informal student of politics, he quickly identified with what he called the "uprising" of 1993 and instinctively linked himself to the events leading to the 1995 strike and its unionizing aftermath.[52] "That day the compañeros in live chicken [weren't allowed] to go to the bathroom. They said we will stop working. [Three] Aguacatecos started the work stoppage. . . . They scolded them and locked them in a room. They didn't have any communication with the others. There began the struggle. We came to see what the situation was with our compañeros. . . . From that day to this we have been in a struggle. . . . We [Aguacatecos] are all united, no one is left behind."[53]

The politics of the López Castro family, on the whole, fit no conventional or predictable ideological map. An abiding idealism salted with individual ambition played off against a cynicism rooted in an extended cycle of national violence and political corruption. José Samuel's schooling in the capital from the age of twelve had been facilitated both by his uncle, Marcelino López Castro, who served with the center-right Unión del Centro Nacional (UCN) Party of soon-to-be-assassinated Jorge Carpio and an older cousin, Marcelino Pérez Castro, who had run for mayor of Aguacatán on Ríos Montt's center-left Christian Democratic (DC) Party ticket in 1974. (In June 1998 Marcelino Pérez was elected assistant mayor of Aguacatán on the National Advance Party—PAN, the centrist, national ruling party—ticket.) That these two relatives (and close friends) joined separate political parties, in fact, was no accident. As Marcelino López explained, both young men initially had hoped to be teachers, "but here in Guatemala to get a job as a teacher is not easy. You have to give money to somebody, to the minister of education. . . . So I said to Marcelino [Pérez], 'You go to this [DC] side, and I'm going to this [UCN] side. If the side you're running for wins, you're going to get a job. If my side wins, I can get a job.' . . . So his organization won, and he got his job."[54]

Like his elders, José Samuel set little stock in party labels or enduring organizational loyalties. He acknowledged that he, like many other

Aguacatecos, expressed early sympathies for hometown hero General Ríos Montt—who, in the exaggeration of popular folklore, derived from peasant stock just like themselves. What had attracted (and still attracted) many Aguacatecos to Ríos Montt was his crackdown on criminals and government corruption. Paulino López readily recalled the pledge that each civil servant took under the Ríos Montt regime: "No robo, no miento, no abuso" (I do not rob, I do not lie, I do not take advantage of the people).[55] What likely also initially appealed to José Samuel's family was the general's very public conversion to evangelical Protestantism in the late 1970s.[56] But after noting President Ríos Montt's *mano dura* (hard hand) toward the Maya, José Samuel became disillusioned with the country's political leaders: "I have observed and analyzed a lot. They always say they are different, but they are not. . . . Democracy is a good thing, but there is no democracy in the Central American states. A country has to be free to have democracy and we do not have this. [Democracy means] to live free, work tranquilly, to have work and enough salary to live."[57] The López Castro family, like other Guatemalan *indígenas* seeking maneuvering room in a restricted public sphere, ended up looking locally to the individual or party label that best seemed to serve the moment, rather than to any grandiose, national vision of sociopolitical redemption. That same spirit of pragmatic commitment to the immediate struggle rather than a transcendent cause conditioned the participation of Paulino López and José Samuel in Morganton's labor disputes just as it did in politics back home. For them, "democracy" was less an abstract *political* principle—let alone a matter of electoral procedure—than an ideal *social* world where ordinary people could live in peace with a degree of economic security.

Another factor affecting the López Castro clan—and certainly distinguishing them from their more pious neighbors—was an eclectic, live-and-let-live religious identity. Paulino, for instance, had converted to the Protestant Church of his mother-in-law in Aguacatán, but he had found no formal church to his liking in the United States. Both for him and for José Samuel, religion had become more of a private than a public force. "I feel," he said, "that the word of God protects us in this world. I feel that this help from God protects us from *las cosas malas* [the bad things]. I am not a proper [Christian], I am not perfect, but I feel part of that [Protestant] church."[58] Back in Aguacatán, Paulino's successful political nephew, Marcelino Pérez Castro, allowed that his family had equally journeyed over the religious as well as the political map. Marcelino's grandmother and mother were Protestant and his father was Catholic. In middle age, Marcelino himself in-

How the Dead Helped to Organize the Living

clined toward the ancient Maya spiritualism of costumbre. Following the Mayan calendar, he anticipated another "great turning" in the world in 2012; in the meantime, he insisted, religious differences did not matter in local political decision-making.[59]

Whereas family ambition and political experience help to account for the prominence of Paulino and José Samuel López and of Francisco and Oscar Fuentes in the events of the émigré Guatemalan community in Morganton, the explanation for others who rose to the fore among the Case Farms workers is somewhat different. For some, education appears to have served as a crucial formative experience. In a country where the Mayan majority comprised only one in four primary school students, one in ten secondary school students, and one in twenty university students, the educated child of indigenous parents owed his gift (for boys were better rewarded than girls in this respect) to determined, and often courageous, teachers both within and outside the local community.[60] Aside from the most basic issue of lack of access to schooling, one of the persistent problems for Mayan children was a national educational system that had long ignored and disparaged their native languages, forcing indigenous students to adjust abruptly to *castellano* (Spanish).[61] Beginning in 1965, after a constitutional revision allowed for using the native languages within a larger Castilianization process, *promotores bilingües* (bilingual promoters or native Mayan speakers who had completed the sixth grade of primary school) were assigned to schools across the country, even though they did not qualify for the salary of *profesores titulados* (certified teachers). Aguacatán was fortunate to be in the front rank of such bilingual initiatives, with schools reaching out to the aldeas with both youth and adult literacy programs as early as 1966. The Bible mission of Harry and Lucille McArthur further aided local literacy efforts.

After setbacks during the civil war, local bilingual initiatives begun in the mid-1980s were institutionalized in 1990 with the creation of the Instituto Mayance, a K–12 secular establishment dedicated to reaching poor children, with classes in Awakateko as well as Spanish for girls and boys.[62] According to the school's assistant director, Víctoriano Rubén Raymundo, the institute had always aimed to build character in its students: "perhaps not to become a leader, for a leader is someone extraordinary, but perhaps as a supporter in an organization, as an *apoyo* [helper]." "Everything is a chain," explained Rubén of the lessons of a Mayan heritage that his school tried to implant. "I don't put myself in my own place but rather I put myself in the place of others. Before making my own decision, I ask for the opinions of others. For that reason we use the [first person] plural and not the singular." The institute's graduates were trained to become teachers, but under the economic pressures of recent years, many had left the country for manual labor in the United States. "It's a shame," said Rubén, "for they are prepared to enter a profession."[63]

Félix Rodríguez (aka Roberto Mendoza), who threw himself into the Case Farms strike of 1995, became a union committee member, and later served as one of three protagonists in a union-led hunger strike a year later, was a product of the chain of Aguacateco bilingual education. Born into a "puro Awakateko" family of campesinos in the aldea of Cantón in 1973, he had begun school at age eight, spending half the day studying and the other half working with his father in their fields. At age twelve, he was able to attend the newly opened Instituto Mayance from which he graduated in 1991. Forced by economic circumstances to suspend plans for a higher degree, Félix, then twenty-one, arrived in Morganton in 1995 encouraged by reports he had received from an older brother. "'It's like in our pueblo at home,' he told me, 'a season of heat, a season of cold, it's almost the same.' 'When you arrive,' he said, 'you're not going to miss [home], for it's the same. Here [in Morganton] there's no big city, no big buildings, it's like Guatemala.' And when I arrived, [I saw that] he was right."[64]

Félix entered Case Farms just as the Guatemalans' grievances had reached the boiling point. "The situation in the plant was hard," he remembered. "If someone got sick, they [the company] didn't care." On the "whole-bird" line where he was working, "there had been two persons, they now put only one. The people started to realize what was happening. . . . Everything started when some of our people who had been working there for some time said that we must change that, and we started to support them. When they stopped the line, everybody stopped work, then [the leaders] said we should leave. When we got outside the only person there to help us was Daniel Gutiérrez, he must have talked to the padre [Father Ken Whittington]. From there we walked to the church. For three days or so we met in the church." Quickly, Félix involved himself in the daily meetings that developed out of the strike into an organizing committee for the union. Previously, he had known "practically nothing" of unions. "I had no idea and no interest until this problem arrived at Case Farms." What he did acknowledge, however, were prior beliefs in "social justice," which came "in part from the family and from the Instituto [Mayance], because there they taught us, they trained us, there they helped us to know what is good for our people. We [Aguacatecos] were formed by our indigenous ancestors

How the Dead Helped to Organize the Living

so that we must give of ourselves for the good of those who come after us . . . so that they can take some advantage of it, because I know that I have children, brothers, and that some day they will come here."[65]

The lament offered by Rubén Raymundo about the social scrambling of educated Guatemalans induced both by a militarized state and a failing economy is an important one. Ironically, however, while inevitably "proletarianizing" Third World émigrés who might originally have anticipated professional positions, the global marketplace also sprinkled the itinerant international labor force with people of considerable wit and uncommon experience. Víctor Hernández, for example, went to Morganton in May 1995 and picked up a job at a local furniture factory, "because it was too hard to live in Guatemala economically, with no land, no house, with illness and other problems." The son of a campesino father scraping a subsistence from a mere three *cuerdas* (one cuerda equals about one-tenth of an acre) of land, Víctor had the initial good fortune to be recruited in the fall of 1983 by the La Salle Brothers School, a Catholic institution in the departmental capital of Huehuetenango, which gave scholarships to indigenous students—a school that was subsequently renamed for its North American director, James Arnold Miller, assassinated in political violence only a year before Víctor arrived.[66] Víctor left Huehuetenango in 1988 with an accountant's degree and, motivated by the spirit of solidarity, worked for five years with a long-standing agricultural cooperative in Aguacatán. The job was "good," but it did not pay enough to support a family of two children. Víctor tried other options in other towns, but "there were too many professionals who could not find work."

On his arrival in Morganton, Víctor was immediately sympathetic to the union cause. Because of the regional tradition of cooperatives and other forms of community self-help, the idea of union was "not new to [the Aguacatecos]." Moreover, the union structure and function, as developed after the strike of 1995, seemed perfectly logical and matter-of-fact: "Yes they [Case Farms Aguacatecos] are very organized. They have a union-elected leadership committee. They organize work stoppages. One time a worker injured his arm and the company did not want to compensate him, claiming it had occurred outside of work. But the committee these people had formed was called and responded. The people united. The people decide whether to organize a work stoppage and thus give the committee the strength to approach management. The people form a completely united group that management cannot ignore."[67]

Most Guatemalan emigrants, of course, had neither the formal educational background of Félix Rodríguez or Víctor Hernández nor the familial apprenticeship to leadership skills of José Samuel or Oscar Fuentes. Yet other forms of modern-day political learning were evident among the worker-émigrés. For Marta Olivia Gálves, a native of Guatemala City who fled the country in 1989 after guerrillas abducted her and other passengers from a bus, practical political knowledge initially derived from events very much "on the ground." Raised by her mother and an uncle in a wood and plastic lean-to shelter, sometimes going without even the daily ration of tortillas and beans, Marta was forced to repeat first grade and then to quit school altogether at age twelve to work in the market. She nevertheless cherished memories of individual freedom and community improvisation from her urban girlhood. A "big talker" who liked to "run in the streets" with her friends after school, Marta also captained her girls' basketball team. Among her prize possessions was a school uniform she bought to wear for parades on the national *día de la libertad* (independence day— September 15); she wisely bought it "big" to last, taking down the hem a little each year and occasionally refurbishing the dress's colors with store-bought paint.[68] But Marta Gálves had her biggest learning experience in the aftermath of the Guatemalan earthquake of 1976, which left 22,000 dead, 77,000 injured, and over a million homeless. For the survivors, co-operative local efforts made up for the government's absent or utterly corrupt rebuilding programs.[69] As Marta recounted: "Many people died and our neighborhood became a ravine and we took a football field, we occupied it. We organized ourselves to keep this land. . . . We struggled with the government. We lived there four years. We improved that land with the help of the government. . . . Later, when the football players returned[,] the government told us we had to leave. . . . We asked the government for other land. They sold us new land. We won. They built us facilities. I have this [property] there today."[70]

Drawing on long-established community survival skills and the leadership of colleagues with a variety of pre-migration experiences, the Morganton workers had already made important organizational gains in the period leading up to the 1995 strike. Their advances were registered on a variety of levels. Guatemalans, for example, enrolled by town of origin in a vigorous, all-Hispanic soccer league. Similarly, Guatemalan religious life proliferated with the establishment of two Hispanic evangelical churches in addition to the growing constituency at St. Charles Catholic Church, where Guatemalans monopolized a weekly Sunday Mass, launched a separate charismatic meeting on Saturdays, and established distinctive Mayan choir groups that practiced at all hours of the weekend.

But one of the more sophisticated signs of community organization emerged only weeks before the strike of 1995 with the formation of an Aguacatán burial society. Common among other "hometown associations" of Central American migrants, the idea of sending bodies home to Aguacatán for burial sprang directly from Paulino López.[71] When his twenty-one-year-old son Remigio died of illness in Indiantown in 1989, "friends, countrymen, Aguacatecos . . . gathered the money to send his remains to Guatemala . . . there began the idea to organize." Following the death of Roberto Vicente Rodríguez in an automobile accident in Morganton in April 1995, Paulino drew on his earlier experience to institutionalize the self-help network through a *directiva* (leadership committee) on which he served as treasurer. From this experiment came the beginning of a nation-wide network of directivas, which regularly responded to local appeals for help: "Here in Morganton we [Aguacatecos] have maybe one hundred apartments. The directiva decides how much we ask from each person. It is an obligation. All the people are in agreement. Twenty-five dollars or twenty dollars from everyone. The money is collected and we telephone other directivas in places like Missouri, and other states; from these places come a list with twenty or thirty Aguacatecos, and it comes with all the money in a money order."[72] The money is sent home to the widow, mother, or closest kin. If there is more than is needed for the transportation and funeral expenses, it is expected to be used for the family's welfare. Paulino emphasized that the sense of mutual obligation is strong among the Aguacatecos.

The bible of the directiva was the *libro de actas* (record book), effectively a census of all community members in good standing, as recorded by the organization's secretary. Inspection of this richly bound volume revealed an introductory section of rules relating to such issues as aid for cases of sickness, accidents, and special status (i.e., lowered assessments) for the newly arrived. Requests for aid from non-Aguacatecos were constitution-ally treated with sympathy but were held to be strictly "voluntary." The first "census" for the deceased Vicente Rodríguez, for instance, raised over $13,000 from 257 persons, with husbands and wives paying separately. Con-tributions were received from ten states as well as Canada. There was no overt penalty for individuals who neglected to make their directiva contri-bution, but symbolically such transgressors alienated themselves in a significant way from their kinspeople. "The community," explained Paulino, "is not obligated to send their remains home, this is our condition."[73]

Back in Aguacatán the burial society created by the émigrés also had a presence in the life of the community. Marcelino Mendoza Velásquez, for example, was one of five people from town district El Calvario who attended to messages, sent through Paulino López, from the Aguacateco network in the United States. In case of a death abroad, Marcelino, who had a laboring job with the town (among other tasks, he helped to organize the weekly market day), received a phone message, collected a wired monetary commission, then picked up the body at the Guatemala City airport.[74]

As the contact center between the home and the diasporic community, the Aguacateco directiva clearly carried an emotional and symbolic significance beyond its practical functions. As such, the fact that the "secretary" of the Aguacateco directiva in 1995, José Samuel Solís López, was also on the strike committee and subsequent union organizing committee suggests the seamless connection between the Case Farms struggle and the "official" interests of the community.

The growing mobilization of immigrant workers thus drew on older sources of allegiance. Among the Aguacatecos, the power of the ancestors—as witnessed both in the formal organization of a directiva and more informally in the mutual loyalty of Aguacateco workers to each other and to a new set of "elders" as community leaders—had, in important ways, survived modernism's "revolt against the dead." The adversity of outward circumstances, the challenge of finding a toehold in a new land, perhaps acted to reinforce communal ties, creating a hedge against an individualism heedless of its effects on one's closest neighbors. In most cases, after all, a migrant's welfare in the United States—finding a job, a place to live, and transportation to work, as well as acquiring a work permit or green card—depended on an interlocking community network. Cemented by a common language, family and old friendship ties, or merely common memories of home, this sense of belonging to a group derived from an identity constructed across generations, an identity that conjured up the dead and made it important for the dead in North Carolina to return to Aguacatán for a final reconnection with their ancestors.

If the Morganton Aguacatecos clearly drew on ties forged in their home country, then the migration experience seems also to have affected the definitions and boundaries of Aguacateco fellowship. In particular, the traditional separation between "pure Awakatekos" and "Chalchitekos" all but vanished in the new land. An older view of ethnic character differences, to

How the Dead Helped to Organize the Living

José Samuel (right) and Mario Ailón on their Morganton front porch, 1998.

be sure, still surfaced in the memory of Paulino López, a local "westerner" or "puro Awakateko": "[Awakatekos] have a calm character. For example, if I have a problem with you, between our sons, or between animals, we say, 'Friend, I have a problem with you' [or] 'How much can I pay you for the damages?' This is the calm way. On the other hand the Chalchitekos are full of rancor. 'You did something bad to me. I am going to take revenge on you.' . . . They like to argue, they are organized, and they easily joined the guerrillas." Yet, even in the Old Country, the divisions, according to Paulino, possessed decreasing significance: "They [the Chalchitekos] are another race [in origin], but they have become Awakatekos." Whatever fine distinctions remained in the homeland simply no longer operated abroad. In Morganton, avowed Paulino, "we respect that we are all Aguacatecos, we are united."[75] Serving alongside José Samuel on the union organizing committee in 1995–96, for instance, was his nineteen-year-old housemate Mario Ailón, a Chalchiteko. The Fuentes brothers, likewise, were Chalchitekos. The Morganton directiva, moreover, made no distinction by ethnic (as opposed to linguistic) origin. "We are in a country that is not ours," José Samuel explained.[76] The sense of immediate solidarity, of mutual support for the self-respect and welfare of family members, fellow countrymen, and other workmates, proved a strong bond uniting the early union partisans at Case Farms.

How the Dead Helped to Organize the Living

At the same time, migration provided opportunities for a break with the community. The individualist (or better, family-centered) quest for the American Dream might easily grate against a larger set of restrictive, collective obligations. Especially within the circuitry of American factory workplaces with their vaunted aversion to unionism, all the more extreme in a southern setting, individual ambition might be satisfied most quickly in defiance if not outright opposition to communal norms. Two competing forms of "Americanization" seemed to beckon to Aguacatecos in Morganton. One brought them into a tight circle of community connectedness and at the same time linked them to a U.S. version, however frail, of workplace mutualism in the form of a labor union. The other drew more on the power of a swaggering individualism and constituted an updated enactment of the "revolt against the dead."

But no simple traditional versus modern, "Mayan" vs. "Hispanicized" or "North-Americanized" identity adequately explains the base of support for the workers' movement in Morganton. The fact that the "modernizing" Aguacatecos forged the path toward labor organization suggests that some degree of socialization in modern-day politics, education, and social relations proved indispensable to the newcomers. One Morganton union activist credited the stress of Guatemala's thirty-year war as a source of newfound solidarity among the indigenous migrants: "We have suffered a lot here in Guatemala, more than the people in the U.S. . . . We have learned how to defend ourselves. Many of the people were members of the guerrillas, they trained them, they taught them how to organize, to fight for their rights. Other people were in the army and there they taught them how to defend their rights, how to organize themselves."[77] Yanira Merino, a former Salvadoran leftist who arrived in the middle of the May 1995 strike to serve as chief union organizer for the poultry workers, was taken aback by the Guatemalans' unpredictable transference of past experience to a new "political" situation. A few workers on the organizing committee, she recalled, had guerrilla experience, but most had been in the army or the civil defense patrols. "Some say that they are anticommunist . . . and many have a high level of understanding within the organization. [For example,] Francisco Ortiz Mendoza Jr. I think he was up to corporal, and he was very proud to have served for the Guatemalan Army. He showed me pictures and everything."[78]

When it came time to support the strike and the subsequent union at Case Farms, both recent understandings of movement and organization building as well as more deeply rooted communal loyalties came into

How the Dead Helped to Organize the Living

Returning home: gravestone in San Rafael la Independencia,
Guatemala, with the inscription, "Santos II died in Lowland, TN,
October 18, 1995, U.S.A."

play. The Aguacateco burial society—at once a cause and effect of community solidarity—fits into a long-held practice of working-class immigrant groups in transition. Though perhaps seldom (for practical reasons) established to return bodies to the homeland, the burial society was a common early assertion of mutualism among other immigrant groups and working people in general. In their classic study *Industrial Democracy* (1897), Sidney and Beatrice Webb noted the almost universal presence of "mutual insurance" within nineteenth-century trade unionism; this "'benevolent' or friendly society side of Trade Unionism" normally covered "the provision of sick pay, accident benefit, and superannuation [retirement] allowance, together with 'burial money.'"[79] In the United States, moreover, many workers' distance from home seems to have added to the importance of proper burial rites. As early as the 1880s, Italian mutual aid societies focused on "free medical assistance, unemployment compensation, and burial."[80] In Ybor City, Florida, Spanish cigar makers enrolled in El Centro Español in 1891 "paid twenty-five cents a week in return for social privileges and death and injury benefits."[81] In function and structure, perhaps an even closer historical match to the relations of Morganton mutual aid society and labor union movement lies in the experience of the Jewish *lansmanshaft* (fellow townsman society). "The many-sided *lansmanshafts*," wrote Moses

Rischin, "uniting the features of the Old World burial, study, and visitors-of-the-sick societies, bound the immigrant to his shtetl [Eastern European Jewish village] and birthplace."[82] In more recent years, the United Farm Workers of the 1960s also started out as a self-help association that offered burial insurance to its members.[83] Among modern-day Central American emigrant self-help groups, the "burial" function has particularly defined the Guatemalan associations.[84] In sum, both the history of workers and the history of immigrants—two overlapping groups struggling for some minimal security and decency of treatment in an often adverse environment—point to the centrality of burial rites as a basis of communal identity and self-protection. The Morganton Aguacatecos reaffirmed a more universal message—the dead not only make demands upon the living but also sometimes serve as their most efficient community organizers.

How the Dead Helped to Organize the Living

4

No One Leader

Marc Panepinto, the thirty-year-old chief organizer for the Laborers International Union of North America, arrived in Morganton on Tuesday evening, May 16, 1995, following the second day of the Case Farms strike. His reactions to what he witnessed the next morning are etched in his memory as "the most exciting day I've ever had in the labor movement." As Panepinto recalled it:

> There were four or five hundred people showing up in front of the plant. The entire Latino workforce appeared with banners and signs and just stood there across the street from the plant in this silent demonstration. They walked out on Monday, and then forty-eight hours later this group of Spanish-speaking workers—actually only about 10 to 15 percent of them spoke Spanish, most of them spoke Indian languages from Guatemala, which I wasn't aware of until that night—I was just awestruck by the fact that this group had organized this strike and demonstration with no help from any sort of institution except the church and a legal-aid attorney in Morganton.[1]

The visitor's amazement continued at the strike organizational meeting he witnessed Wednesday night at St. Charles Church. "I'm still under the impression that these people speak Spanish," Panepinto replayed the scene,

> and this meeting starts and I see the room begin to break into clusters—there's like fifteen or twenty people here, there's thirty people there—and I start asking what's going on. Well, the meeting was being translated into seven or eight Guatemalan dialects. Oscar [Fuentes] and Marta [Gálvez] and other workers are speaking, and there are little leaders of each group who are translating from Spanish into native dialects. I'm just blown away. I'm walking around the room trying to listen to these native dialects, and I'm thinking where am I? Here we've got people who are indigenous people. These are people who are not sophisticated to any level at all and who are in this country, a foreign country.

They are two languages removed from speaking anything close to English, and they are fighting this employer. I just couldn't believe what I was seeing.[2]

As the union professional recognized, he had entered a social movement already in midstream. Indeed, his own challenge over the next few weeks would be less one of organizing workers than whether he could sell LIUNA's potential services as a strategic ally to an already-constituted local leadership. For their part, Case Farms worker-leaders, together with a few key community allies, faced the inverse question: Should they transform a local workplace-related protest into a union drive, and, if so, was LIUNA the right union to bet on? Both points came down to organizational leadership. As it happened, the struggle at Case Farms generated some extraordinary leaders—and some extraordinary conflicts of leadership. What is more, a movement begun among indigenous Guatemalans quickly blossomed out to affect a larger workforce, in the plant and beyond. While the Maya remained at the core of the struggle, as the irreducible rank and file of the unionizing drive, other agents—including LIUNA organizers, the union's local attorney-advocate, Mexican émigrés, and even a few native-born workers—emerged as key contributors to the local workers' movement.

The 1995 strike at Case Farms was formally triggered when three workers from the "live bird" line—Francisco Vicente (age nineteen), Juan Mendoza (age twenty-two), and Víctoriano López (age twenty-one)—complained to management about poor working conditions at the plant and were summarily fired. "It's the same situation as [three] years ago," a representative explained to the press, citing problems of line speed and inadequate bathroom breaks. According to the reported remarks of a translator brought in to deal with the Mexican and Guatemalan workers at Case Farms, the incident began Wednesday, May 10, when Juan Mendoza asked to go to the bathroom. "The supervisor said he didn't want to let Mendoza go, but he could have 30 seconds. [Mendoza] said the supervisor timed him. . . . He made it back to the line OK; but it upset him to be treated like that." Mendoza told his friends about the experience and found they had complaints about the pace of the production line that led to a group grievance session with management on Thursday. Personnel director Ken Wilson maintained that company officials only ordered the men arrested when they refused to return to work or leave the plant. "There were about 10 employees involved in the incident, and these three were the only ones who refused to go back to work or leave the premises," Wilson explained. "We had no choice but to do what we did."[3]

The next step from labor's side occurred outside the workplace over the weekend after the dismissal of the trés muchachos. A growing mobilization gathered strength at meetings on the property of Francisco and Oscar Fuentes and subsequently at St. Charles Church. Attorney Phyllis Palmieri's notes from that period indicate that by the beginning of the following week, she was summoned to offer legal advice to a brewing rebellion:

> It was explained to the workers that work stoppages and strikes inside the company were not protected activity under the [National Labor Relations] Act. The activity on Thursday could be in a gray area. Deciding to strike on company property would clearly be a prohibited sit-down strike and would not be protected activity. This could result in mass arrest such as occurred in 1993. The workers decided to elect a committee and requested that this attorney go with them to the office of Case Farms and meet with Ken Wilson on Monday, May 15, 1995. At approximately 10:30 P.M. on Sunday, May 14, 1995, I received a call from Daniel Gutiérrez indicating that the workers had decided to strike and would be demonstrating outside the Case Farms plant on Monday, May 15. The workers requested that I be present to meet with them and company representatives, if the company agreed to do so.[4]

It is not surprising that the Case Farms workers called on Palmieri for assistance. Not only did she have practical legal advice to offer about the extent and limits of the rights of workplace picketing and protest, she had more experience with labor organization than did almost anyone else in Morganton. Born in eastern Pennsylvania in 1948 to a blue-collar family, Palmieri identified herself as an "ordinary working-class kid" who married a "UMW [United Mineworkers Union of America] lawyer" and raised three sons. Less ordinary was the fact that in 1979, after briefly pursuing a career in social work, Palmieri began a dual life as law school student by day and coal miner by night. While completing her law degree in 1984, she continued to work, in the footsteps of her Sicilian grandfather, a full ten years in the mines as a belt operator. One of a dozen women in an eight-hundred-person workforce, she emerged as a strong union advocate as well as a feminist and all-around "progressive" in her politics. Separated from her husband by the early 1980s, Palmieri ultimately faced a choice, she explained, "between coal mining and the law." She chose law, finding work in New

Mexico and Martinsburg, West Virginia, before an advertisement for a prisoners' rights project ultimately drew her to Morganton in 1989. Within a year she had moved to Catawba Valley Legal Services, the place from which she was first summoned to what would become a nearly consuming practice on behalf of the Case Farms workers. Palmieri first established sympathetic contact with her new Central American neighbors not via legal issues but through two of her sons. In the spring of 1990 their classmates included a son of Pancho José and a daughter of Andrés and Juana Pascual.[5]

Advocacy for working people seemed to come naturally to Palmieri. "I went to Catholic school when I was young. It's something [Legal Services director] John Vail and I used to talk about, that people in legal services are either Jewish or Catholic. Where does this heat-seeking-missile approach to finding justice and fairness and equality come from? I've long thought that it comes from Catholicism and also from a working-class background. . . . The Gospel of St. Matthew, the activist among the apostles, that is a guiding force in my life, both how I try to work in the union and how I practice law." Active recommitment to Catholicism in her case, in fact, derived from two relatively new influences on her life: spiritual counsel from Father Ken and a psychological battle with the effects of multiple sclerosis, the disease with which she was formally diagnosed in March 1996. "[Father Ken] brought me back into the church. I wanted to do that for my sons, so they could learn how to be who they were. . . . Father Ken was very supportive. He wants to expand the parish and include Guatemalans and Mexicans as well as divorced Catholics."[6]

Palmieri likely planted the first seed of unionism among the Case Farms workers. As she remembered, "it [unionization] was one of the options discussed on Mother's Day—Sunday night, May 14, 1995. Daniel [Gutiérrez] had asked me to come; the idea was to let people know what their options were. . . . People were saying, 'What can we do?' And all that could be said was, 'Well, you can go back to work. You can *not* go back to work. Or, you could organize yourselves into a group to negotiate the terms and working conditions under which you will work.'" In support of the union option, Palmieri contacted AFL-CIO attorney Michael Okun in Raleigh and asked him to dispatch a representative from the UFCW. In rapid succession, first UFCW and then LIUNA organizers arrived in Morganton, and by the end of the week, when the Case Farms employees returned to work, their leaders had already voted to organize themselves into the LIUNA-led National Poultry Workers Organizing Committee.[7]

It was a remarkable group that assembled at 7:30 A.M. on Monday, May

Flanked by strike leader Oscar Fuentes (left) and Morganton police chief Robby Williams (right), Daniel Gutiérrez interprets for striking Case Farms workers. Photo by Jeff Willhelm, *Charlotte Observer*, May 15, 1995.

15, to plan the strike. Palmieri's contemporary notes on the meeting mention the presence of translator Daniel Gutiérrez, Oscar Fuentes, Francisco Fuentes, Marta Gálvez, José Samuel Solís López, and unspecified "others."[8] Among these critical early actors in the workers' campaign, perhaps the Fuentes brothers most clearly signaled the complexity of such an effort. To be sure, their initial support proclaimed to the surrounding community that the grievances at Case Farms were recognized by the town's most powerful Guatemalan family.

Yet, Francisco Fuentes quickly disappeared from the ranks of the strikers. Though testimony varies as to whether he ever stopped work (he claimed that he did, but union loyalists insisted that he did not), by all accounts he had concluded his association with the protest by the end of the first week's action.[9] Fuentes himself has offered two, slightly differing, accounts of his behavior. In one explanation, he suggested that, unlike his spontaneous participation in the 1993 protest, he could not openly lead a workers' organization because of his dependence on company personnel manager Ken Wilson, who had helped him secure credit at a local bank and continued to subsidize his Florida recruiting runs. Once the strike was on, Francisco left

No One Leader

his brother Oscar, who had already displayed formidable oratorical gifts, "in charge" of the events. Things might have worked out well, he insisted, if only the union had not stepped in to inflame the situation.[10] However unorthodox the arrangement, even a skeptic like Phyllis Palmieri acknowledged its initial effectiveness. "[Oscar's] brother is Mr. Inside, he doesn't show up at any union meetings and works during the whole strike. And [Oscar] is Mr. Outside. Pretty powerful—we [the Fuentes] control what this workforce will do."[11]

With the passage of time—and his own departure from Case Farms—Francisco Fuentes adopted a more sweeping and categorical judgment about the entire "upheaval" at the poultry plant. It was a doomed effort from the start, the ex-leader mused. Though a "militant" and "unified" action might have extracted a real victory from the company "within two weeks," such discipline was never in the cards given the ignorance and inherent mutual suspicion among his own Guatemalan people. "As soon as the strike began, they were divided. The night shift crossed the picket line from the beginning. . . . It was just like in Guatemala. [They] offered corn to the guerrillas one week and [paid tribute] to the Army the next." "I had enough of them," Francisco, who had himself felt compelled to switch sides in Guatemala, thus explained his estrangement from the movement that he helped to create in Morganton.[12]

However the Fuentes brothers anticipated that their protest might end, events quickly developed beyond their control. Probably most important was the fact that Case Farms management showed no initial willingness to meet with the strikers or reconsider the dismissal of the trés muchachos. With the company standing firm and openly threatening to hire replacement workers, Oscar Fuentes and his compatriots on the strike committee began to look elsewhere for a solution to the conflict. Their objectives, they realized, would require more than a single protest or a one-shot walkout. Certainly by the third day of the strike, the leaders' thinking had coalesced around the objective of unionization. The increasing social polarization wrought by a continuing strike had, in fact, made impossible the kind of controlled negotiation among leaders that Francisco had counted on. Instead, once talk of a union began in earnest, Francisco, strike instigator, emerged as one of the strike's biggest and most aggressive foes.[13]

The loss of Francisco Fuentes to the community struggle was a bitter blow. His reputation quickly suffered as workers tried to account for what many regarded as a betrayal. "In the last hour he sold himself to the company," declared Mexican union stalwart Carlos Alberto Salido. "The first thing Francisco saw was the money," said José Samuel. "To be bought is the . . . devil. He sold his people and continued working." "He lied and deceived the people . . . it is his character to organize and then abandon the people," added Paulino López. "Before he was Señor Francisco, now he is different."[14] Félix Rodríguez indicated that the Fuentes' behavior cast a pall on the entire Aguacateco community. "We felt bad, *casi es como ver-guenza* (it's almost like shame)," he said. Then, in a way that suggested how fragile were the bonds of intercommunal unity among the indigenous Maya, he added: "The Fuentes are Chalchitekos, they're willing to fight for something but they also change their principles just for the money."[15] The common epithet hurled at Francisco behind his back was *vendido* (sellout).

In the aftermath of the 1995 strike, Francisco's relations with the sur-rounding community of Aguacatecos he had once led deteriorated further. A union partisan swore out a legal complaint that Fuentes had thrown a punch at him at work.[16] More significant, the Aguacateco *directiva* filed charges against him for insurance fraud following the death of Case Farms worker Juan Marquín Vicente, killed when struck by a van in his drive-way on September 4, 1995. Vicente, who regularly wired payments back to Guatemala for his wife and three children, was his family's sole means of support. Records show that Vicente was one of several Case Farms em-ployees whom Francisco had persuaded to list himself as the beneficiary on a $12,000 life insurance policy offered by the company to its employ-ees. A suit brought by Vicente's widow—prepared by Paulino López's son, Felipe, who entered Phyllis Palmieri's office as a legal assistant in 1998—alleged that Fuentes regularly recruited employees for the company at fifty dollars a head and told them "that since they were not U.S. citizens, they must designate [Fuentes] as the beneficiary," but that he "would be sure that their families received the money." The complaint noted that within a month of Vicente's death, Fuentes cashed in the policy for his own benefit, and that the company itself recognized the wrongdoing by subsequently removing Fuentes's name as beneficiary on other employee policies.[17]

While admitting no wrongdoing, Francisco readily acknowledged the personal cost of repeatedly cutting against the grain of community feeling. A formerly Protestant churchgoing family now found it more comfortable to pray at home rather than face the disapproval of fellow Aguacatecos. Francisco's son Max, a high school junior in spring 1998 who hoped ulti-mately to enter the Morganton police force or the U.S. armed services, stated that he had occasionally incurred scorn from other Aguacatecos on Morganton's city streets. "Well, see, they know my dad, they don't like my dad, and some, they don't like me either. Kids don't really care about it, it's mainly the adults."[18] As for the Vicente case, Francisco claimed that he was merely protecting the insurance money for the deceased's eldest son before "union lawyers" intervened and made communication with the widow "impossible." Francisco felt himself to be the victim within the transplanted Aguacateco community. In the midst of his poststrike and legal conflicts, he charged that vandals—whom he identified with the union and the directiva—cut down six fruit trees in his yard and stole a CD player from his car. "They humiliated him in the Guatemalan way," explained his son Max. "But my dad doesn't get intimidated easily."[19]

Aside from the problem of Francisco Fuentes, a unionizing strategy among the foreign-born Case Farms strikers was complicated by the fact that they were confronted with two unions to choose from. Of the two, any knowledgeable insider might have expected the United Food and Commercial Workers to prevail. After all, it claimed nearly 60,000 poultry workers already under contract in the United States and Canada, whereas the Laborers International Union of North America was brand new in the poultry sector. In addition, the UFCW had a base in North Carolina and prior knowledge of the Morganton poultry workers' problems, whereas LIUNA was not even an affiliate of the state's AFL-CIO. Finally, UFCW was not tainted, as LIUNA was, by federal monitoring for alleged mob influence.[20] Unfortunately for the UFCW, however, most Case Farms workers knew nothing of U.S. geography or of the history or current status of the U.S. trade union movement. What mattered in Morganton was who was talking to them and what he or she had to say. It did not help the UFCW, for instance, that its first envoy to town reportedly did not speak Spanish.[21] Though the two unions briefly attempted to cooperate, from the beginning there was no getting around a spirit of invidious distinction between the respective organizers. Marc Panepinto remembered his first encounter with the local organizing committee of Case Farms workers:

A guy from UFCW, a Spanish-speaking guy, gives a little pitch. People clapped and applauded. I don't know, I can't really recall what I said. I like to think of myself as an eloquent speaker, someone who can incite the crowd, and I gave a little five-minute talk. I just tried to convey to people the awe and wonderment I had had at what they had done, and how proud I'd been to be a part of it. I also said that my role there was to work for them: my closing was, "I'm here to help you and to work for you." I ended and I got tremendous applause. People clearly liked me as compared to the UFCW guy. So the Laborers' endeared themselves to them by what I had to say that night, and it was really heartfelt.[22]

In explaining their alliance with LIUNA, Case Farms workers spoke less often of Panepinto than of commitment to the union organizing process itself, a process that began even as employees returned to work on Friday, May 19, and Monday, May 22. On the advice of organizers from both unions, in fact, the workers had heeded the company's warning that failure to report back to work would lead to massive new hires. In turn, the company offered the mild concession that it would suspend trespassing charges and rehire the three workers whose arrest had triggered the strike. In addition, it promised to create a check sheet to ensure equitable distribution of bathroom privileges and announced plans to install new microwave ovens and drinking fountains. Finally, newspaper reports credited the subsequent dismissal of one particularly obnoxious supervisor to the strikers' impact.[23] On the one hand, the company had endured a walkout without once meeting with worker representatives, without addressing pay or benefit issues, and without making a substantial change in the break policy, which still placed crucial discretion in the hands of supervisors. On the other hand, workers had shown that they could stand up to the company with impunity. The struggle, for many of them, had not ended; rather, it had just begun. As early as Thursday, the fourth day of the strike, petitions circulated among the workforce calling for a National Labor Relations Board (NLRB) election to certify union representation for the strikers.

The move from organized protest to the sustained commitment required for a union drive also entailed a subtle shift in local leadership. The workers' testimony indicates that after the initial test of self-respect manifest in the walkout, the union organizing strategy beckoned as a higher, political project evoking ideals of justice and democracy even as it summoned its advocates to renewed struggle and sacrifice. At Case Farms, moreover, the union ideals were not associated so much with an office or emissaries based in Washington as with the charisma of one Spanish-speaking organizer on the ground. The initial shift in leadership at Case Farms thus involved a diminution of the role of the Fuentes brothers and simultaneous confidence in a crucial LIUNA representative—not Marc Panepinto but Yanira Merino, a volunteer, apprentice organizer "imported" on May 20 into the campaign from California. As Panepinto admitted, "Yanira brought it home for us."

Because of who she was as much as what she said and did, Yanira Merino raised the political stakes of the workers' strike in Morganton. Born in 1964 to a poor family (her father was a delivery man, her mother picked coffee and took care of the house) in a small town in El Salvador, she experienced at age twelve as a junior high student an all-too-quick immersion in the political violence of Central America:

> He was a math teacher. Very straight but he really helped us. He had ways to make us really want to study. He always encouraged us to try to see the history of our country, of our people. He used to say, "Don't just read the history that is in books, because that is controlled. Talk to your grandparents." He would always encourage us to go and help the community, collectively to do things. We never knew anything about him, just that he was strict but yet a good teacher. And one morning he was getting his classes [ready], and two, three men walked into our classroom and told him to go outside. He acted very calm, and the next thing we heard was shots. We ran out and he was there. I think that was a big impact on my life.

Soon, both Yanira and her older brother had become involved in the student associations surrounding the guerrilla resistance movement (FMLN) in El Salvador. "In my neighborhood I was part of the association, and from then on I participated in . . . demonstrations and doing graffiti." In 1979, fearing for their safety, Yanira's parents sent her and two younger siblings to live with an older sister already in Los Angeles. A year later, however, she returned to El Salvador to rejoin her older brother who was now a full-time revolutionary. In 1981 her fiancé was killed after being "disappeared" by right-wing death squads. Yanira spent the next several years in support work conducted variously in her home country, Mexico City, and Los Angeles. In 1985 she gave birth to a son. Two years later she was in Los Angeles training a group of American university students preparing to visit El Salvador when she was abducted, raped, and tortured by Salvadoran men who "wanted to set an example for other activists in LA." Determined to remain in the struggle, she returned to El Salvador, until—as a single mother of two in need of an income—she moved to the United States for good in 1992, the same year that the Peace Accords ended the civil war in her country. Yanira returned from El Salvador an FMLN partisan but educated more in the "slogans" of socialism and struggle than in any extended political understanding. "I came out of El Salvador at a time when you had to think with your own head, apply things to your own situation."[24]

As tough and experienced a political organizer as she was, Yanira had, in fact, just completed her first bit of union organizing USA-style when she arrived at Case Farms in 1995. She had taken a job at the Los Angeles's Ore-Cal shrimp-processing plant, a workplace filled with Hispanic immigrants. Given her strong English-language skills, she quickly worked her way up to quality control technician. Her unionizing efforts began, oddly enough, after she complained about a male worker with nine years' experience and he was summarily fired. "I was very, very unhappy," Yanira remembered, "because they used my complaint against the worker." Her breakthrough in organizing in 1994 was not with the female shrimp processors but with the skilled male machine operators. An unpopular company bonus plan combined with nepotism in the appointment of supervisors touched a raw nerve among the operators. "That was enough. After that, I said, 'Well, I keep saying union. This is the only way. I don't know what union means in the United States, guys, but I know union means that we're going to be united.' And so, there was a group of five of us and we got together and said, 'Well, they're going to fire us if they find out, but it will be worth it.' And that's how we started." As one of her early recruits later told a reporter: "When she speaks, you feel she means it. Not only that, she gives you a big smile that sends you into a trance." On November 18, 1994, two days after Yanira had returned from her sister's funeral in El Salvador, the Ore-Cal workers voted 89 to 14 to join the Laborers union. Then, seemingly flush with victory, Yanira recalled, "something funny happened, and this was how I learned how unions work in the United States. The company started pressuring us. They cut [our] hours. They moved me from quality control to clean the bathrooms; I cleaned bathrooms for six months. They moved the people they thought were ringleaders. You know, the misconception of management. They think that the workers don't think, that it's always the leaders; that without the leaders, the workers are nothing. So they put us in that situation." Against the advice of their own union representative, the Ore-Cal workers decided to raise the ante. About fifty workers descended upon an upscale restaurant owned by Ore-Cal in downtown Los Angeles. "There we were, about fifty of us, having lunch for hours at their tables. And all we were drinking is Coke and water, and we were making noise, talking union for four hours." Shortly after this confrontation, the company came to terms; by that time, however, the union had already dispatched its new star organizer to North Carolina.[25]

Yanira Merino arrived in Morganton with the task of recruiting strikers for a union drive. After huddling with the organizing staff—which included Southeast regional vice president Orlando Bonilla, a native of Nicaragua; and Case Farms worker Valentín Velásquez, an Aguacateco and former Guatemalan schoolteacher whom the union quickly enlisted on its side—she made her way to the Sunday soccer fields, where one could expect to encounter much of the local Guatemalan community. "I also like soccer, so I sat there with the guys and started talking with them about soccer. Then I asked some of them, how was the strike? Everybody was so happy, it was good, it was fine. . . . I got them to let me talk to one of the leaders, Oscar Fuentes. I met Oscar there and he gave the appearance of being a very strong leader. . . . He's tall, well-built, and he knew how to talk. He knew how to put the fire. So we arranged a meeting of Valentin and Oscar that night. The next day I went to visit [leaflet] the plant, then I started house-calling."[26]

With one eye on Oscar Fuentes and other Case Farms activists and the other on five UFCW organizers temporarily stationed in town, Yanira sought to consolidate striker loyalty for LIUNA. From the beginning it was obvious that Oscar would be difficult to corral. Yanira remembered him as "volatile," and she treated him with kid gloves: "I took over the [workers' organizing committee] meetings to answer questions, but I always allowed Oscar into the meetings." According to Yanira, a turning point in the wooing race between the two unions came when the UFCW circulated a leaflet linking LIUNA officials with the Mafia. The message, which suggested that the unions were more intent on destroying each other than fighting the company, apparently backfired. "I told the workers," Yanira related, "let's not lose focus. I don't know if Mr. Coia [LIUNA president Arthur Coia] is Mafia. He might be. Mr. Coia is not your problem, your problem is how much they're paying you."[27] To counter "corruption" images from another source, LIUNA organizers also made sure to refer to their affiliate as "la union," not "el sindicato," the latter term summoning up the state-endorsed labor organizations in Mexico that frequently collaborated with employers.

At a pivotal meeting at which they talked sequentially to LIUNA and UFCW representatives, the Case Farms workers posed a Solomonic question to Yanira:

They said, "If you were to have an election where you had the Laborers and the UFCW, the two unions and the company [i.e., no union] as options, what would you tell me [sic] to vote for?" I said, "You guys, I'll tell you this, vote for the UFCW but never vote for the company, because if you vote for the company they will screw you." The UFCW organizers had told them they had better vote for the company, because the Laborers were so bad that it was better to vote for the company than vote for the Laborers. . . . So I remember Mateo [Quinones] said, "You know, she told us because she thought first what would be best for the workers, not what would be best for her union." So the next meeting they came and told me that they asked the UFCW to leave. . . . The main thing was that the leadership was seeing that the workers were being divided. . . . You're talking with leaders; you're not talking with people who don't know, you're talking with leaders. They might not all know how to write and read, but they were natural leaders.

In the end Yanira's cultivation of Oscar Fuentes had paid off, for it was Oscar who reportedly barred the door to UFCW delegates at subsequent organizing meetings, a bias that, among other things, permanently alienated community mediator Daniel Gutiérrez, who had urged a position of nonpartisanship in the intra-union wars, from the strikers' cause.[28]

By the time of the NLRB union representation election in July, LIUNA had the field to itself. Within a few weeks of the end of the May 1995 strike, the UFCW had backed away from Morganton, at once recognizing LIUNA's better-consolidated position with the rank and file and apparently accepting a consolation prize of a deal at the top between the two unions: in exchange for "giving up" the Morganton plant, the UFCW acquired "sole rights" to a Perdue plant then under joint investigation. Facing a simple yes or no vote, workers handed the LIUNA a narrow but convincing victory, 238 to 183, or 57 percent to 43 percent.[29] A correspondent from the *Charlotte Observer* relayed the majority decision that "voting for the union was the only way to convince company officials to take their demands seriously." A pseudonymous worker representative emphasized that the main issue was "lack of respect": "When we would ask for something it would be ignored. They didn't care what workers needed to do their job well. We hope the union can force them to care. . . . [We] want to be paid a decent wage, be able to work in a safe environment and be able to do things like go to the bathroom when [we] need to."[30]

Although no one recorded it at the time, subsequent impressions suggested that the union electoral victory also reflected the continuing ethnic differences within the plant. Yanira Merino, for example, broke down political sympathies by place of origin as follows: Aguacatán (the single biggest group in the plant) was "overwhelmingly pro-union"; Q'anjob'al (the second largest group in the plant) was "mostly negative, didn't want to talk to us"; other, less numerous Mayan groups were "split," including K'iche'-Totonicapán ("mostly positive") and Mam–San Marcos ("mostly negative"). In addition to the more numerous Guatemalans, the Mexican workers ("very supportive") initially provided another key pro-union bloc. North Americans, approximately 20 percent of the workforce—or about one hundred workers evenly split between blacks and whites—and generally uninvolved in the May 1995 strike, likely also contributed little to the pro-union vote. White workers, bunched in slightly better-paid maintenance department jobs, proved especially difficult to reach.[31] Whereas local and ethnic markers helped to direct worker sympathies at Case Farms, gender apparently did not. "They were the same as the men, though I didn't talk much to the Guatemalan women," stated Mexican activist Juan Ignacio Montes, who arrived at the plant shortly after the union vote.[32]

For all the centrality of the Aguacatecos in the election victory, one who was missing from the union celebration was young Oscar Fuentes. Between pressure from his older brother and his own entrepreneurial ambitions, Oscar had dropped out of the organizing ranks shortly before the final balloting. Yanira Merino reconstructed what to her mind was a touch-and-go struggle for Oscar's soul:

> Oscar was younger. I think it was the first chance he had to work away from his brother. His brother had been like the figure, he controlled everything. This time was Oscar's turn though. He said, "[Francisco]'s wrong, we need the union." And he was a good speaker. . . . But in all the time we were with the committee and in general meetings, I kept saying, "Oscar, this is not a one-man job. This is everybody. You get tired. Most go back to Guatemala. So everybody has to be involved." That was the message that we had. Leaving everything to Oscar was not a good idea. You're always afraid to build that *caudillismo* [boss control]. Three weeks before the election he came and told me he didn't want nothing to do with it, and people started telling me he was spending a lot of time inside the office of the company. He didn't have nothing to do; the people in his trailer would not even open the door for him. [Once] he came out and told me, "Yanira, I'm not saying nothing against the union. I'm not saying go for it or go against, I just want nothing to do with it." And then the workers started thinking that he was bought; that the company gave money to him. Right after [the vote], he did have money to go back to LA.

Aside from direct company influence, however, it is possible that Oscar Fuentes misinterpreted certain signals coming from the union organizers he had initially befriended or even that he was caught in a union con game. Both unions, according to witnesses of the time, were at least holding out the possibility of economic rewards if not out-and-out cash offers to the rank-and-file leaders. Marc Panepinto remembered an informal bargaining session at which Oscar, in particular, demanded the high price of going on union salary as an organizer, a demand that was politely rebuffed:

> When I was trying to woo the committee early on I told Oscar and Francisco point blank, "You work in the plant and are a [rank-and-file] organizer. Our policy is that if you work in the plant we aren't going to pay you, but if something happens and you think you want to be a [professional] organizer, you can come with us." I clearly made that offer to them, but it was predicated on the fact that I didn't want them to get fired in order to get a job with us. Well Oscar wanted more than that. Oscar thought he was better than the people he was working with. He was clearly a leader as an individual but he didn't have the class consciousness that Yanira or Marta [Gálvez] had. For him this became sort of a grandstand; he was getting to do something cool that got attention. He wanted more—he wanted to be put on staff and he wanted money, and I was unequivocal about that. I said, "That's not going to happen. I'm not going to pay you to give me these workers." If you want my jaded perspective, Oscar was looking for a supervisor's job from the very beginning.[33]

In the end—whether feeling betrayed by a supposed promise not kept, paid off by the company, or simply pushed by his brother but unwilling to follow him into the face-to-face ignominy of vendido status—Oscar Fuentes had effectively abandoned the Morganton struggle to new blood. Once Oscar left town, Yanira recalled, "we started saying, 'No one leader, no one leader.' Everybody had to be a part of it. That's how we're going to come to have something, not have one person have it all. I remember [after he left] we had a meeting and [somebody] said, 'You know about Fuentes?' 'Yeah [I said], we know about Fuentes. But he's out of here.'"[34]

Even as a six-year, multipronged campaign for a contract opened in the wake of the victorious NLRB vote in Morganton, the workers left on the ground struggled to sustain their collective presence both in the plant and in the larger community. In the workplace, a combination of "quickie strikes" and work slowdowns combined with an extended two-week strike for recognition in August 1996 testified to the vigor of a movement otherwise officially ignored by the employer. Such events also reflected a de facto shift in the ranks of worker-activists. While a few of the original Guatemalan strikers continued to contribute to the unionizing effort, others left the plant, and in some cases the region or even the country, in response to personal imperatives. Among the workers who stepped forward in this often dreary period of meetings and more meetings punctuated occasionally by more dramatic actions was an eclectic, racially and ethnically mixed group that had its own distinct reasons for "sticking to the union."

Perhaps the most notable change in the postelection period of union activism was the disproportionate number of Mexicans versus Guatemalans in the rank-and-file leadership, a phenomenon variously attributed to several factors. Among the Aguacatecos, in particular, defection of the Fuentes brothers left both a temporary loss of confidence and a practical lack of English-language speakers who could interact with the union's newly appointed local legal counsel, Phyllis Palmieri, as well as other LIUNA emissaries from Washington. Though fewer in number (estimated at 10 percent of the workforce), Mexican and Mexican American workers operated with comparative confidence in the Case Farms multilingual, multicultural environment, stepping forward as natural intermediaries between Anglo authorities—in the union as well as in the plant and town government—and a "Hispanic" laboring class. In the subsequent rounds of company-union battles, therefore, the Guatemalan majority in the plant (including the union's Aguacatecan stalwarts) spoke less clearly in their own name than they had at the beginning of the conflict.

The most influential of the new additions to the union fold was undoubtedly Juan Ignacio Montes or "Nacho," as he was known to his friends. Born in a small town in the northern state of Durango, Mexico, in 1965, Nacho grew up in a campesino family of nine brothers and sisters. At sixteen he moved to Mexico City to attend high school, from which he graduated in 1985. With little economic incentive to seek a university degree, Nacho followed many of his friends as well as an older brother to the United States, initially taking a job as a dishwasher in San Diego. Over the next ten years, during which he returned to Mexico to marry and became the father of two daughters, he continued working in restaurants. But fear of gang violence led Nacho to look for alternatives. From a brother-in-law who had worked briefly at Case Farms, he learned not only of employment possibilities but also of a calmer community with comparatively cheap rents. Nacho and his family arrived in Morganton in January 1996, and he took a position at Case Farms as a quality inspector, a job not only with a few more cents in hourly compensation but also with the added advantage (especially for a future organizer) of comparative mobility within the plant. Nacho had arrived at a critical moment for the fledgling union movement. The company had ignored the union election vote and brushed aside workers' claims regarding a recent snow-induced shutdown.[35] Among workers, gnawing

94   *No One Leader*

Former Case Farms union leader, Juan Ignacio "Nacho" Montes,
at home in Valdese, North Carolina, 2001.

frustration at the lack of tangible results and continuing bitterness at the
defection of the Fuentes brothers left a leadership vacuum. Practically from
the moment of his arrival to his election as local union president in 1998,
Nacho emerged as perhaps the single most steady and dedicated union en-
thusiast at Case Farms.[36]

Despite the generally unfavorable circumstances, a few clues help explain Nacho's unshakable commitment to the union. A green card (or permanent residence status) acquired with the assistance of attorney Palmieri
in 1996 provided him from the beginning with a secure sense of rights
in his adopted country. But there was surely something more that motivated Nacho's activism. He reported, for example, that as soon as he joined
the union committee, he twice received supervisory offers but declined
them: "It's more important for me to be something for the workers than
be a supervisor." Whereas Nacho, like practically every other Case Farms
worker, had had no prior industrial experience, he had participated in a
strike—in his case, as part of the student movement in Mexico. The students had shut down the Collegio de Vachilleros twice in the early 1980s "to
demand books for the library and material for the labs." In these actions,
Nacho edged up to the leaders "so I could get the kind of experience of
being in the front." It was also in high school where he first encountered the

works of Karl Marx and other socialist writers. Though his direct exposure to left-wing groups dried up on arrival in California, Nacho, with a strong command of English, continued to seek out newspapers with a distinctly anticapitalist viewpoint. Interviewed in 1997 after continual stonewalling of the union by the company, he remained resolute: "The people are asking for more money. We want free safety equipment, more vacations, more sick days. The company is going to fight back. But we're going to make them sign the contract."[37]

Among those who would remain with Nacho and the union project through the 1996 strike and after were two other workers who had grown up in Mexico, Carlos Salido and Luís Alberto "Beto" González. Salido's contact with Guatemalans had begun as soon as he entered the United States at age nineteen, following high school graduation in Oaxaca in 1994. "Everybody was always saying, 'Let's go see El Norte.'" As he crossed the border with a group of friends at Nogales but with no particular destination, an Awakateko-speaking Guatemalan directed them to Indiantown, Florida. There, Salido worked briefly in agricultural and construction labor, sharing a house with six other Mexicans and thirteen Guatemalans, until another Aguacateco spoke of job openings at Case Farms in Morganton. Salido, who had joined the 1995 strike a mere five days after arriving in town, neatly captured the subsequent cycle of depression and renewal in the union ranks. In his view, "many people drifted from the course" following company recriminations against union activists. Salido himself was refused reemployment at Case Farms after he took a two-month work leave in Alaska in the spring of 1996. Nonetheless, he remained on the union organizing committee and was ultimately put on paid staff by LIUNA until he returned to Mexico in early 1998. As others either left the plant or defected from the union after the NLRB vote, it fell to a few stalwarts to maintain an organization. "Thanks to Juan Ignacio," said Salido, "we returned to raise up the people."[38]

Beto González, of Guatemalan birth and passport but raised in Mexico, rose to prominence in the local workers' ranks beginning with the 1995 strike. Arriving in Morganton from Indiantown, Florida, in search of an alternative to farm labor, he jumped into the worst job in the plant—"live bird"—in January 1995 at age twenty-eight. After several early arguments over mistreatment by a supervisor, he was transferred to "whole bird," where he discovered that other workers were also complaining about "injustice" in the plant. As it happened, the first day of the 1995 strike Beto was "on holiday," for his birthday. But he quickly learned of plant events from the "whole-bird" strike leader, Carlos Salido: "'Listen Luís,' he told me, 'we're on strike, no one's going to work.' I said, 'Well, alright, I'll help you, I'm not going to work either.' I began to get interested until little by little I became completely involved [in the workers' movement]. The struggle was on."[39]

When the workers staged another strike in August 1996—this time to force the company to sign a contract—Beto had already entered the re-shuffled union organizing committee. To bring "greater pressure" on the company, Beto said, he took the lead in organizing a hunger strike in front of the plant that also enlisted the Aguacateco Félix Rodríguez (listed in the press as "Roberto Mendoza") and Neil Pezzulo, a visiting Glenmary priest-in-training. Beto learned of the hunger strike in Mexico, as one of many tactical options in an uphill struggle. For him, the tactic carried no particular spiritual inspiration ("I'm Catholic but not very religious"). Nor was Cesar Chavez, the Mexican American farmworker leader who perhaps most famously wedded the hunger strike to the U.S. union cause, a model for Beto. He had barely heard of Chavez: "I remember a little that he made a hunger strike, but I don't know what it was about. The [hunger] strike was my idea."[40]

Despite union claims to the contrary, the 1996 work stoppage and accompanying hunger strike mainly bred frustration and disillusionment within the worker ranks. As the company was unyielding in its refusal to bargain and threatened to hire replacement workers, there was a steady drop in worker support. The strike was called off in eight days. The failure of direct action placed union leaders in a strategic quandary. On the one hand, they showed that they could rattle the company's chain (indeed, Case Farms offered a fifty-cent hourly raise—the last across-the-board increase Morganton poultry workers would receive through the spring of 2001). On the other hand, they had not found the magic bullet to bring the company to contract terms. What was worse, in the immediate aftermath of the workers' reluctant return to work, the company was able to "pick off" a few key union supporters. In particular, three former union committeemen (all Mexicans) took supervisory positions at a salary of two thousand dollars a month—effectively jumping sides in the union battle for a 25 percent difference in pay.

The case of one of them, Francisco Ramírez, illustrates the larger challenge facing the union. Ramírez, according to those around him, was "a leader," a man who "spoke very well with the people," and who could carry the workers' grievances effectively to management.[41] It was Ramírez who directed the in-plant stoppages in 1996, handing out assignments to both English and Spanish speakers, then beginning the stoppage himself by having the packing room workers on the bottom floor quit work and conspicuously walk up the ladder to signal that the strike was on.[42] His organizing skills had been honed as a loan and insurance salesman in Mexico, where he had learned to knock on doors and literally "stand in the way" of the customer until a deal was made. As the example of Ramírez indicates, the very talents needed for movement building (communication skills, independence, and ambition) were also the qualities that might, under the right inducement, separate the worker from his or her workmates. Worker Katherine Harbison, one of the few African Americans among the union partisans, recalled the bitterness she felt after Ramírez "went and got himself a yellow hat" (a supervisory position): "I called him a traitor. I said, 'You was our leader and we done what you told us to do and now you turned your back on us.'" Local Spanish-speaking unionists tended to lump the three new supervisors together as "los vendidos."[43]

Aside from the political challenge facing the union forces after the 1996 strike, the case of los vendidos illustrates the volatile mixture of family, class, and ethnic loyalties operating within a small-town immigrant community. Perhaps most intriguing to the outside observer is not merely that Ramírez was the brother of union stalwart Carlos Salido but that Salido and fellow union stalwart Beto González continued to share a house with the two other vendidos—"Fofo" (Rodolfo Gómez) and "Chapino" (José Luís Hernández)—for more than a year after the strike. Such divergent reactions on the part of paisanos or even family members on the issue of union loyalty were reportedly not uncommon in Morganton. Pressed for an explanation, Carlos Salido framed such situations as part of a larger cycle of individual adjustment to an alien world. As he put it (pointedly avoiding mention of his own brother): "Work is work, friendship is friendship, I believe. People know that [with] Chapino it is work from Monday to Friday; if we go out on Sunday he is my friend." In Chapino's further defense, Carlos observed that "he has been a supervisor only six months. I believe we have to wait and hope." Acknowledging that when it came to Case Farms business, "Luís and I talk alone." Salido also found it important to distinguish among supervisors: "The people like Chapino, they don't quarrel with him. . . . He did it [took the promotion] to make more money, not to take advantage of the people or treat them badly."[44]

Nacho, who spurned similar offers to become a supervisor, was somewhat less forgiving. As he saw it, the company "tries to split the people and they'll be more easy to break." At the time, he chose not to speak to these ex-workers, but he acknowledged that for others family and friendship ties transcended workplace loyalties. Nacho conceded that the Hispanic ex-worker supervisors "may still be sympathetic to the union, but they are thinking of themselves and how they can make more money." A similar spirit, he suggested, guided his own brother-in-law, Maximo Hernández—whose presence had originally drawn the Montes family to Morganton—when he crossed the picket line in the 1996 strike. "We live in a free country," explained Nacho. "He's more conservative. . . . We stopped writing each other for a while, but [now again] we're still friends."[45]

For an old union partisan (especially one who grew up in coal country) like Phyllis Palmieri, such day-to-day fraternization among workplace antagonists was unfathomable. She speculated that in Morganton there might even be cases of family or friendship groups with a calculated approach to workplace conflicts: "There are several guys living in a house, and maybe one says, 'You take the vacation [strike] this time, and I'll go out next,' who knows?"[46]

Essentially, local union leadership depended on close working (and social) alliances and informal hierarchies. Phyllis Palmieri (in regular local consultation with sympathizers like Father Ken Whittington) constituted the official pipeline to LIUNA leaders in Washington, D.C. In turn, Yanira Merino, or occasionally more senior LIUNA staff like Marc Panepinto or Washington emissary Pat Moran, would arrive at more or less regular intervals to inspect and reinspire the local campaign. Such visits would bring the outsiders together with Nacho and an organizing committee composed of Mexicans and Guatemalans, the latter of whom included Aguacatecos José Samuel and Félix Rodríguez, plus a stray exception like Marta Gálvez. In practice, however, especially when a confrontation or other demonstration of strength beckoned, the multicultural net around the Morganton union supporters was wider than has yet been conveyed.

To illustrate, among the workers in regular attendance at organizing meetings were Dora Martínez and Julia Luna, two Ladina immigrants from coastal Guatemala. With a sixth-grade education and few economic prospects, Dora had left her homeland along with most of her family in 1981 and worked in California for fifteen years as a hotel maid in addition to one stint in a salsa manufacturing plant; she also married and had a son. Following the breakup of her marriage, she "discovered" her lesbian sexual identity in 1993 and soon established a long-term relationship with Julia, whom she had met in California. The complications of "coming out" amid disapproving family members persuaded the couple to seek a new start else-where; word of mouth led them to Morganton, a place, Dora said, where there were "mucha gente que me quieren, que me aprecien" (many people who like me, who appreciate me). Though Dora had no prior union experi-ence, her brother had spoken highly of his contact with the United Farm Workers in California. Of influences affecting her strong union loyalty, she cited the rhetorical magnetism of Yanira Merino, the communal unity of the Aguacatecos ("they always help anyone who needs it"), and the shop floor influence of Nacho ("people seek him out at lunch with their prob-lems, whether or not they are in the union"). Overcoming the fears that she said prevented many other women workers from openly declaring their union sympathies, Dora made a decision for "a future for our children." Yet, even as the union officially "[showed] respect" to Julia and Dora, the female partners could not take a climate of tolerance for granted. A super-visor once told Dora that other women workers had complained about the presence of "lesbians in the bathroom." By 1999, for reasons unknown, Dora and Julia had left town.[47]

Also notable for their "exceptional" social identity among the union partisans was Katherine Harbison, one of two or three African American women who publicly backed the union cause, and Mark Michaelis, the lone Caucasian receiving the spotty English-language translations at union com-mittee meetings. Katherine, who had worked in Breeden's Poultry after high school in the late 1970s and staged her own workplace protest, had returned to the plant following jobs at Broughton Hospital and Hardee's in 1995.[48] Like Dora Martínez, she quickly responded to the organizing ap-peals of "Juan Anoches" (Juan Ignacio) and "Anita" (Yanira Merino): "I had this friend, Harry Davies, he was staying with me, and when the first strike started, he was involved, you know, and they would come here and pick him up and I wanted to get involved. So every time they would come to pick us up we would go to the church and we'd talk, and I decided, yeah, it's about time. And I said, well, it took these people to come over here to really do something about this plant. Because they [Case Farms management] really thought these people was ignorant. These people was not ignorant; they've got more sense than we have." Unlike most of her English-speaking coworkers, Katherine Harbison had no trouble identi-fying with the Hispanic union activists: "We wasn't special and they ain't special. We all got mistreated the same way."[49]

In June 1997 Katherine was fired from Case Farms for absenteeism. She blamed the problem on a difficult work schedule: "We get off work like

No One Leader

5:30 and I don't have time to pay my bills. Living in the housing authority, you've got to pay your rent plus extra. I called them first and told them, 'I'm going to be late, I gotta go pay a bill, I'm going to pay my rent, light bill, cable bill, and then I go into work.' I said, 'If you let us off at a decent time, I wouldn't be coming in late to pay my bills.' I have to pay my bills." But she was also convinced that the company was looking for any excuse to get rid of her. "Every time something would happen, you know when everybody would walk off the line, I would walk off the line too, and they'd give me a mean look and they'd watch me all the times because I was upstairs [organizing], you know . . . when I knew there was going to be a strike I would have to go around and tell the workers what time we was going to walk off this line, and they would watch me." After formal separation from the company, Katherine continued her activism with the poultry workers' union, an association that expanded her own geographic horizons: "Like when they [the union delegation] go out of town they come and get me too. We was in Greensboro . . . and we going to Alabama. And I still get letters and stuff and put them in a manila envelope. . . . I might not be there [in the plant] but I'm sure someday I can do something."[50]

When Mark Michaelis arrived at Case Farms in the winter of 1995, he was down on his luck. Mark was born in 1962 in nearby Valdese, North Carolina, after his parents moved south from Michigan. He had held, and lost, a string of jobs in Morganton: "a lot of restaurant work," employment in two furniture factories, and housekeeping assignments at both Grace Hospital and the Western Carolina Center. "I experienced God and salvation when I was fifteen years old," he said of his Primitive Baptist faith, "and when I was growing up I was basically a good churchgoing kid. I didn't go out and drink or party like the other teenagers, pretty much until I got out of high school. Then my father died and my life went all to pieces after that. I had a lot of ups and downs; I couldn't hold down a job or seem to stay in the same direction all the time. I also had a lot of other problems; I'd been involved in drugs and whatnot. [Then,] I moved to the place where I'm living at now, and I went to Case Farms because I didn't have a car and it was the closest place for me to work at."[51]

Unlike the other white workers around him, Mark, always disposed toward unions, quickly joined up with the Case Farms campaign:

I'd heard about what was going on at Case Farms before I went to work there and I was already curious about it. I got to talking to people in the cafeteria, and they asked me what I thought of it. I said, "I support unions. I think a union would be the best thing that ever happened to this company." So some-body invited me to a meeting . . . then they asked me to be on the negotiating committee, and I've been working with them ever since. . . . You know, I could see God working in this; I could see why God brought me to Case Farms—both for myself and to help these people too.

As Mark saw it, the union was contending not only with management but also with the dual prejudices of native-born workers, white and black, against both unions and Hispanics. In the former case, he explained, "it's [a matter of] job security. . . . Some of them are loyal to the company, having been there for twenty-five or thirty years. Some people in there are just content with their jobs; a few people are grateful just to be working, and they've got the attitude that they shouldn't bite the hand that feeds them. This is alright but when that same hand is slapping you in the face all the time it's kind of hard not to fight back once in a while." Both in town and among the tiny minority of "American" workers at the plant, he noted a deep resentment toward the "Hispanics." "[People] just don't like them. They feel that they're coming in here and taking American jobs; they're displeased with the fact that—well, I don't know if it's a fact, but a lot of them have the understanding that they [the Hispanics] don't pay taxes like we do."

In assessing the union's conflicts with Case Farms management, Mark tried coolly to assess the roots, and potential resolution, of workplace problems. Though caustic in his criticism of "abuses" he alleges were rife in the treatment of ill and injured workers, for example, he found enough blame to go around in the constantly contested matter of bathroom breaks. "They [management] try to be as good as they can about letting people take bathroom breaks when they need to, but they're simply short-staffed. . . . It's just supposed to be a ten minute break to go to the bathroom, but you have a lot of people who take advantage of that time. . . . A lot of people take fifteen, twenty, thirty minute breaks, and then you got folks stand-ing there complaining because they can't get to the bathroom." Under the circumstances, he believed, individual arrangements for breaks only raised frustration levels. "They need to designate a fifteen minute break period in the afternoon. The most effective way to do that is to shut down one [pro-cessing] line at a time and send them to the back to take a break." Mark, moreover, did not blame the supervisors for workplace tensions. "They can't keep any decent supervisors because they really don't treat them any better than they treat the workers. They work them to death; a lot of them come in at five or six o'clock in the morning and don't get out until seven o'clock at night."

Sporting a "Promise-Keepers" T-shirt, Mark Michaelis attempted in 1998 to reconcile the twin commitments in his life: the union and the church. Acknowledging that most of his fellow congregants saw unions as "troublemakers, because as you know unions have a bad history of violence and corruption," he was confident that they would come around "once they understand the whole aspect of it." "The Bible," Mark explained of the book that he carried to work every day, "says that if a man has people working for him, he's supposed to pay him a just wage. When you're paying people barely enough money to live, I don't see that as just. They do not treat the workers with the respect they deserve. I mean, if it wasn't for us, the company would not be making their money. I feel like anytime you're doing anything in an effort to make things better for people, that that's a lot of what Christianity is about. You know, Christ was always concerned for the welfare of the people."[52]

All in all, the union campaign at Case Farms had generated a remarkable dynamic among a diverse group of working people. Individual personalities had at once stamped the movement in their image, but momentum developed beyond the power of any one person or even any one preestablished group. Rather, the possibility of change—of tangible improvement and empowerment—in a central aspect of daily life had stirred a host of people to assert themselves in ways they had not done before. For the moment, at least, they had become leaders. Yet, for all the excitement generated by the union drive among employees, the campaign's outcome depended to a considerable degree on the workers' allies outside the plant, far from Morganton.

5

The Workers Are Ready

The immigrant workers who walked out at Case Farms were risking a great deal to create a second chance for themselves and their families. In many respects, however, the American labor movement and the specific union the workers joined had also traveled far from their home bases and were equally desperate for success. Though it proved a far more complicated and difficult struggle than anyone might have forecast at the beginning, the forthright stand of the Case Farms workers in 1995 came at a propitious moment in U.S. labor history.

The previous twenty-five years, to be sure, had not been the headiest times for organized labor. The AFL-CIO had adopted a generally bunker-like posture toward the threats of a changing economy and political climate: before his death in 1979, for example, federation president George Meany had brushed aside concerns about the spreading unorganized sectors of the workforce with the comment, "the organized fellow is the fellow who counts."[1] Yet, no one could deny the once-powerful movement's steady loss of both economic clout and political influence. The unionized proportion of the total American workforce dropped from 35 percent in 1955 to a mere 15 percent—and just 10 percent in the private sector—by 1995, and the unions had proven toothless before employer hardball tactics once President Ronald Reagan fired striking air traffic controllers en masse in 1981. What is more, the post–New Deal political coalitions that had made labor the fulcrum for progressive social change in America had become badly frayed by the federation's preoccupation with anticommunism abroad and a reluctance to rock the boat at home. The fact was, no major worker-oriented social legislation—outside of President Richard Nixon's signature setting up the Occupational Safety and Health Administration (OSHA) in 1970—had been passed since the 1930s, and the limitations in both coverage and enforcement of national labor law were legion. With the exception of significant inroads among public sector workers (such as the explosive growth of teachers' unions) and a few heroic stands for those left out of economic prosperity (the Farmworkers' successful grape boycott and the rise of hospital workers' Local 1199 offer perhaps the most prominent examples), the unions appeared to be standing pat with a shrinking hand. In retrospect, the assassination of Rev. Martin Luther King Jr. while he was aiding an African American garbage workers strike in Memphis in 1968 sadly highlights a path not taken toward the reinvigoration of labor as a social movement.

Yet, something of a sea change for labor was under way by the mid-1990s. Appropriately, an end-of-the-decade commentary on organizational developments involving the unions was entitled "A Second Chance: The New AFL-CIO and the Prospective Revival of American Labor." A bare three months after the July union vote in Morganton, in fact, the "new AFL-CIO" leadership determined to change the public persona of organized labor in the United States. Led by John Sweeney, president of the Service Employees International Union (SEIU)—itself a sign of needed organizational reorientation to a postindustrial economy—a "New Voice" insurgent slate proclaimed a commitment to aggressive organizing, political confrontation with corporate power, and broader coalition building with other "progressive" issue-oriented organizations. The positioning of Executive Vice President Linda Chávez-Thompson, a Mexican American born to Texas sharecropper parents, on the New Voice slate was a dual symbol of the enhanced status of women in the federation leadership as well as a welcoming signal to the rising tide of Latino workers in U.S. industry. But the federation also promised to back up its words and symbols with action. Encouraging its affiliated unions to augment their individual efforts with coordinated industrywide drives to match employer power, the AFL-CIO immediately stepped up support for strawberry pickers in California and hotel and restaurant workers in Las Vegas and began a cross-industry campaign among low-wage industrial workers in Los Angeles. In the workplace, the biggest initial success for New Labor came with the Teamsters' nationwide United Postal Service strike in the summer of 1997, a publicly militant show of force led by New Voice stalwart Ron Carey. In addition to reinvigorating domestic organizing, the new leaders spoke of constructing a "new internationalism," responding to the globalized economy and its spreading Third World sweatshops with a determined effort to organize "across borders." After decades of Cold War–dominated international work aimed mainly at combating communist influence within worker movements, the AFL-CIO set its sights on the overwhelming influence of multinational corporations over worker movements everywhere. The new leaders thus cheered the example of the 1994–95 Bridgestone-Firestone tire strike in which the United Steel Workers of America (which had absorbed the fading remains of the United Rubber Workers) derived critical leverage from the actions of Japanese and other labor federations abroad, as well as the initiatives of other member unions in opening a dialogue with their Mexican counterparts to the south.[2]

In some respects, labor's rank and file exhibited the spirit of the "new unionism" even before the triumph at the top of the AFL-CIO. Sweeney's October 1995 victory at the AFL-CIO convention, in fact, reflected a subtle shift in power and strategy among many of the federation's affiliates. Perhaps most apparent in Sweeney's own successful SEIU campaigns like Justice for Janitors, an organizing drive beginning in the late 1980s among long-ignored service sector workers, the new spirit attempted to harness innovative techniques of publicity and consumer or stockholder pressure ("corporate campaigns") to older forms of shop floor mobilization. In their uphill battles with big employers over the previous decades, some sections of a labor movement otherwise steeped in inertia, old-boy leadership networks, and instinctual defensiveness had, in fact, experimented with new techniques. A new breed of organizer—younger, college-educated, often experienced in a host of "new movement" political issues—poured out of the federation's Organizing Institute (OI), an in-house academy launched in 1989 under AFL-CIO president Lane Kirkland. Determined to match "brains" (particularly the arts of publicity, mass communication, and political networking) with the traditional "brawn" of factory floor confrontations, the OI sought to counteract management's application of specialized expertise in labor disputes. In addition, well before the federation's turnover at the top, a combination of radical necessity and rank-and-file insurgency had infected affiliates like the Textile Workers, the Mine Workers, and the Teamsters with an uncommon creative ferment.[3] By the mid-1990s the interlocking obstacles facing the labor movement—an anti-union offensive of employers and "union-busting" law firms, ineffectual sanctions of illegal employer behavior afforded by the governing National Labor Relations Act, the nearly automatic resort to replacement workers in the case of strikes, the growing downsizing of a globalizing economy, and general congressional kowtowing to corporate pressures—convinced even the most hidebound unions of the need for a change in direction.

Yet, to understand how LIUNA got involved in a poster-child campaign

The Workers Are Ready

for new immigrant workers requires more than a general acquaintance with the state of the labor movement around 1995. If any trade union in America needed a "second chance" to recover its vitality at the beginning of the 1990s, that union was the Laborers. Not that it was weak in material resources. Nor was it a stranger to the world of immigrant workers. Indeed, the International Hod Carriers and Building Laborers Union of America, which gave birth to what officially became LIUNA in 1965, initially rose with the support of European, especially Irish and Italian, immigrants. Longtime general secretary-treasurer Arthur E. Coia, for example, who joined the union in 1933 at age twenty-five, poignantly remembered a generation that "had to work for slave wages from morning to night": "I know those people because my father was one of them. He was an orphan when his parents were killed in Italy, but he came to this country, worked very hard and raised a family. He worked as an accordion player, and I played the tambourine for him when I was young. But he was also a laborer and an organizer, and I followed in his footsteps. After I finished grammar school, I went to work in a macaroni shop in Providence. I really had ideas of becoming a priest, but then my brother died and I went into construction to help support the family."[4] Buoyed by the post–World War II building boom, LIUNA, once a struggling stepchild of the more skilled construction trades, emerged as a powerhouse in its own right. Despite a relatively decentralized leadership structure, major financial resources accrued to the national union through a set of joint labor-management job-training funds. These trust funds, together with a political action committee created in 1965, provided dual testimony to the robust health of an organization representing about four hundred thousand members by 1996.[5] Adopting a statesmanlike, even conservative public posture of "labor-management cooperation" while pressuring employers and the government to grant union contracts, the Laborers avoided the destructive confrontations with corporate power that befell many other AFL-CIO affiliates.

Unfortunately, the Laborers suffered from a significant problem of their own: corruption. The union leaders offered a classic model of autocracy. For thirty years, they had held no elections or conventions but simply "self-appointed and reduplicated themselves as one or another died or retired." They also curried notorious connections to mob bosses.[6] Since the days of "Big Jim" Colisimo, a gangster in pre-Prohibition Chicago, union executives had regularly associated with known criminals. Joseph Moreschi, International president for four decades, was indicted in 1944 on charges of embezzlement. According to a Justice Department memorandum, Peter

Fosco, who succeeded Moreschi, had "ties to organized crime" that dated back to Al Capone. When Fosco's son, Angelo, took over in 1975, his "election," too, was reportedly engineered by Chicago crime boss Anthony Accardo. On Angelo Fosco's death in 1993, Arthur A. Coia, who had succeeded his father as secretary-treasurer in 1989, all but inherited the presidency, even while vowing to clean up the union and restore its public reputation.

Raised far from the hardscrabble world of the construction site, Arthur A. Coia possessed an articulate and even elegant presence. A college and law school graduate who had been admitted to argue before the U.S. Supreme Court, he had also found time to cultivate a competitive golf game and a taste for Ferraris. Yet, although he preferred to present himself as part of a "new generation of North American labor leaders," Coia could not easily escape the union's seamier past.[7] For years, his father, Arthur E. Coia, had drawn police scrutiny due to his close personal association with alleged New England crime boss Raymond Patriarca; indeed, both father and son escaped prosecution in 1981 for a kickback scheme only because the statute of limitations expired. Police authorities suspected the younger Coia of continuing ties to the Patriarca family. Despite close associations with the Democratic Party (including distinction as the single biggest union donor to the 1996 Clinton reelection campaign), the Laborers, particularly its president, could not escape public attention as the federation's enduring "rotten apple." To preempt a full federal takeover of LIUNA finances under the antiracketeering RICO (Racketeer Influenced and Corrupt Organizations) statute, which had been previously invoked against the Teamsters, Coia reached an unusual agreement with the government in the summer of 1995 to establish an autonomous in-house prosecutor to investigate all allegations of corruption.[8]

"Reform—of necessity" was effectively Coia's watchword as he tried to reshape the Laborers' affairs in 1994–95. Whatever his personal motivations—and observers continue to debate the sincerity of his convictions—Coia moved dramatically to drag the once-conservative Laborers into the forefront of dynamic and progressive change within the AFL-CIO.[9] As he wrote in May 1995, "All of us know that business-as-usual is not getting the job done. Attitudes and practices have to change, and change greatly to meet the challenges of a very different economy and broader social contract."[10] As evidence of its changed direction, LIUNA trumpeted new issue-oriented partnerships with such organizations as the Coalition of Labor Union Women, the National Rainbow Coalition, and Navaho

Nation, while Coia publicly championed issues like defense conversion and expanded public housing. Most importantly, Coia drafted top Textile Workers' organizer Duane Stillwell and two of his assistants, David Kiefer and Marc Panepinto, to create an organizing department where none had existed before. When the newcomers chose to probe the food-processing industry, Coia lent the effort enthusiastic support, recruiting further talent from the AFL-CIO Organizing Institute. Within three years, LIUNA's investment in organizing went from practically nothing to an astounding $10 million.[11] Moreover, following the practices of other progressive unions like SEIU and the Union of Needletrades, Industrial, and Textile Employees (UNITE), LIUNA added both a "corporate campaign" capacity to the organizing department and a volunteer organizing program. Coia foresaw "hundreds of LIUNA members volunteering their time to organize their fellow workers throughout North America." Finally, he announced the initiation of a new organizing crusade. "These committed volunteers will participate in a massive organizing campaign in the poultry and food processing industry. This campaign is coordinated by the North American Poultry Workers Alliance, an unprecedented organizing effort involving LIUNA, the UFCW, and partners in the civil rights, consumer and economic development communities. It promises to be one of the largest social change campaigns in recent history." As if to punctuate Coia's enthusiasm, newly elected AFL-CIO president Sweeney would soon appoint the Laborers' leader chair of the federation's prestigious Organizing Committee.[12] Organizer Marc Panepinto, for one, gave Coia credit for wanting to make something happen:

> He came into office with a lot of big ideas. He wanted to change a tremendously moribund international into a vibrant place. And he had good ideas: he created an organizing department, a PR department, an international affairs department, and a research department. All those things were new. He was willing to spend money to do things. Now . . . did he do that because he was interested in helping the workers of the world? Probably not. Was he interested in creating a persona for Arthur Coia? Definitely. In doing that, did he really help workers? Yes, he did.[13]

Within weeks of Coia's May declaration, the Case Farms workers in Morganton emerged as the centerpiece of both the Laborers' New Union image and New Union reality. "Poultry sort of launched the successful portion of my organizing career," recalled Panepinto. "We were able to organize probably 2,000 poultry workers in Mississippi out of 2,500 in a very short time, in less than a year." Flush with victory in Mississippi in 1994, LIUNA's organizing team fanned out into other sections of the "broiler belt." While Panepinto himself focused on Alabama, another LIUNA operative, Bill Goodrich, was probing several Perdue Farms plants, including one in the North Carolina town of Robersonville. "While [Bill] was driving down the highway headed to the [Robersonville] plant and was listening to the agricultural report on the radio . . . he hears this report of Case Farms workers walking off the job in Morganton. So he immediately pulls off the road and calls me in Alabama to say, 'These five hundred workers just walked off the job on a wildcat strike. We've got to get up there.' This is like ten o'clock in the morning [on Monday May 15, 1995], we hear about this walkout, and we just bust on up there."[14]

Despite the moderate size of the Case Farms plant and its remoteness from other LIUNA outposts (the Laborers had no organized local in North Carolina and relied on a regional headquarters in Virginia to service the operation), the Morganton campaign quickly absorbed a disproportionate share of energy and resources not only from field organizers but also from the research and legal departments of LIUNA's national headquarters in Washington, D.C. It was in Morganton, in short, that the once-staid construction union would try to apply many of the lessons of John Sweeney's new playbook for a revival of the American labor movement.

The strategy began with the raw enthusiasm of the organizing team that entered Morganton in the midst of the 1995 walkout. "We didn't choose poultry," said Panepinto, "poultry sort of chose us." While watching and waiting for workers' "action," the New Laborers' organizing team led by Duane Stillwell and Marc Panepinto soon found itself up against the southern poultry business. "I was there one day in D.C., just got hired on, and this rep in Mississippi was saying: 'We need help here. We've got an election in eighteen days. Give us help.'"[15]

The career trajectories of the Stillwell-Panepinto leadership duo suggest the dynamism that initially infused the Case Farms campaign from the outside as well as from the shop floor. Born in 1960 to a lower-middle-class family in Denver, Duane was initiated into the labor movement in a McDonald's restaurant organizing campaign as a teenager. A graduate of the state university at Boulder, he went on to get a law degree but soon switched career tracks to become an organizer for the Textile Workers' union and a charter member of the AFL-CIO's Organizing Institute in 1989. From the excitement—if inevitably mixed success—of textile campaigns in Dallas, Kannapolis (North Carolina), and Monroe (Louisiana),

Duane gained a reputation as an aggressive organizer who "could move the ground." The fading domestic textile industry, however, looked less and less like the place to do it. Marc Panepinto, the son of a Buffalo, New York, construction worker and grandson of Sicilian immigrants, also came from a union background. While working his way through college, Marc had joined his father's local of the Laborers union. Following graduation at SUNY-Buffalo, he chose a more professional route back into the labor movement. With a master's degree in labor and industrial relations, Marc was just thirty years old in 1995 when he suddenly found himself in charge of LIUNA's newly constituted Southeast poultry drive.

Duane and Marc hoped to bring the same energy and success to the Laborers that had earlier characterized the Textile Workers and SEIU. "They imported this new aggressive organizing [model]," recalled one initially admiring staff member. "'Hotshop' organizing, combined with a political [or public relations] strategy, trying to get longterm advancement. [Duane] was pretty much all over the place—California, the Midwest, etc., wherever was hot."[16] Marc looked back on his mission with Duane and the Laborers as a laborite version of the French Foreign Legion. "There are the big thinkers in the labor movement," he said, "there are the people with good politics; and there are the people who want to do the work. . . . We like to win, and we like to organize workers. People can put down beautiful plans for their organizing program and think about this stuff, and they can talk about the utility of rank-and-file organizing and how it's got to be done, but all of that doesn't lead to a lot of action. Duane and I are on the side of, 'The workers are ready, let's go with them.'"[17]

To be sure, from the beginning, LIUNA's Case Farms organizers had to overcome the skepticism of the union's more conservative Old Guard. In particular, the Laborers' mid-Atlantic region, headed by its vice president Jack Wilkinson in Virginia, only reluctantly lent support from its construction worker base to the new organizing crusade.[18] Marc remembered that Wilkinson's representative in Morganton, conservative Nicaraguan émigré and former construction worker Orlando Bonilla mixed with Salvadoran activist Yanira Merino "like oil and water." In the course of the campaign, Orlando showed up as seldom as possible.[19] To make its mark, the Stillwell-Panepinto team clearly needed both on-the-ground results and continuing indulgence from the union's national executive.

At Case Farms, the first phase of organization went swiftly and relatively smoothly except for one hitch on the union side. Notwithstanding the fact that LIUNA was essentially handed an already-organized rank-and-file base mobilized by the 1993 and 1995 strikes, the Laborers initially faced the fairly common problem in U.S. industrial relations of an intramural rival—in this case, the UFCW. With a long-established foundation in the food-processing industry—nearly sixty thousand poultry workers under contract nationwide and several local affiliates in North Carolina, including one turkey plant—the UFCW had reason to feel that Morganton was its "natural" turf. Yet, after some higher-level attempts at multiunion cooperation fell through (among them, formation of an on-again, off-again national poultry workers alliance), LIUNA gave full license to its aggressive team of organizers. As Marc Panepinto related:

> There was negotiating at headquarters level . . . but what was really going to happen was going to happen on the ground. We were trying to maintain some congeniality so it didn't look like we were fighting. Phyllis Palmieri and Father Ken were continually counseling the two groups of union people to behave themselves. We got people signed up on petitions that night [Thursday, the last day of the strike] and we were fighting over wording—both the general counsels in DC and us on the ground. We circulated one petition that night that angled out the UFCW—after it got about fifty names on it the UFCW realized what we had done and tried to stop it. So we took that petition back and circulated another one associated with the National Poultry Workers [Organizing Committee]–AFL-CIO. Everybody up there [in Washington, D.C.] signed on, but there was ongoing acrimony between the two unions.[20]

By the end of May LIUNA prevailed, winning a vote of allegiance within the eleven-member local workers' organizing committee. This was followed by an NLRB ruling giving the laborers sole claim to a place on the election ballot.[21]

The honeymoon phase of the Laborers' campaign lasted through July 1995 as the union prepared to demonstrate its strength in a formal vote. LIUNA did everything it could to make Case Farms a test case of its new organizing resolve. Among a series of support efforts, about twenty-five union "volunteers" from Local 362, Bloomington, Illinois (they were paid their weekly base rate plus room and board), were bussed in for a two-week stint of support work. The encounter may have had more effect on the visitors than on the new immigrant workers themselves. As Mike Matejka, Bloomington labor editor and activist, remembered: "Most of the folks were shocked at the living conditions and working conditions of people in the poultry industry. You heard over and over . . . 'Boy, I didn't realize I had it so good,' or 'I don't have to ask permission to go to the bathroom,

I don't have to worry about feeding my family.' The stories of abuse were shocking to the majority of our folks involved." In addition to home visits encouraging a union yes vote, the out-of-state Laborers offered the Morganton workers social services such as helping them with driver's license applications and immigration forms. Matejka said that the workers were used to being charged, and often exploited, for such services. "When the workers reached for their wallets, we said, 'No, this is a union. We take care of each other here.'"22

Aside from the call for solidarity, Mike Matejka and the leaders of other self-styled "progressive" LIUNA locals placed the Case Farms campaign in a framework of internal union politics. They were aware, for example, that more conservative LIUNA members were saying, "Hey, how come you're out putting all that energy into organizing those folks down there when you're not organizing that non-union [construction] contractor across the street? There's a risk there for the union in terms of its own constituencies." For Matejka and his colleagues, the Case Farms campaign—like the lure of the southern civil rights crusade a generation earlier—was just the opening the Laborers needed to expand their organizing ideal. "The folks that came back from [North Carolina] started doing organizing around here in non-traditional units. Throughout the state of Illinois now, we've got Laborers organizing nursing homes, small factories, public employees. . . . That experience going South . . . helped change the framework for Laborers who were receptive to the idea of 'We don't just organize construction workers anymore.'"23

Two nights before the Case Farms vote, LIUNA president Coia himself journeyed to Morganton to rally the troops. For those who had watched the union boss on other occasions, something seemed different about his demeanor in North Carolina. Matejka, for one, remembered:

I saw a copy of his official speech, and he didn't follow it. We were in the church, and he was really touched by the minister [Father Ken] doing the program there, or allowing his church to be used. . . . I think being around [these] workers called this Catholic spirit out of him. . . . He began to talk about his own immigrant background, and the Laborers as a union of immigrants. He then went into his own physical experience with cancer and that he went to Lourdes and these other Catholic shrines in Europe to pray for his own cure. I had his official speech laying there in front of me, and I'm looking through this and thinking, "This is nowhere in here." A number of other organizing folks—particularly the Anglo ones—were like, "What do you think about that? How do you think people handled that?" But I thought it was great. I don't think it would have worked in front of Southern Baptists, but here it was quite appropriate.[24]

As John Jordan, special projects coordinator for LIUNA, saw it: "[The workers] all stood up and cheered. Coia was very affected by it. He's one of these union guys that lives a pretty isolated life. This was one of the few times that he got out and sort of mixed it up. He hung out late, going around shaking hands, he was like the last to leave."[25]

Following the July 1995 election victory, LIUNA strategists faced the second phase of its Case Farms campaign. Almost every union organizing effort confronts two major formal challenges: first, the effort to be officially recognized as a bargaining agent, a process normally routed through an NLRB election; and second, the struggle for a contract. Nationally, a dramatic rise in employer opposition across all industries since the mid-1980s substantially raised the bar for union success in both halves of the organizing process. During the period 1986–95 the number of employers running aggressive anti-union campaigns, including the use of tactics such as discharges, threats of plant closings, captive audience meetings, and electronic surveillance, increased from 22 to 42 percent. One result was a national union win rate in NLRB elections of less than 40 percent, a figure that dropped further in right-to-work states like North Carolina.[26] Nor was a collective bargaining contract assured for those workers who secured union recognition. According to U.S. Department of Labor figures, unions received a contract after their initial election win in only 60 percent of the cases from 1992 to 1995, a drop of 15 percent in one decade. Altogether, the odds were clearly stacked against the unionizing forces. At the national level fewer than 20 percent of private sector workers who attempted to organize under the NLRB were able to gain representation under a union contract.[27]

Case Farms followed the modern-day union avoidance script to the letter. It formally disputed the NLRB election results, resisted all entreaties to meet with union representatives, and in the ensuing months selectively threatened or fired several union activists. Altogether, the Case Farms legal challenge began with an appeal to the NLRB immediately following the July 1995 pro-union vote, continued into the Fourth Circuit, U.S. Court of Appeals, in August 1996 as well as a subsequent petition to the U.S. Supreme Court in 1998, and extended into further wrangling during 1999–2001 after the company cancelled contract bargaining sessions. Such recalcitrance continually put the ball back into the union's court. For LIUNA

The Workers Are Ready

organizers, therefore, stage two, or the contract quest, comprised three related operations: vigorous legal assertion of the union's legitimacy and demand for good-faith contract talks; activation of a larger political support network, including a corporate campaign aimed at the company's public reputation and consumer market; and active display of union power "on the ground" by worker rank and file.

In its original legal rebuff of the union election results, Case Farms ingeniously connected a local dispute involving Hispanic workers to international ethnic conflicts contemporaneously capturing public attention. In particular, the union campaign in Morganton coincided with the escalation of violence in the former Yugoslavian province of Bosnia-Hercegovina. The early months of 1995 had witnessed rising public concern over the issue of "ethnic cleansing," highlighted by brutal massacres of Muslims by Bosnian Serbs in Tuzla and Pale in May, and growing reports of human rights violations by a newly appointed United Nations war crimes tribunal.[28] The employer's argument in both its NLRB and federal court appeals accused the union organizers at Case Farms of creating "ethnic fear" among the Hispanic workers at the plant, thus making the pro-union vote of the workers invalid. As Ohio attorney David P. Hiller argued for the company, "the election at Case Farms must be set aside because the purpose and likely effect of the Laborers' misconduct was to instill *fear* in highly vulnerable alien voters."[29]

Indeed, the growing presence of new immigrant (and especially Hispanic) workers in American industry—not to mention earlier cases of black-white racial hatred—had established recent precedents to which both Case Farms company and union counsel appealed in court.[30] The company's argument against LIUNA made several specific accusations. On July 7, 1995, as workers left the plant at the end of their shift, union organizer Yanira Merino accused anti-union Mexican employee Jesyka Martínez of being a "traitor" to her ethnic group by "looking down" on Guatemalans and calling them "lazy bums." According to Case Farms, the resulting commotion "*stirred ethnic sensitivities* and *set the stage* for the Union's effort to instill ethnic fear" by means of a controversial leaflet that accused Case Farms of having "*fired* the entire Amish work force" at its Winesburg, Ohio, plant, replacing the employees with lower-wage Hispanics. Insinuating that Hispanics would themselves be in danger of being fired if the union did not win the election, this "Amish handout," the company argued, contributed to a "terror campaign" based on ethnic fears. For good measure, the Case Farms brief referred to an African American woman who accused Guatemalan workers of calling her "nigger" and throwing chicken wings at her during worktime and a white woman who complained that she did not receive the union handbills and was not invited to union meetings.[31]

LIUNA's response to the company's accusations fell to forty-two-year-old counsel Lawrence Gold, a litigator with a lifelong passion for labor's cause. Raised in a New York City Jewish immigrant family, Gold was influenced by his mother's employment as secretary for the National Maritime Union and his grandfather's experience as a textile worker organizer. With a B.A. from Amherst College (1975) and a law degree from Cornell University (1980), he briefly joined a union organizing campaign in a Boston bookstore chain before settling in with a Washington, D.C., labor law firm with strong ties to the Laborers union. Once Arthur A. Coia became president, Gold was regularly dispatched as the union's senior litigator in organizing cases. Indeed, in the union's campaign at Virginia's Smithfield Packing Company in 1994, he encountered the legal intricacies of "ethnic hatred" for the first time when the company pinned its objections to a pro-union vote on the exact translation of a Spanish-language leaflet.[32] For Gold, work on the Case Farms campaign held a special appeal:

> I viewed it as an archetypical example of the kind of organizing that is necessary. It has so many elements of what is happening with American workers and culturally in the United States as well as with the labor movement. . . . It's an industry that's historically dangerous in a state historically non-union and anti-union. The large employers—Perdue and Tyson's—are virulently and successfully anti-union. Case Farms was an off-shoot of Perdue, and more and more the poultry industry has turned to immigrant work forces. . . . For the Laborers it was a very significant move in a new direction. And the way the company waged its anti-union campaign—it's [also] an archetype of what's wrong with American labor law. . . . It's a textbook-type approach they took: You lose the election, you file your objections, and everything is a stall. You take it through hearings, you appeal to the full NLRB. You lose there and you refuse to bargain; you force the board and the union to go to the court of appeals, and you play out the string as long as you can.[33]

With both legal erudition and logical precision, Gold picked apart each of the company's objections to the union election. Stressing the universality of the union's message, he argued that the campaign's fifteen leaflets, typically bilingual, were regularly distributed to all workers and in no way singled out Hispanics as the only workers the union was interested in helping. Likewise, the controversial Amish leaflet (which he subsequently

The Workers Are Ready

admitted was factually inaccurate as well as a generally "ill-advised" and "unnecessary") had not inflamed ethnic tensions since it argued (accurately or not) that Case Farms mistreated its Ohio as well as its North Carolina workers, was focused on "economic fairness and unity issues," and, in any case, Case Farms workers likely had no idea who the Amish were! In the incident involving Jesyka Martínez, the union argued that Yanira Merino was justifiably upset by the aspersions cast by Martínez on pro-union Guatemalan workers and that the argument they engaged in contained no "impermissible racial appeals." With regard to the chicken-throwing accusation from the black female worker, Gold elicited testimony from her that the offending workers "were just acting up" and that, as part of a stressful work culture, "they throw chicken wings at each other all the time." On balance, Gold deftly cleared the decks of any comparison of events in Morganton to those in previous cases where union actions had been held to have been aimed "solely to make a sustained [ethnic] appeal" to "exploit ethnic fears of the Hispanic employees."[34] In reaching a decision with regard to the complaints about union leaflets, the original NLRB hearing officer drew on a compelling fact dropped by an employer witness before the board: Most Guatemalan employees at Case Farms "did not read or write English or Spanish and thus could not have been harmed by the union message."[35] Gold's legal victory survived a lengthy appeals process. Following the U.S. Supreme Court denial of Case Farms's last appeal, the NLRB ordered the company to sit down with union representatives beginning in May 1998 and engage in good-faith negotiations in pursuit of a collective bargaining contract. The labor board used its maximum power to require the company to negotiate for a period of up to one year.

Even as attorney Gold pursued Case Farms in the courts, LIUNA organizers in Morganton and in the union's Washington headquarters fashioned a political offensive against the company. Thirty-three-year-old special projects coordinator John Jordan took on the latter task. An idealistic, politically minded union staffer, Jordan had worked in Democratic Party campaigns, organized chemical workers in Georgia, and spent a year with the Geneva-based trade secretariat of the International Union of Food, Agricultural, Hotel, Restaurant, Catering, Tobacco, and Allied Workers Associations (IUF) before joining Coia's New Laborers in 1994. The Laborers' organizing plans sounded "exciting," remembered Jordan, "and for a couple of years there, it was." To new staffers like Jordan, Case Farms was just the bogeyman that the new AFL-CIO aimed to topple. "It had all the elements: the South, immigrants, low wages, you know, the whole bit."[36]

Jordan turned to labor and Central American–oriented solidarity networks, to religious leaders who might respond to a social justice theme, and in the end to any group, regardless of its politics, that could be prodded to help. Seeking to "impress a relatively small company with our reach and keep morale up in Morganton," Jordan contacted Kurt Stand, North American liaison to the IUF.[37] Stand, in turn, chartered an anti–Case Farms letter-writing campaign from IUF affiliates around the world and worked through the U.S./Guatemala Labor Education Project (US/GLEP) to facilitate ties with Guatemala City Coca Cola workers' leader Rodolfo Robles. Robles's union, an IUF affiliate, had endured a courageous struggle despite multiple brutalities at the hands of the Guatemalan military and gained worldwide attention when its yearlong factory occupation led to a contract in 1985.[38] Ultimately, a Guatemalan organizer, Humberto Escobar, spent three weeks aiding LIUNA campaigns in Morganton and Gadsden, Alabama.[39] To further promote the cross-border exchange, LIUNA arranged for Father Ken to visit the families of Morganton workers in Guatemala (timed to coincide with a papal visit there), but the venture was canceled due to the death of the priest's mother.[40]

The Contract Task Force that Jordan coordinated also sought ways to place direct pressure on Case Farms. But because it was privately held, the company was not an easy target for a "corporate campaign." Pioneered by the textile workers in their 1970s struggle with the J. P. Stevens Company, the corporate campaign classically targeted company investors.[41] Although the union did arrange a token picket at New York banks with which Case Farms did business, political strategy focused from the beginning on getting to the company's consumers for a potential boycott.[42] In a supercompetitive industry, one might expect that any bad publicity would affect the company's bottom line. There was also the Russian connection. In February 1996 the Russians, who constituted the single largest market for U.S. chicken exports, suspended imports, citing bacterial infection and inadequate inspections in the processing plants.[43] In North Carolina, prices were reportedly already dropping for the dark meat that the Russians favored in contrast to white meat, which was preferred by American consumers.[44] "Surely you can make use of this in some manner," John Jordan wrote campaign director Duane Stillwell.[45] But there were complications on the consumer front. The Morganton plant produced no one brand-name product; rather, it sold primarily to wholesalers, who then resold the product to restaurants and retail chain stores. A potentially more promising target was the Case Farms plant in Winesburg, Ohio, which pro-

The Workers Are Ready

duced a well-marketed "Amish Brand" chicken. Though this would likely require some coordination with the UFCW, which was the only union pursuing the Ohio plant, the idea was pushed in strategy sessions.[46] Among other bits of intelligence, the union had received information that in big-city advertising Amish Brand was being falsely touted as a "natural" and an "organic" product.

In one or more ways, then, it first appeared to the Case Farms organizers that a consumer-oriented publicity effort could prove a "powerful component" of the larger campaign.[47] As a first step, in July 1996 the union warned some twenty-two Case Farms customers—mostly small meat and poultry wholesale markets and a few restaurants—spread out across the country of the "volatile situation" in the North Carolina plant.[48] With help from Citizen Action, a state-based consumer and worker rights network, the union staged protests in Ohio and Michigan and demonstrated at the industry's National Broilers Convention in Atlanta. As late as January 1997, Jordan was still arguing for "high-profile" public events around the "fakery" of Amish chicken: "This could be their Achilles heel."[49] In the end, however, the consumer focus—due to the diffuse trajectory of Morganton's product, the political complexity of dealing with the firm's two plants, or simple failure of nerve among the union high command (in retrospect, it is hard to know which)—proved a nonstarter. Defending the union's strategic decision-making toward Case Farms, Marc Panepinto simply concluded that "they really had very few vulnerability points."[50]

Without an obvious opening for attacking Case Farms financially, the union forces resorted to a more general political exposé to attract outside attention and to shame owner Tom Shelton and his company into a settlement. The most important player in this respect emerged in the National Interfaith Committee for Worker Justice (NICWJ), an organization established in Chicago less than six months before the Case Farms union vote. With her own roots in the evangelical Church of Christ, NICWJ director Kimberley Bobo had worked for twenty years in hunger and housing coalitions and as a staff member at Chicago's Midwest Academy, a training center for community organizers. In 1990 a speech by Mineworkers leader Richard Trumka led her to volunteer to coordinate religious support for the union's militant stand at Pittston, Virginia. Bobo said that she was shocked at how few formal ties had been cultivated between the churches and the labor movement. By the time of the Case Farms campaign, she had succeeded in knitting together a coalition of Chicago clergy around worker rights issues and was reaching to establish a more national profile for the labor-clergy coalition. As the wife of US/GLEP organizer Steve Coats, moreover, Bobo was already fully sensitized to Guatemala-related issues.

From the beginning, the poultry industry beckoned as an obvious point of entry for the religious community. As Bobo explained: "It doesn't take a genius to understand that the conditions for poultry workers are horrendous, and that they would be well served by some form of union organization. Our basic view is that it is not our job to tell people whether they should join a union, our job is just to protect their rights to do that. We figured this was an area that would be relatively easy to build religious support for; it's a lot easier to build support for poultry workers than for a basketball union." Although connection to a poultry-centered campaign was still a talking point within her fledgling coalition, Bobo received a plea for help from LIUNA's John Jordan. "I had no money and no staff," she said, "so I was sort of like, 'It's not an ideal time, but what the heck, let's do what we can.' I literally put my first staff person in place as a temp employee to help work on putting together the delegation to go to Morganton. It just seemed like it was the right thing to do."[51]

The Interfaith Committee's first act was to send a fact-finding delegation of twenty-five religious leaders to Morganton in late April 1996. Among the leaders were committee chair and retired Methodist bishop Jesse De-Witt; Rev. Jim Lewis, an Episcopal priest already well known for his activism among poultry workers in the Delmarva Peninsula; and Rev. Jimmy Creech, program associate for the North Carolina Council of Churches. Creech had pastored migrant farmworkers and protested the wars in Central America before becoming alternately celebrated and reviled by his congregations in North Carolina for his gay rights advocacy.[52] "The Case Farms situation challenges the moral conscience of the nation," Creech told the assembled visitors in Morganton. "These workers are struggling against all odds to realize the American dream."[53] "Lord, we cannot say grace over chicken while workers are being oppressed," declared Lewis, as he knelt in prayer on the public street outside the entrance to Case Farms. "You opened the Red Sea and led your people to freedom. You rolled away the stone and led us to new life. We pray that you will open the doors to this plant." In one crisp sentence, directed not to the visitors whom he warned not to trespass on company property but to a beckoning reporter, personnel manager Ken Wilson answered Lewis's plea: "There isn't going to be any meeting."[54] With equal terseness, Ken Sehested, executive director of the Baptist Peace Fellowship of North America, summarized the clash at

The Workers Are Ready

National Interfaith Committee for Worker Justice mobilizes
outside support for Case Farms workers on the second anniversary of
the union vote at the Morganton plant. Photo by Jeff Willhelm,
Charlotte Observer, July 14, 1997.

Case Farms: "Worlds colliding. Peasant farmer of distant land, meet small-town USA. What twist of fate has brought you together? The world's plant managers know. They have their hands around both your throats."[55]

The Interfaith Committee followed up its trip to Morganton with a devastating report on abuses of worker rights at Case Farms which was distributed through union and church circles around the country. The report criticized management on several grounds. The most frequent complaint of workers, according to the investigators, concerned the "dangerously high speed" of the production line. Combined with the rigidity of work assignments (there was no rotation of jobs at the plant), the line speed only exacerbated repetitive motion injuries frequently reported in most poultry-processing plants. Also negatively affecting working conditions were high carbon dioxide emissions, a by-product of the packing process, which caused eye problems. The committee also accused the company of illegal acts, including firing several dozen workers for union activity, making paycheck deductions for basic safety equipment including plastic gloves and boots, and cheating on wages owed for cleanup time at the end of the day. Finally, the report condemned the general lack of respect for the workers as people, exhibited at once in the arbitrary denial of bathroom breaks, the lack of a Spanish-language version of personnel and safety guidelines, and the intimidating closed-door meetings that the company had begun conducting to "talk about how bad unions are." "As people of faith who believe that each person is a child of God who deserves to be treated with dignity, and as Americans who believe in democracy and workers' rights to bargain collectively," the Interfaith Committee pressed Case Farms chief executive officer Shelton to arrange a "just resolution of concerns."[56] Conscience-struck supporters of the North Carolina workers reportedly demonstrated outside Shelton's Salisbury, Maryland, home.[57]

In addition to winning media attention on behalf of the workers, the Interfaith Committee hoped to build bridges to local clergy in Morganton. This second goal proved more difficult. A blanket invitation to the town's one hundred churches in early June 1996 turned up only six respondents for a meeting at St. Charles Catholic Church. One of them, a female minister from Grace Episcopal Church, questioned the meeting's sponsors: "Why do we want to be bedfellows with the labor union?"[58] Determined to reach a wider audience, Kim Bobo made a special return trip three months later to meet with the Clergy Association of Morganton:

> Father Ken went with me and it was absolutely one of the more interesting places I've been. I wish I could have tape-recorded the entire meeting, because there were just classic statements. There were some people who said things like: "Don't they already make better wages than other people in the area?" Father Ken was really superb, and said, "That's not really the point is it? If they were asking for Cadillacs and ten-weeks vacation, they'd still have the right to organize." Then there was a bunch of stuff like, "Well, shouldn't we just let the laws and the courts play themselves out?" But there were other people within the assembly that answered, "Hey, if we'd done that with civil rights, no one would have gotten anywhere." Also, a bunch of the clergy said to me, "Look, I personally would like to do more but I can't. My congregation won't let me, and I'm not like Father Ken—my congregation hires me, and they can fire me." We ended up having a very good meeting. They made some commitments in terms of trying to get a meeting with the company, and about a broader forum where they hear from the workers. But the guy who agreed to do all this stuff left town, and no one followed through.[59]

Although black ministers (Father Ken remembers two or three at the meeting) generally expressed more sympathy than whites for the workers' plight, they, too, chose not to get involved in the labor dispute.[60]

Altogether, despite some show of interfaith concern, religious support for the workers in Morganton relied overwhelmingly on the Roman Catholic Church, a fact not lost on certain unsympathetic observers. A letter to the local newspaper bristled with pent-up spleen at the union, the Chicago-based Interfaith Committee, and, most of all, the Catholic Church's entanglement with the new immigrant workforce:

> The very same papist sanctuary who ran ads way down South to entice the flood of migrants here now import paid activists here, from Chicagolia, to tell the hand that feeds the migrants to give more, so the workers can in turn give money to the church, its paid action organization, and the union, thereby granting power to the undeserving instigators. . . . We are an immigrant nation. European and African slaves along with the free poor, and the landed wealthy alike have all earned our proud places in American society. These Mexican, Mayan, Hmong, and other recent immigrant groups want a guaranteed place with unearned rights that would give them the same status as those whose blood, sweat, and tears have taken three centuries to achieve. Well it doesn't work that way in North Carolina. Here one, or a group, earns their station.[61]

Although they largely drew a blank from both company representatives and the wider religious community in Morganton, the Interfaith Committee and its allies continued to press its case across the country. Adopting a model that the International Ladies Garment Workers Union had once used with the apparel industry, a national poultry alliance called for a "code of ethics" among processors, including a living wage, safety on the job, and workers' right to organize. Representing fifty organizations from Citizen Action to the National Contract Poultry Growers Association, this labor-centered coalition backed by John Sweeney's new AFL-CIO attempted to intervene in specific labor disputes like Case Farms as well as to influence national labor and regulatory policy. Its biggest victory came in November 1996, when President Bill Clinton's secretary of labor, Robert Reich, agreed to investigate the poultry industry, declaring that "sweatshop conditions, whether in garment factories, fields or poultry processing plants, will not be tolerated."[62] Reich acknowledged that his decision was prompted in part by publicity about the Case Farms conflict.[63] Unfortunately for the pro-union forces, the promised federal action was both delayed and muted. Secretary Reich's successor, Alexis Herman, held off on the implementation of Reich's investigatory promise due to the reported pressure of industry lobbyists including Arkansas powerhouse, Tyson Foods (a major Clinton backer), and nine southern U.S. senators, who wrote an explicit letter of opposition.[64]

While LIUNA and its allies were applying legal and political stratagems to bring Case Farms to the bargaining table, rank-and-file activists and organizers on the ground struggled to prove to their fellow workers that a union presence could indeed make a difference in day-to-day work life. In effect, the two wings of the movement were interdependent. On the one hand, the workers did not have the leverage to beat the company on their own. On the other hand, if the middle class–dominated poultry alliance were to grab national attention for the plight of poultry workers, it needed tangible evidence that workers themselves were prepared to do battle for their rights. And, in what LIUNA's poultry task force leaders acknowledged was a "make-or-break" campaign, they knew that in Morganton they were battling against time.[65] Elapsed time meant more labor turnover, the dismissal or demoralization of worker activists, and the reassignment of union campaign coordinators (like Yanira Merino) to "higher-yield" projects.

So it was that in the spring of 1996, nearly a full year after the union vote, with no sign of movement from the company, LIUNA—fearing a loss of morale within the unionized ranks—again cranked up its pressure tactics at the workplace. Relying on the new group of Mexican in-plant leaders around Juan Ignacio Montes, organizers Marc Panepinto and Yanira Merino devised a number of actions to attract both their members' and the company's attention. More than eighty workers walked out in late June, for example, to protest the firing of a new employee after Ken Wilson refused to meet with a union grievance committee.[66] Demonstrations of an estimated one hundred workers outside the plant followed.[67] Another "quickie" strike—this one lasting a mere forty-five minutes—followed in early July, warning the company that the union was gearing up for a more serious, long-term confrontation.[68] "During that year," remembered Nacho, "we started organizing inside the plant, having stoppages, and demanding things. Inside the plant we were having good support."[69]

A warning to the company of a different kind came with the announcement in late July of the creation of a giant "food bank" for Case Farms workers to be housed at Father Ken's St. Charles Church. The food shipment, about forty thousand pounds of it filling a tractor-trailer truck, came from a surprising source—Operation Blessing, the philanthropic arm of conservative Virginia televangelist Pat Robertson's 700 Club. The shipment was a personal coup for John Jordan, who had learned that Operation Blessing had played a similar role in helping out many of their members

The Workers Are Ready

during the Mineworkers' prolonged Pittston strike in 1989–90.[70] "They're exceptionally nice people," Jordan said of the evangelical operation. "For them, it was a sob story [involving poor immigrants], it had nothing to do with labor."[71]

Then, on Thursday, August 8, workers struck plantwide with the sole aim of forcing management to the bargaining table. Led by the local organizing committee and coordinated by a visiting Marc Panepinto and Yanira Merino, the strike began with defiant words. "Case Farms is going to the bargaining table this time, period," declared Panepinto.[72] Pointing to LIUNA's food reserves and assurance of strike funds, Panepinto held up the union as the immigrant worker's primary lifeline: "We are here to support these workers. They are isolated here in Morganton, the community has not embraced them. We have embraced them as union brothers and sisters."[73] In a similar spirit, Father Ken again turned St. Charles's parish hall into a meeting room and strike kitchen. "Oh yes," he wrote in a call for food and spiritual support for the workers, "St. Charles will be their headquarters while they seek justice."[74] On the third day of the work stoppage, the workers themselves upped the ante of confrontation by means of a selective hunger strike. Five days later, the three hunger strikers were still only sipping liquids when the union used a march and protest rally— complete with giant papier-mâché puppets, a guerrilla theater, and a show of support from assorted visiting union representatives and a smattering of sympathetic townspeople—to reassert the workers' demands for a contract, including a wage increase, seniority pay differentials, and paid medical or maternity leave.[75] For his part, personnel manager Ken Wilson continued to refuse to meet with worker representatives, insisting that the company must wait for the court's ruling. "We will abide," he promised, "by the court's decision." Even more ominously, Case Farms took the first steps to hire replacement workers.[76]

Despite its logistical preparation and impressive pageantry, the 1996 standoff proved an uncertain affair and, in the end, an unhappy turning point for the union. Outwardly, the union preserved a confident face when, following the parade and rally eight days into the conflict, it officially called off the strike and accepted a simple company offer to rehire the strikers. "The workers were willing to stay out for as long as it took, but [union officials] thought we had made our point," Marc Panepinto insisted to the news media. "We had to convince workers to return." The statement hid more than it revealed. Even union leaders admitted that they had cut production during the strike by no more than 50 percent, a testament to a

Case Farms–LIUNA hunger strikers Luís Alberto "Beto" Gonzalez (left) and
Félix Rodríguez, August 1996. Photo courtesy of Beto Gonzalez.

problem of mass defections from early on. Jean-Claude André, a LIUNA
"student organizer" who spent two-and-a-half months in Morganton during the summer of 1996, remembered the problem of company "scabs." According to André, Case Farms avoided the union pickets by transporting
strikebreakers into the company parking lot and then building a staircase
directly over the fence into the plant proper. "That really crippled us," he
concluded. Even Guatemalan workers, with a less visible presence among
the union leadership, were decidedly less "solid" in 1996 than they had been
the previous year. One Q'anjob'al employee who crossed the picket line
later insisted that the strikers were all Mexicans![77] However exaggerated,
the claim likely signaled a serious problem for the union among its would-
be constituency. André, moreover, recalled that many Latino workers were
"drunk" or "hungover" when summoned for early-morning picket duty.
Under the circumstances, a return to work beckoned as the union's only
tenable option.[78]

Though masked by official union rhetoric and vigorous pursuit of other
pressure points against Case Farms, failure of the 1996 strike proved a severe
blow to worker morale in Morganton. The earliest and most tangible sign
of demoralization came in the defections, shortly after the strike, of union
committeemen Francisco Ramírez, Rodolfo Gómez, and José Luís Her-

The Workers Are Ready

nández to the rank of company *mayordomos* (in-plant supervisors). Nacho recalled the early poststrike general union meetings, the air thick with talk of company deception and worker demoralization, and the organizing committee in a sad state of disrepair.[79]

But the repercussions of the 1996 stalemate went deeper than the loss of a few individuals to the union cause. On the ground in Morganton, the union forces, despite a continuing up-and-down cycle in local activity and outside injection of funds and technical support, refrained from any job action longer than a shutdown of a few hours at the Case Farms plant. Perhaps even more telling was a subsequent, initially subtle change in the priorities and commitments of LIUNA itself. Organizing the poultry industry was proving more difficult and slow-going than originally contemplated by the Stillwell-Panepinto team. Indeed, whatever its problems, the Morganton campaign remained a greater success story than most other hotshops LIUNA had visited. To consider one example, the campaign at the Perdue plant in Robersonville, North Carolina, had come to a dead halt with an overwhelmingly negative vote on the very day in 1995 when Morganton voted pro-union. The fact was, if LIUNA could not face down a comparatively small employer like Case Farms, it was not likely to get far with the equally anti-union industry giants.

Indications grew by late 1996 and early 1997 that LIUNA organizers were rethinking their poultry crusade. To their credit, there was no backing down from the formal commitments they had made in Morganton. They vigorously contested the company's delaying tactics in the courts and continued to "service" the Case Farms local through a retainer to Phyllis Palmieri's law office and a salary to a local worker-organizer. Yet, the visits by Merino and other national staff became less and less frequent after the 1996 strike. Within LIUNA, the stalemate at Case Farms only enhanced doubts about the wisdom of the campaign that had existed in some quarters from the beginning.

If there were tensions from the outset between LIUNA's new organizing department and its older regional leaders, the demands of the Case Farms campaign had done little to relieve them. Coincident with the August 1996 strike in Morganton, the Laborers were preparing for a national convention, the first in their history where officers would be elected by a rank-and-file ballot. The union's vice president Jack Wilkinson, it happened, was being challenged by Panepinto's old friend, Michael "Bud" Corsini from Buffalo, and both Stillwell and Panepinto publicly backed his insurgent bid. "It was a very high risk strategy," recalled John Jordan. In his view, the

1996 strike got caught up in intramural union politics, a test of one style of leadership versus another. "It became a kind of competitive thing . . . Bud Corsini ships down a busload of people [to help with the strike], all the way from upstate New York. . . . And Wilkinson ships in a bunch of people from his local. So they're all in this thing. [Stillwell] thought that this would bring the company to its knees. Corsini, as the more explicit backer [of the campaign], would get the credit." Whether or not there was such a strategic linkage between the Morganton strike and the union election (and Panepinto, for one, categorically denied it), the LIUNA election results, in which the incumbent Wilkinson soundly trounced Corsini, did not reinforce the position of the organizing team. If anything, it strengthened the hand of those in LIUNA who questioned the union's recent lateral organizing initiatives. Similar second-guessing of the "new union" strategy broke out at the national AFL-CIO convention in Pittsburgh the following year. "Don't they realize," an American Federation of Teachers (AFT) delegate reportedly scolded the Sweeney team, "that if they really push this organizing, the labor movement is going to wind up being a movement of strawberry pickers and chicken pluckers?"[80]

In fact, the AFT critic need not have worried. By the time of the fall convention in 1997, Stillwell and most of the rest of his poultry organizing team had been severed from LIUNA. The last straw, to be sure, had nothing to do with Case Farms and nothing to do with poultry. In January 1997 Stillwell had entered a high-stakes, competitive drive to sign up thousands of public workers in Riverside County, California. In the midst of a feverish campaign schedule, a majority of about twenty union staff members complained of overwork; when LIUNA rebuffed them, they escalated their protest into a weeklong strike demanding *their own* recognition as union staff employees. As the chief scapegoat for this organizing debacle, Stillwell was forced to resign in mid-March, and Panepinto, David Kiefer, and others associated with the union's new wave soon followed.[81] LIUNA's ambitious entry into the food-processing and other low-wage, labor-intensive industries was effectively over.

What was left of a once-promising organizing crusade was the union's foothold at Case Farms. Like a tar baby that first beckoned to the touch but then refused to let go, LIUNA—for the good of its reputation both inside and outside the AFL-CIO—was "stuck" with its lonely Morganton outpost. While minimally discharging its commitment to service the local (formally chartered in 1998 as Local 700, apparently with only coincidental connection to the role of the 700 Club in the group's history), the international union basically awaited the appellate court's decision on the company's seemingly interminable legal maneuverings. As Interfaith Committee director, Kim Bobo analyzed LIUNA's internal calculations in 1998: "They've invested hundreds of thousands of dollars in this campaign with nothing to show for it. There's got to be people saying, 'Do we pour [more] money into this, or do we just bag it? Now to their credit they've continued to put resources into it, but probably not enough to get them over the edge. On some level, it only makes sense to do it if you have a long-term commitment to poultry. Given that they don't, the fact that they've put resources in at all is a tribute to their commitment to do the right thing."[82]

But soon it was not just LIUNA's original organizing team that had left for (or been redirected to) other pastures. The international political campaign waged on behalf of the Case Farms workers through the IUF came unglued when IUF organizer Kurt Stand's international credentials proved to carry an unwelcome edge. In October 1997 Stand was arrested along with his wife, a former Pentagon lawyer, and another accomplice—all three "former campus Marxists" at the University of Wisconsin who had allegedly spied on the United States for twenty-five years for East Germany. Stand's secret career—which, it turned out, he had been recruited into by his own father, an East German intelligence officer—came to an inglorious end when, seeking new outlets following the collapse of the Soviet Bloc, he and his wife sought to sell their services to the South African government of Nelson Mandela, which turned their names over to U.S. officials. Stand's friends in the U.S. labor movement and elsewhere were flabbergasted. "This business of spying for East Germany," sighed one incredulous friend from Madison, "and doing it after the cold war was officially ended. . . . The Japanese soldiers who hid out on the Pacific islands all those years at least had the excuse of not knowing the war was over."[83] In January 1999 Stand and his wife were found guilty of conspiracy and attempted espionage; they were sentenced, respectively, to seventeen years and twenty-one years in jail.[84]

For LIUNA, the prosecution of Kurt Stand was insignificant compared to the renewed legal setbacks of Arthur A. Coia. In the same month as Stand's arrest, the in-house union prosecutor announced plans to charge the union president with malfeasance. Although a two-year investigation had formally cleared Coia of mob connections, it faulted him for fraud in avoiding tax payments of $100,000 in the purchase of three Ferraris worth more than $1.5 million. After initially contesting the finding, Coia agreed to step down as union president in December 1999—remaining as president emeritus at a salary of $250,000 per year—and to pay his back taxes.[85] By late 1997, in short, Coia's whiz-bang organizing initiatives—whether conceived from political idealism or for political cover—had largely run their course. Between the dismissal of the original organizing staff and Coia's own troubles, according to attorney Lawrence Gold, "there was a real change in the direction of the Laborers. Poultry was no longer a goal or a target." In the changed circumstances, the Case Farms campaign "became kind of an orphan."[86]

A final political setback for labor's would-be new turn occurred at the top of the AFL-CIO hierarchy. Ron Carey's recent "reform" victory over James Hoffa in the pivotal Teamsters union was thrown out by federal investigators in January 1997 on grounds that unauthorized outside funds— engineered through Citizen Action (whose Ohio affiliate had coordinated consumer pressure against Case Farms)—had found their way into Carey's war chest. Soon, not only would Carey be forced to step down as union leader (ultimately to be replaced by Hoffa in a special new election) but also the financial chicanery involved in the Teamster case appeared to implicate John Sweeney's right-hand man, AFL-CIO secretary-treasurer Richard Trumka. All in all, it was a calamitous turn for the federation's new guard, one that forced it on the defensive and ate into its capacities for aggressive national organizing.

Although the shakeups in the labor movement's front office disrupted a chain of command that had previously provided Morganton workers a powerful lifeline of outside support, they did not in themselves spell defeat for the local labor effort. Indeed, with on-again, off-again bursts of energy and initiative, union activists dug in for the long haul. Represented by Nacho as in-plant leader, Carlos Salido as paid organizer, and legal adviser Phyllis Palmieri (and aided by legal assistant Felipe López, Paulino López Castro's well-educated, English-speaking son who arrived from Aguacatán in 1998), Local 700 determined to make its presence felt. In addition to closely monitoring company behavior, the union fielded a soccer team and provided immigration and naturalization services, as well as other legal advice, to the larger Latino community. "We fought hard in '97 and '98," asserted Beto González. "With Nacho we were always making plans for how to get a contract." No doubt, the union local's most impressive weapon remained its ability to rally workers at a moment's notice over in-plant grievances. A brief walkout in 1997, for instance, restored the job of Manuel López López, an Awakateko who had named his new daughter "Yanira"

The Workers Are Ready

after the 1995 strike leader. More effective than plantwide stoppages, however, union-based pressure provided a check on arbitrary supervisor authority. One day, workers were told that the plant would be closing an hour early and, therefore, there would be no early afternoon break. When complaints echoed up the line to Nacho, he quickly responded. "I said, 'Let's stop one line and everybody goes on break ten minutes. Then when you guys come back, we stop another line.' And the Supervisor said, 'Hey, hey, what happened[,] why do you stop the line?' I told him, 'Do you want me to stop the whole department or the whole plant?' He said, 'No, no, no, we want to try to work something.'"[87]

Ironically, by the time Case Farms workers got their day at the bargaining table, few of their erstwhile allies were paying much attention. In June 1998—with the air long since removed from LIUNA's national organizing balloon—Case Farms exhausted its final legal appeal and sat down, under court order, for a required year of contract bargaining talks "in good faith" with union representatives. What might have been a period of celebration and rejuvenation of local union energies, however, in the end proved the opposite. The negotiations, run on the company side by Ohio labor lawyer David Hiller (who had handled Case Farms's earlier legal appeals), in association with Ken Wilson, and on the union side by contract specialist Richard Beck, supplemented by a committee of eight local worker representatives, including Nacho, Beto, Marta Gálvez, and Guatemalan legal specialist Felipe López, dragged on for weeks and months.

Richard Beck called the Case Farms conflict "one of the more bitter disputes I've ever experienced." A native of Henderson County, Kentucky, and a construction laborer who rose up through the ranks of LIUNA as steward, foreman, and local business manager to international representative and contract specialist, Beck had officially retired after thirty-five years of service as a union administrator but was still summoned to handle selective negotiations. Having earlier negotiated poultry contracts at Sanderson Farms and other plants in Mississippi, Beck initially approached the North Carolina situation with guarded optimism. The Laborers union, he noted, had tried to avoid conflict; through labor-management "cooperation," "we believe you can usually strike some type of happy medium." But at Case Farms, the two sides never really communicated. The company's instinctual anti-unionism, in Beck's view, had only hardened in the face of previous work stoppages and the union's corporate campaign. Management lawyers told Beck that Case Farms president Tom Shelton had been personally angered and insulted when protesters had appeared outside his church in

Salisbury, Maryland. "I tried to change the climate, to install labor peace," said Beck with apparent exasperation at attitudes on both sides of the dispute. Given the polarized climate, the protracted negotiating sessions made little progress. The fact was, the union was not looking for dramatic material breakthroughs from the contract. During the previous year, Case Farms had already given a $0.45 hourly increase to its workers in Winesburg, Ohio, and Goldsboro, North Carolina (a new plant it purchased in late 1997), while the prevailing Case Farms wage was stuck at $7.05 per hour since 1996, far below industry standards.[88] Although union negotiators formally demanded a modest $0.50 hourly raise (a symbolic "nickel" above the company's nonunion plants), Beck believed that the union would, in fact, have willingly settled for a $0.25 per hour "token" settlement in Morganton. But Case Farms merely offered an insulting $0.15 per hour increase to the overwhelming majority of production workers while singling out a few skilled maintenance workers (who happened to be disproportionately white and heretofore only weakly involved in the union) for bigger bonuses. In addition, it proposed an incentive bonus based on a quota of pounds of chicken run per day that the union feared would only exacerbate line speed complaints. In an internal union vote in January 1999, the company proposal was overwhelmingly rejected. "They tried to divide us," Beck recounted. "It was totally ridiculous."[89]

In May 1999, following its mandated one year of negotiations and weeks of postponed union-management meetings, Case Farms abruptly announced that the parties had reached an impasse and that it would no longer meet with union representatives. Local 700, which had refrained throughout the negotiations from any job actions lest it create an excuse for the company's withdrawal from the talks, tried to reassemble its workplace pressure. But it could muster only a lackluster, ineffectual work stoppage. "The majority were just not willing to stand up," observed Richard Beck. Rapid turnover in the plant combined with the presence of an increasing number of immigrant workers without legal work permits accentuated the organizers' problems. Sensing its opponent's growing vulnerability, Case Farms then fired an even bigger gun. "It's time to bring the bargaining process to a conclusion," read a May 28 memo distributed to all employees. "In an effort to break this logjam we have decided to withhold work and initiate a partial lock-out. Commencing next week the work week will be reduced to four days. We will be closed on Mondays starting this coming Monday, May 31. If the four-day work week fails to bring the bargaining process to a prompt conclusion, we will decide whether to reduce the work week further."[90] The warning, coupled with rumors that the Morganton plant was shifting production to the newly acquired operation in Goldsboro, set off a panic among the Spanish-speaking workers.

By the end of the next week a group of anti-union workers, reportedly at the initiative of the plant supervisor, circulated an English-language petition that a majority of workers signed.[91] According to union representatives, most workers thought that the petition supported reopening the plant on Mondays, and they were not shown the document's heading, which declared a vote of no-confidence in the union, effectively a formal mechanism of union decertification under NLRB rules. With the petition in hand, Case Farms (though choosing not to file formally for decertification) declared that LIUNA no longer represented its workforce and that the company was no longer bound to recognize the union. Local 700 representatives quickly filed unfair labor practice motions with the NLRB. Not only was the Monday shutdown a brazen scare tactic, argued attorney Phyllis Palmieri, but also the company had unfairly intimidated workers from expressing themselves by hiring a former Burke County sheriff as an armed and very visible head of plant security.[92] As was typical, the union's complaints rested for months, unresolved, in a backlog of NLRB cases. At most, the NLRB might argue before a special master of the circuit court that the company had evaded its responsibility to "bargain in good faith" and ask the court for redress in the form of a contempt citation ordering Case Farms back to the negotiating table. By the fall of 2000, the NLRB determined to initiate such proceedings. But no force on the horizon appeared capable of compelling a formal agreement from the company to do business with its organized workers. "I think they never had any intention of signing a contract," reflected Palmieri. "To drag it out the way they did over the course of a year was a tremendous opportunity for them to undermine the union's strength. . . . It was a case of a cat playing with a mouse until it was weak enough, and then cutting its throat."[93]

A year and a half following the dissolution of the initial round of collective bargaining talks, LIUNA and Case Farms remained as far apart as they had ever been in five years of skirmishing. There was no question—notwithstanding the fraudulence of the decertification petition—that the union had lost substantial strength, perhaps even the capacity to re-win an electoral majority if put to the test.[94] Across the lengthy negotiating period and its aftermath, key local leaders departed from the front ranks of the struggle. Roger Nuñez, a Nicaraguan with strong Sandinista sympathies, was fired after an altercation with his supervisor. Marta Gálvez, exhausted from work and depressed at the union's prospects, quit the chicken plant even before the end of the bargaining sessions.

The case of the local union president, Juan Ignacio Montes, was more poignant still. In spring 1999, following the removal of a tumor in his back, Nacho learned that he had bone cancer; soon, he was forced to quit work to begin treatments that stretched from chemotherapy through a bone marrow transplant in January 2000. Although both the union and his church (St. Charles) rallied around Nacho and coordinated private relief efforts for his family, his medical expenses would undoubtedly have been overwhelming were it not for the catastrophic benefits available under his employer-paid medical insurance. (The bone marrow transplant alone cost $70,000.) On this issue, what separated Nacho and his family from destitution was the charitable act of Ken Wilson, who privately saw to it that Nacho was not dropped from the company's insurance rolls. Whether an act of respect for a longtime antagonist, a simple case of human sympathy, or a more strategic demonstration of paternalism, Case Farms's role in "protecting" the welfare of the local union president speaks volumes about who had power and resources in Morganton and who did not. Nacho's forced withdrawal from the fight deprived the workers of their single most powerful symbol as well as active center of resistance. His inability to return to work was the major factor convincing Luís Alberto González to leave Case Farms after five years' employment for a higher-paying job in a local furniture factory. "He is the one who kept us together," explained Beto.[95] Nacho himself confirmed that for the moment (early 2000) there was "no one who can say, 'We gonna stop the line.'"[96]

Against the backdrop of union incapacity in Morganton—a condition apparent to some as early as the 1996 strike but more universally recognized after the company's demonstrated refusal to bargain—various union partisans engaged in a game of second-guessing about the Case Farms campaign. There were clearly some LIUNA officials, centered in the union's Mid-Atlantic regional headquarters, who believed that Case Farms—so geographically, occupationally, and politically secluded from the union's base of support—was a "bad target" from the beginning.[97] Even former organizing director Duane Stillwell acknowledged that LIUNA's early enthusiasm for a poultry campaign was probably "wishful thinking—we should have handed it off early on to UFCW."[98] At the other extreme were advocates like Kim Bobo and John Jordan, who believed that LIUNA was too tepid in its strategy and commitment. Bobo thought that serious preparation for an extended strike might have spelled the difference be-

The Workers Are Ready

tween victory and defeat. "Could they shut down the operation to do a strike for two months? That would require strike pay for everybody, but they could do strike pay for two months and shut the operation down. . . . [Or] there are certain days that chickens come in, and then there's no place and way to store them. So let's say they strike every day that chickens come. That would work."[99] In his own list of might-have-beens, Jordan put more emphasis on union-community ties. LIUNA, he asserted, never established a permanent presence in Morganton that the people could believe in: "They shuffled people in and out with no strategic vision. And this whole notion of branching out into the community, it was foreign. I remember [Marc] Panepinto saying, 'We organize workers, not communities.' If you're going to go in, if you're going to get 300 or 400 people all wound up, and you're going to make promises to them, you'd better stick with it. Put two people in there and just keep them there long-term, working with [the local people]. To assist with the spontaneous stuff. Just to be there."[100] Although Panepinto bristled at Jordan's critique—"[somebody] with the right politics but not a thinker or a doer"—he too faulted LIUNA for lack of follow-through at Case Farms. "I'm not satisfied we did everything we could, just because the region disavowed itself of this thing and really never wanted to invest in it. That was a racist decision on [their] part. You know, 'these little Guatemalans in Morganton'—it was never their [the regional affiliate's] baby and they sort of got dragged into it."[101]

Disillusionment after 1996 spread among key community supporters as well. Father Ken Whittington, whose commitment from the beginning was crucial to building up the union, perhaps best reflected the subsequent letdown. Local people, he suggested—seemingly including himself—felt that they had been exploited by the company and by the union. "[The workers] are fed up with people coming. Any outsider is seen as just that, an outsider. They don't understand who is there to help them or the ins and outs of the struggle. They want better conditions. They were organized before the union came along. Then the union sailed in and promised them things, and the promises are not there. . . . The theological term for my feelings about the union just now is 'pissed off.'"[102]

Immigrant worker activists like Nacho and Beto tended to be less categorical in their judgments. Committed to union principles and grateful as immigrants for an uncommon helping hand extended toward Latino workers, they measured their words carefully before finding fault. More in sorrow than anger, for example, they sensed the slow withdrawal of LIUNA's support. One specific criticism they agreed on centered on the tactical decision by national union leaders, as communicated by Richard Beck, to cease and desist from in-plant actions during the extended negotiations with the company in 1998–99. Unable to witness a union presence, they suggested, the workers—themselves constantly turning over through geographic mobility—lost confidence in the union as an alternative to company authority. "[Richard] Beck," said Nacho simply, "didn't want to fight."[103] "I didn't understand him well," echoed Beto. "He said we had to respect the rules [*los convenios*] but the company never followed the rules."[104]

Former LIUNA counsel Lawrence Gold, who now worked for the AFL-CIO, called the Case Farms situation "tragic and maddening." On the one hand, he was critical of certain decisions taken by the union. Clearly, he believed, the union had bitten off more than it could chew in Morganton:

> If the Laborers' organizing program had grown and continued as it seemed like it was going to . . . there might be a corporate campaign going on now. . . . I think it's an absolutely ideal case to bring public attention: here's an example of a lawless company and an exploited labor force. It's got everything and would be a very appealing example. . . . But the Laborers never really had the internal capacity to wage something like that. They just didn't have the experience or the personnel. The AFL-CIO would have been a good partner, but that was not pursued. It's a lesson in how as a labor movement we have to be more strategic in how we organize. We [the AFL-CIO] are now encouraging unions to focus their organizing energies on their core industries, on what they know best and where they have the most density. . . . From that point of view the Laborers doing Case Farms made no sense. I wish it could have reached some kind of accommodation for a joint action with UFCW.

But Gold also raised doubts that *any* strategy—including a well-endowed corporate campaign—undertaken in the contemporary period of U.S. industrial relations would have led to a workers' victory in Morganton. "It requires a public climate that finds employer opposition and intimidation and the firing of workers—that looks at that in the same vein that race discrimination and sex discrimination is looked at. So that there is some general public opprobrium directed at it. Right now the right to organize and rights in the workplace don't have the same stature in our culture." Might it take nonviolent resistance after the manner of the civil rights movement to force a change? Gold was dubious. "It doesn't seem practicable. We're not talking civil disobedience against Jim Crow laws here. Can you do civil disobedience over the fact that the law permits the company to petition

The Workers Are Ready

to review an NLRB decision no matter what, and it happens to take the court of appeals years to resolve those cases? It's not the same."[105] Given the structure of industrial relations, even a reenergized organizing mission by the new AFL-CIO failed to arrest the steady decline of unionization in the private sector.[106]

Typical also was the frustration of Case Farms workers, who, even after winning an organizing drive, could not get their employer to take seriously the formal obligation to bargain for a contract. Particularly after 1980, employers and their legal advisers regularly confounded the spirit of the nation's labor laws, originally passed to ensure the speedy institutionalization of collective bargaining once employees have indicated a union preference. Extended appeals and challenges of NLRB or other judicial rulings became the standard modus operandi to withstand a union campaign.[107] By delaying union recognition and serious contract bargaining for months or even years, a company was able to take advantage of worker turnover as well as fatigue, demoralization, and the exhausted organizing budget of the participating union. Indeed, in the 1990s an estimated one-third of the workplaces where workers voted for a union never achieved a first contract. In one of the most notorious cases, three thousand workers at Avondale Shipyards in New Orleans were stymied for seven years in their effort to institutionalize an original pro-union vote.[108] By way of comparison, it is worth speculating what would have happened to the Case Farms workers had the same company located its plant in Canada rather than in the United States. Unlike the United States, Canada gives provincial labor boards the authority to impose first agreements when the parties are unable to reach a settlement on their own.[109] In the United States, whereas an executive caught stealing trade secrets or manipulating stock may face the wrath of the state, the law appears comparatively feckless in dealing with employer abuses of rules meant to encourage union representation and collective bargaining. In terms of labor rights, immigrant workers would have been better off seeking a more northerly El Norte.

By the spring of 2001, about six years after the original union vote, it seemed that only an epitaph was needed to mark the end of the extended struggle at Case Farms. The company had regularly played its hand of punish, ignore, or delay until it had good reason to suppose that the union forces would fold their tent. The law had languished, as was its wont in American industrial relations, as a frail and almost irrelevant instrument of justice. Public attention had also wandered: without strikes or dramatic clashes, no press came to the Case Farms workers, while social justice activists equally were drawn to more heroic battlefronts. Even the national union, absorbed for years in other business, paid scant heed to Morganton except as a kind of perpetual mortgage to good intentions gone awry: practically speaking, a monthly retainer to Felipe López and the occasional visit of an organizer—in the manner of a country doctor paying respects to a dying patient—was all that was left of the Case Farms "campaign."

Yet, for diverse reasons, the Morganton dispute refused to go away. In the first place, although U.S. labor law was weak and slow, it nevertheless afforded to the persistent a formal base of legitimacy. Second, for all their setbacks, a core of Guatemalan workers—gathered around Felipe López and a reconstituted organizing committee—continued to look to the union for workplace protection. Picking up the pieces of a fractured leadership structure, Felipe and a few union volunteers went back to the business of weekend house calls, methodically reestablishing union representatives in each of the plant's main departments. Although shunned and stymied on the big issues, the union forces continued to pester the company at every turn. When, in March 2000, for example, Case Farms issued sweatshirts bragging about its accident-free record, a union leaflet retorted, "What a joke! Do we need to die to call it an accident? Many of us have had accidents but they never call it accidents. . . . Brothers and Sisters don't be fooled by a sweater! Let's stand up and fight together for a fair contract that will give us: some respect, dignity, a safe workplace, fair wages." The fact was that, however bleak its bargaining position, the union's institutional persistence in Morganton lent it a continuing legitimacy within the immigrant workers' community.

Local hopes thus rose on April 17, 2001, when—rather than face further legal delay and attendant court costs—the company agreed to settle with the NLRB over its contempt citation for refusing to bargain in good faith. The settlement mandated an "intense" new three-month round of negotiations as well as company payment of $130,000 (or roughly $200 per worker) as "compensation" for its prior transgressions.[110] On the rank-and-file union negotiating committee (supplementing the "professional" counsel of Phyllis Palmieri, Felipe López, and an attorney from LIUNA's Washington, D.C., headquarters), a half-dozen workers representing the three major Guatemalan sending communities in town—Aguacatán, Totonicapán, and San Marcos—joined Francisco Aguirre, the Q'anjob'al-speaking (from San Miguel Acatán by way of Guatemala City) successor to Nacho as in-plant leader. With negotiations about to open, veteran activist José Samuel Solís López was pleased. Although most of the "new committee" members were "recent employees," he noted, "the rest [of us] initiated them into the struggle, they learned what the problems are here." While taking nothing for granted, José Samuel seemed confident that the company would finally accept a union presence. "We're not asking for much and they don't want to go back to court," he reasoned.[111] After many winters of discontent, by early summer of 2001 José Samuel and other union stalwarts remained hopeful that justice would in the end be theirs. They sensed that they could not enact it on their own, but when outside help came, they would be ready.

6

Changing Places

Outside the drama of the labor conflicts, Morganton's immigrant workers tried to make the best of their individual situations. In their struggle to get by day-to-day and as they faced uncertain futures in terms of work, residency, and citizenship status, the general tone among the transplanted Guatemalans was not pessimistic. In 1999, for example, I received a letter that began, confidently, "Greetings from this little Maya Community in Morganton."[1] The message bespoke both pride and purpose. Barely a decade removed from the arrival of the first migrant worker in town, it required an act of imagination to reconstruct an entire Mayan social fabric amid the uncertainty and dislocation of a job-driven transplantation. Yet, even as the restricted property of local organic intellectuals, the vision of a transplanted "Maya Community" suggested the ready adaptability of immigrant aspirations and identities.

Let us begin with four quick impressions of Guatemalans whose lives have interacted with a larger world. The first image is of Gaspar Francisco, a Q'anjob'al Case Farms worker from a tiny aldea outside San Miguel Acatán. In discussion, it was quickly obvious that, for Gaspar, Morganton (and, indeed, the whole world outside San Miguel Acatán) was but a means to a paycheck, a way to make ends meet for his family back home. Gaspar, who had lived in the United States since 1985, was among the first twenty-five Guatemalans to settle in Morganton in 1990. Despite a decade of residency, however, he had precious few friends in the town; in fact, he knew little about the people or place in which he currently lived. Of the English language, he had learned *casi nada* (almost nothing). The mammoth share of what he earned, he sent back to Guatemala monthly in $500 or $1,000 increments. Outside work, he rarely indulged in pastimes other than rest. Each year, with the company's permission, he spent up to one month in his native village. Only occasionally frequenting the Catholic church, Gaspar watched Univision, ate tortillas, and dreamed regularly of one day going home with enough money to buy land (his family had always rented) near San Miguel. A man of simple tastes, he would have liked nothing more than to return to his *milpa* (corn patch) to continue, if slightly less desperately, the life bequeathed to him by his ancestors.

The second image is of a sidewalk conversation outside the private mail service office of King Express in San Miguel Acatán during the summer of 1998. Marcos Miguel González ran the office, and he warmly greeted the North American travelers who had been deposited on his street after a long bus ride from the regional capital of Huehuetenango at the end of the working day. The big news from "Huehue" was that the Volcano Pacaya (one of three that ring Guatemala City) had erupted the previous day, spilling gray ash over the streets of the capital. The story was all over the country's newspapers and national television channel. Yet, Marcos knew nothing of the story. None of the metropolitan dailies had yet arrived in San Miguel (in retrospect, I am not sure how often they ever appeared there), and his own satellite TV did not pick up the signal from the capital. While Marcos pumped the North American visitors for news about his native country, he had exciting news for us as well. He knew that Reggie Miller had helped the Indiana Pacers defeat the Chicago Bulls, 107-105, in an NBA (National Basketball Association) Eastern Conference semifinal game the previous evening.[2]

The third image summons up Justo German Castro Lux and his wife Tránsita Gutiérrez Solís Castro, K'iche'-speaking immigrants from the Guatemalan department of Totonicapán and two of the most devoted Pan-Mayanists in Morganton. It was a letter from Justo that evoked "this little Maya Community in Morganton." Appointed to a Glenmary community development project in the summer of 1998, Justo and his Chilean-born "co-missioner," Francisco Risso, a Catholic Worker, charted a local Consejo Maya (Maya Council) that worked at several levels: provided English-language classes, an alcoholics' self-help group, support work for the Case Farms union and immigrant rights, and a class in leadership training, as well as sponsored a Mayan cultural group featuring poetry declamations and the music of the *marimba*.[3] In addition, future plans for the Consejo mentioned "promotion of the four Maya languages in Morganton [Q'anjob'al, Awakateko, K'ich'e, and Mam]," building a network with other Latino and Mayan organizations in the United States, "a small project to support the organizations and poor communities in Guatemala," and social services outreach in Morganton, such as providing transporta-

Tránsita Gutiérrez Solís Lux and daughter Ixchel
in Morganton, 2000.

tion, interpreters, and job placement assistance.[4] This local effort was
linked to a national Pan-Mayan movement, concretized at North America's
First Maya Congress, in Lake Worth, Florida, on December 3–4, 1999.
Justo emerged from the event as a member of the congress's governing
council.[5] To celebrate their commitment to tradition, Justo and Tránsita
chose names for their four children—Tojil, Canil, Ixchel, and Chilam—
from the pantheon of Mayan literature.[6] For her part, Tránsita always wore
her native *traje* (traditional clothes), even while working in a local convenience store.

The final image is an exchange with three daughters of Q'anjob'al strike
leader "Don Pancho" José in the library of Morganton's St. Charles Church.
Of the three, Ana, then twenty-six, was the only one who had even a faint
memory of her life in Guatemala. Yet Ana, Petrona (twenty-three), and

Changing Places

Isabel (seventeen) all very much identified as "Guatemalans" and "Q'an-job'al," as well as "Hispanics," though not as "Latinos" ("that's the Mexi-cans"). All three daughters were more comfortable in English than Span-ish, though frequently among themselves and in their parents' home, the lingua franca for all but the grandchildren was Q'anjob'al. Isabel, the only one of the three with U.S. citizenship, avidly watched *Who Wants to Be a Millionaire?* and was proud when she correctly guessed a right answer. She was considering joining the ROTC and entering the U.S. Army with the thought that this could be a path at once toward professional training as a nurse-midwife and a down payment on a house. Ultimately, she wanted to live in Hawaii, for there, she dreamed, were "Americans" who "look a lot like us!" Ana, for her part, took pride in wearing her native traje; un-fortunately, however, she had "never learned" to put it on correctly, so she simply threw it around her as a "jumper" when she went to church. At the end of our interview, when they had answered all my questions, Petrona interjected, "Tell us about Guatemala! What is it like?"[7]

These stories only begin to suggest the complexity of identity among the contemporary Maya, whether in their native Guatemala or transplanted to the United States.[8] Within the space of the four examples, we meet in Gaspar a classic "bird of passage," a temporary migrant worker who identified overwhelmingly with his home country and was culturally all but unaffected by his economically forced emigration. Meanwhile, Don Pancho's daughters betrayed both the power and the ambiguity of assimi-lation—on the one hand the pull of a U.S.-centered consumer melting pot, on the other the unmistakable sense of difference, bred at once by loyalty to one's roots and imposed by racial/ethnic discrimination in the United States. Arguably, such contradictory tugs of "outsider" identity and second-generation assimilation repeated in barely altered form a pat-tern well established by earlier immigrant generations.[9] But Marcos's story —the only nonimmigrant of the bunch—suggests something rather differ-ent. By tuning into a globalized communications network, he points to a new "transnational" reality affecting Guatemalans, to a greater or lesser degree, in both host and sender countries. If globalization had not quite taken command in San Miguel, it certainly had made a difference, reori-enting a tiny provincial town to events thousands of miles away, short-circuiting national identity for a specified global sports partisanship, and, of course, via mail services like King Express itself, providing a new local eco-nomic base from "remission" payments sent from abroad. Yet, rather than simple absorption into the logic of the global marketplace, the case of Justo and Tránsita suggests an alternative form of transnational identity. Exemplifying what anthropologist Diane Nelson calls the "Maya hacker," Justo and Tránsita used the tools of the computer and internet access precisely in order *not* to be appropriated into a Ladino (or otherwise westernized) nation.[10]

The Maya of Morganton present a fascinating case of cultural collision. How do we make sense of the entry of some of the world's most traditional (by any definition) agricultural producers into the epicenter of the world's consumer economy? Better yet, how did *they* make sense of it? Long consumed with the question of disruption (or "uprooting") versus continuity (or "transplanting") of group identity, immigration history here appears to demand a kind of conceptual hybridity.[11]

In this instance, one of the newest buzzwords of social science, "globalization," will have to serve alongside one of the oldest, "community." As sociologist Malcolm Waters defines the term, *globalization* is "a social process in which the constraints of geography on social and cultural arrangements recede and in which people become increasingly aware that they are receding."[12] Extending the boundaries of a world capitalist economy first evident in the nineteenth century, today's economic revolution has drastically reduced the costs of transportation and communication so that people, ideas, products, and finance capital literally circulate around the globe.[13] Other commentators readily speak of a "global culture," an arena of identity where national boundaries mean less and less and transnational connections or "diasporic public spheres" prevail.[14] One of the more schematic of recent forays on the subject, in fact, distinguishes four variations within the new global culture—"Davos" (or business) culture, "faculty club" (or international human rights) culture, "McWorld" (or commercial pop) culture, and evangelical Protestantism. Yet, even as Guatemalan migrant poultry workers reflected an increasingly globalized world of investment and labor markets, they also defined a fifth variation on what anthropologist Arjun Appadurai calls the "global cultural economy."[15]

If the new Morganton immigrants beckon, on the one hand, as subjects of globalization, they are also quintessential representatives of a very different concept, *community*. In recent times, community has regularly appeared as something "they" (the primitive, premodern, or non-Western "other") have, but that "we" have lost or perhaps are struggling to renew.[16] Moreover, preoccupation with the decline of community—an issue at the root of much modern social science investigation—has functioned as a kind of permanent malaise. Reiterating the community breakdown thesis, for example, political scientist Robert D. Putnam argues that civic engagement in the United States has dangerously declined over the past thirty years. Contending that trust and reciprocity among friends, neighbors, and fellow citizens—what he calls "social capital"—has frayed within a consumerist and individualistically ambitious culture, Putnam sums up his central concern in the title of his book, *Bowling Alone: The Collapse and Revival of American Community* (2000).[17]

The appearance of the Maya in the heartland of solitary (or at least unorganized) bowlers in and of itself constitutes a kind of interpretive provocation.[18] With all the resonance that the concept involves, there is probably no people more closely linked in academic scholarship to "community" than the Maya of Mexico and Central America. As early as 1937, anthropologist Sol Tax stressed the "local nature" of Mayan cultures and defined their basic unit not as a "tribe" or language group but as the territorial *municipio* or township dating to pre-Hispanic times.[19] Drawing at once on his own Mayan field studies and early ethnographies like E. E. Evans-Pritchard's work among the Nuer of the Upper Nile, Robert Redfield by 1955 framed the classic conceptualization of "the very predominant form of human living throughout the history of mankind," "the little community."[20] Aside from their distinct language and dress, perhaps the most striking feature for anthropologists about the Mayan communities was the tightly knit structure of obligations, or "cargos," owed the community by the individual, a system more or less connected to the post-Conquest *cofradías*, local religious fraternities that supervised the veneration of the saints on fiesta days.[21]

Though modern-day scholars have largely rejected an older "essentialist" view of a pristine and exotic culture uninfluenced by modern life in favor of a "historicist" recognition of an oppressed class of peasant cultivators, they continue to emphasize the distinctiveness of Mayan community patterns.[22] Even after world-historic changes including war, rebellion, religious factionalism, economic decline, and mass emigration that would seem to have eroded the "material" or structural basis for such identities, the salience of the Mayan "little community" remains. In the municipio of Totonicapán, for example, where the cargo system had disintegrated by the 1920s and few households depended on agriculture by the 1970s, and where a once-unified ancestral faith had fractured into competing religious frameworks, anthropologist Carol A. Smith nevertheless discovered that the "cultural conception of community remained a [powerful] force" in

Indian social action. Seeking an explanation for this puzzle, Smith located it in a more strategic (and less primordial) understanding of "communities of interest": ongoing struggles against a Ladino-controlled state endowed the tight connections within the Indian community with a continuing, substantive political meaning.[23] Smith's findings coincide remarkably with Douglas Brintnall's study of Aguacatán: in that future port of embarkment for North Carolina, although an older communal authority had all but broken down by the 1970s, Indian political identity was on the rise, not in decline.[24] In many cases, communal discipline seems to function less as an uninterrupted chain of tradition than as one selection within a larger cultural repertoire—a selection conditioned by the call of the present moment rather than the distant echo of the past.

At the same time, recent studies of immigration—rejecting one-way models of cultural adaptation implied by older concepts like "the uprooted" or "the assimilation process"—emphasize cultural continuity across spatial boundaries. Late-twentieth-century scholars speak of "multi-locality, transnational affiliations, and the simultaneity of daily experience in places separated by large physical distances."[25] "Complex connectivity," concludes John Tomlinson, "weakens the ties of culture to place." For Tomlinson, the process is best summed up in the concept of "deterritorialization."[26]

We know, in short, that Mayan "old ways" were not necessarily so old or pure and that immigrants may simultaneously live and identify with at least two diverse social locations. Still, was there something distinctive—and distinctively "Mayan"—in the attitudes and understanding that Mayan worker-immigrants brought with them to Morganton? Beyond a strictly economic and political calculus, in other words, were there traditions and values that help explain the behavior of these globalized workers in foreign lands? Here, most assuredly, we will require the testimony and perspective of the migrants themselves.

Félix Rodríguez, an early stalwart of Morganton unionism, offered a common response to the question of identity. "I feel 100 percent Aguacateco and Guatemalteco," he insisted. "I haven't changed."[27] Echoing Rodríguez, Felipe López's sister Katarina, who had remained in Aguacatán since her brother Felipe left for Morganton in 1997, maintained that Felipe had not "changed." "He promised us, 'I was born here and I am Aguacateco, and even if I go to another country, I am not going to change."[28]

Perhaps not surprisingly, it was at first in relatively simple matters of food, clothing, language, and rural folkways that the Maya stood out—both in their testimony and in the observations of strangers—from their non-Maya neighbors. Ask a Guatemalan in Morganton what he or she means in declaring, "I am Guatemalan/Maya/Aguacateco/etc.," and the first answer was likely to be, "I eat *comida típica* [traditional food]," meaning corn tortillas and beans. First available in a little local Mexican grocery, these basic elements of the Mayan diet soon were readily purchased at any area Bi-Lo or Food Lion supermarket. Chicken was also a staple in Mayan immigrant diets, as it was for North Americans. Víctor Hernández, for example, proudly related that he fixed his own dinners, often combining tortillas and fried chicken in the same manner he was used to at home. Likewise, Tránsita Gutiérrez Solís declared that her family was "never without" tortillas and frijoles at mealtime in Morganton.[29]

Reverence for the Mayan traje was another important symbolic link to the homeland. Gaspar Pascual, who returned to his village of Lajcholaj in 1996 after working nearly ten years in the United States, thus summarized the differences in the two cultures: "The [North American] women are different: *se ponen puros pantalones* [they always wear pants]; here the way is *puro corte* [always wear skirts] and no shoes."[30] Though the cost on a tight budget is steep, first-generation Mayan women in Morganton seem to have had at least one full set of traje (blouse, skirt, belt, and head scarf); some stay-at-home mothers wore it on the street, whereas others saved it for Mass or more infrequent special occasions. Typically, when a family photo was planned (particularly one that might find its way back to relatives in Guatemala), time was required for the adult women of the household to don traje. At any rate, connection to the female dress of one's *pueblo* remained an important badge of identity. As the Awakateka "Marga," who had worked at Case Farms since 1996, explained in a July 1998 interview:

> We don't wear [traje] right now because it's so hot, but when it gets cooler we wear it almost every day. Me, when I first got here, I wasn't used to wearing pants and I really wanted to wear my traje, but I didn't have it [with me]. After a year they mailed it to me [and even though] I got used to pants, I was really glad when they sent it. Almost all the women from Aguacatán here wear traje, including the *cinta* [elaborate native scarf]. People from here do stare, but they generally appreciate *cosas típicas* [native things]. My daughters don't wear traje, the oldest one wants to, she wore it in Aguacatán, but here, it's so expensive to get it sent. . . . My husband and I have talked about it and we decided that when our daughters grow up they can decide if they want to wear traje or not.[31]

The continuing popularity of natural medicines marked another example of the hold of traditional values. While using well-baby clinics or the emergency rooms of local hospitals (only a minority of immigrants had access to Medicaid) in acute cases, many Guatemalans continued to rely on natural cures for minor ills. A Mexican-owned store in Morganton sold homeopathic herbs, and some residents grew a few herbs, like cilantro, for both cooking and healing purposes. Making use of folk wisdom accumulated across generations of family practice was at least one *curandera* (traditional healer) who was regularly sought out by her Q'anjob'al neighbors as an alternative medical adviser. That such contacts were cloaked in secrecy—for fear of prosecution for practicing medicine without a license—to be sure, set a different tone for traditional treatments than was the case "back home."

Language, not surprisingly, was another key ingredient of indigenous Mayan identity and continuity. Despite the fears of intellectuals that the Mayan language would be lost, it has, in fact, remained a vital, and relatively effortless, feature of immigrant life. Both families and single male households in this study were almost universally defined by common language groups, that is, a group of Awakatekan workers would rent a house together, and—at least for the immigrant generation and their children—the indigenous language remained the basis of intimacy even as Spanish and English vied for supremacy in more public spaces.

Until recently, one vital component of the "rhythms" of Mayan life that was missing in Morganton was a marimba. Hailed at home as an "ancient" indigenous instrument (though musicologists convincingly point to its Afro-Caribbean origins), the alternately lighthearted and mournful beat of a solo "marimba pura" regularly punctuates traditional Mayan fiestas. It was a day of celebration in 1998 when a full-sized wooden marimba arrived at Morganton's St. Charles Catholic Church on top of a station wagon. Used both in Guatemalan church choirs and at secular concerts and community meetings, the marimba lends solidity, authenticity, and permanency to the Guatemalan diaspora presence.

There was another commonsensical meaning that the Morganton migrants lent to the assertion that they remained "Maya." It was their identification with a life of physical labor and poverty—at least compared to that of most of their non-Mayan neighbors. The fact is, between the duress of the working day and the pressures to provide for family far away, there was little time or money left for the "consumption" of a radically new lifestyle. Indeed, by one measure the Guatemalan community was more "tra-

Marimba players at "graduation ceremony" for leadership training
class at Morganton's Consejo Maya, 1999.

ditional" in North Carolina than it was back home. "Here," noted one migrant, "we are all *naturales* [native people]."[32] With few Ladinos and no
wealthy landowners, and without the mosaic of a Guatemala City to com-
plicate the social space of this indigenous ethnic enclave, it was possible
to believe in a home away from home. "People live here [in Morganton]
the same as they do in Guatemala," proclaimed Víctor Hernández. While
trying over the past six years to save up to buy a few *cuerdas* in Aguacatán, his own ambitions for what he might bring back from the United
States were typically modest—"some dollars, a jacket, and maybe a little
English."[33] Francisco Mejía Chávez, who hoped to return to Aguacatán at
least once every three years from his Morganton job, had managed so far to
add only *lamina* (corrogated metal frame) to the front of the family's two-
room adobe structure. Félix Rodríguez, with a brother, sister, parents, and
wife all living in Aguacatán, summarized the hopes of many: "to make a
little money, then to return to my pueblo to be together with my family, to
return to be with all my community, to work together, that's what I want
to do in the future. Because if I think of being rich . . . I am never going to
be rich. . . . We are born poor and if we are here it is only to help ourselves
a little."[34] The view of such emigrants as Rodríguez was not in the end

so different from the Trixano laborer whom anthropologist Kay B. Warren interviewed in the western Guatemalan highlands in the mid-1970s: "One works here [in the fields of the plantation] because it is the work of the Indian. If I were not an Indian I would be a *patrón* [landlord]. But as I am an Indian, I have to work under the command of a patrón."[35] The initial impulse of newly arriving Guatemalan emigrants, and one that continued as the norm even after several years of expatriate residency, was to return to the *campesino* life, but with the prospect of economic self-sufficiency.

Aside from direct continuities of practice and identity among individual migrant laborers, this narrative of labor protest and union organization at Case Farms also points to a more subtle connection in patterns of community mobilization between the Mayan homeland and the diaspora of emigration. The union, for one, succeeded to the extent that it inserted itself (however unconsciously) as a kind of *comité cívico* in the lives of the indigenous community. Trusting in the union leaders—and the union's strike votes—as they might honor a traditional comité's verdict on a water or road-building decision for their pueblo, the workers (or at least a solid majority of them over several years) assumed an obligation to act together for the common good. It is a stretch, but not an unwarranted one, to link the union discipline among Guatemalan workers in Morganton to the sense of togetherness and practice of community self-help—extending over centuries in Guatemala—manifest in the community comité, the religious cofradía, and the cargo system associated with earlier civil-religious hierarchies.[36]

From this angle, their very distance from the host culture may have served as the basis of unity within the expatriate Mayan community. Back in Aguacatán, for example, Rev. Gabriel Yol L'un "Padre Gabriel" Rodríguez (who visited Morganton in 1996) was not surprised by the union movement among those he called his *paisanos*. "The lifestyle of the U.S. is much more individualistic, the community is different. . . . [Here] a person doesn't want to be separated from the group. . . . For us, life is 'par' [pairs], just 'you' does not exist. . . . We don't use the word *sindicato* [trade union]. Here we use the word *comunidad* [community]. The idea is the same, no? . . . Build a bridge, it is community. Build a school, it is community. If there is a disgraceful event in a neighborhood, the community has to fix it. For us all is 'par,' two, three, or four, they are the same."[37] In the same spirit, Jésus Acevedo, a Spanish-born United Nations peacekeeper stationed in Huehuetenango in 1997, explained the indigenous resistance to the Guatemalan military in terms of "a spirit of *grupación* [*sic*—literally, grouping together].

. . . They have a concept of justice, not so much Judeo-Christian, through which to resolve conflicts and they have, although we still have to discover this, leaders with the talent for this. Theirs is a code to which an individual submits himself."[38] The emphasis on the group, embedded in both language and behavior, was central. From this perspective, the union—like the *directiva* or the widespread Guatemalan participation in local churches— was simply the latest means of maintaining a moral order within a traditional community.

If the union movement in Morganton was able to draw on a long-established Mayan tradition of solidarity, however, it also reproduced some of the discordant elements that have long dogged Mayan struggles in Guatemalan history. Thus, while the indigenous Maya can justly lay claim to a majority of the population in Guatemala, their own division into some twenty-one language groups makes it difficult to unify around any common agenda. Aguacatán, with its *five* ethnic groups—Awakateko, Chalchiteko, K'iche', Mam, and Ladino—may be more heterogeneous than most; still, its variety points to a larger reality and a major source of division in the Mayan cultural landscape. In classic Mayan accounts, for example, the first *vendidos* were the Kaqchikels who helped Pedro de Alvarado and the invading Spaniards defeat the valiant K'iche's (who happened to have earlier run roughshod over their Indian neighbors).[39] The history of modern-day Mayan communities is equally replete with inter-Indian disputes over land claims and water rights, as well as ongoing conflict between indigenous groups and Ladino officialdom. Even local, indigenous-run jurisdictions— the municipios created by Spanish authorities as a way to bring bureaucratic order and a measure of control to the countryside—were rarely the islands of corporate communal unity first pictured by anthropologists. In the public controversy surrounding the authenticity of Nobel Peace Prize winner Rigoberta Menchú's account of her own life, one of David Stoll's main criticisms of Menchú's testimonial is that she transformed a messy local land conflict among competing Indian claimants into a revolutionary polarization between Mayan campesinos and Ladino plantation owners.[40] Kay Warren refers to such disputes as aspects of "the issue of cultural distrust . . . endemic in Guatemala."[41]

A background of comunidad might well serve as a brace for movement building in a *gringo* factory; yet the inheritance of the rural peasant indigenous past was not one of easy and total cooperation. The evidence suggests that in Morganton, even as the Aguacatecos moved as a group to support the union, many other Mayan workers tended to see the movement as "someone else's"—not a Guatemalan-wide—affair. At one extreme, for example, Q'anjob'al worker Diego de Diego distanced himself from the strike and unionizing campaign of 1996 by insisting that it was "pure Mexicans" who were instigating all the labor troubles at Case Farms.[42] More than LIUNA organizers realized at the time, the Guatemalan workers' community remained divided by important linguistic and localistic identities.

Indeed, there is reason to suspect that local loyalties become not less but more important across the process of migration. After all, immediate survival, let alone prosperity in El Norte, depends to a great extent, on kin and friendship networks. Discovering employment possibilities, arranging transportation, successfully crossing the border, finding housing, actually getting a job, and then "learning the ropes" at work and outside work—finessing each of these crucial steps requires connections. For many workers "legal" passage to the country adds one final stage of dependency on one's fellow villagers. Back in Aguacatán, Francisco Mejía Chávez described a process of "borrowing" papers from a cousin home on the immigrant worker's version of shore leave.[43] Similarly, Francisco Risso, who directed the local Catholic Worker house, regretted that one Morganton activist who had returned home to Guatemala in early 2001 could not come back under the same name.[44] The intricate logic of migration—which became all the more desperate after September 11, 2001—pointed to the necessity of reliance on close friends and family. And, of course, the connection to kith and kin is not just economic but emotional. Entire new mail services have sprouted to respond to the demand for rapid communication—and cash—between distant friends and family members; a woman in Aguacatán complained of the long weekend lines in front of one of the town's few public telephones.[45] At both ends, one might suppose, the narrow communalism and extended family dependency traditionally associated with the peasant community assume a new functionality in the globalized world of migrant labor.

However we mark its influence, positive or negative for the union cause, a notion of cultural *continuity* will only take us so far in illuminating the behavior and attitudes of the Maya in Morganton. The immigrants themselves were quick to note important changes both in their everyday lives and in their longer-term accommodations to a new social order. They often began such commentaries by emphasizing physical and material differences. Juana Pascual, for instance, observed that there was no hand-ground *mixtamal* (corn/lime paste for tortillas) in the United States. And several Guatemalans commented that even if they ate the same foods, they did not taste the same. The produce was not as fresh as that from a local market or one's own field, and the meat (usually chicken) was not the same as when freshly skinned and prepared. Don Pancho José's wife, María, thus regularly skirted the regulations at her housing project by killing chickens in her backyard. Another basic domestic routine was also missing here — the *pila* (the stone basin for washing clothes). As preparation for a possible if unlikely return to the homeland, Juana Pascual taught her daughter how to do both basic tasks — that is, make tortillas and wash clothes — by hand. Though women's dress remains an important symbol of continuity, everyday comfort (particularly in North Carolina's hot summer months) and convenience (especially for those in the workplace or in school) may dictate a change. Less problematical are those new amenities that do *not* conflict with hallowed folkways. A social worker who coordinated aid to many Guatemalan families in Morganton said, "They use Pampers, for example — I don't think I've seen one child with a cloth diaper." She also noticed various modes of baby transport even among traje-wearing women: "I see moms come to [well-baby] classes with their babies [wrapped on their backs]. I also see moms in their traditional dresses pushing a stroller. It's a mixed thing."[46]

Affecting both women and men immigrants is the relative disappearance of "public space" in their adopted homes. In Guatemala, as in other Latin American countries, one is used to a central plaza, with space to walk and talk, and time to sit and "hang out." San Miguelense Félix Miguel, who left Los Angeles for Morganton following the Rodney King riots, liked the comparative friendliness and peacefulness of the North Carolina town. "But there are no public places, you can't *pasear* [walk around], that's just not possible here," he sighed. "Marga," a Case Farms worker from Aguacatán, regretted the same change in customs: "There [in Guatemala] you have more chance to walk outside, go out more and be with people, and here it's hard to adapt . . . at times I feel like I'd like to spend time with you people [North Americans], but I can't, it's very difficult, there's a different rhythm to life here."[47]

Encompassing the domestic routines cited above, the Mayan way of life is in the end linked to the *activity* of a peasant-based, subsistence-oriented agricultural economy, and that connection is largely severed upon migration. Many of the Maya who went to Morganton had already tried, and rejected, agricultural labor as organized in the United States. As Allan Burns found in his study of Mayan refugees in Indiantown, Florida, the pace, repetition, and constant mobility required of migrant farm labor—not to mention the physical dangers and illnesses associated with that work—makes it inimical to the peasant cultivator.[48] Still, many Maya experienced their separation from the land as a distinct loss. As a Mayan refugee in Mexico City has written: "Our whole worldview, our way of thinking, is related to nature; it is related to the land. When we leave and forsake this land, when we are forced to go to other countries, a great number of our traditions can no longer be practiced."[49] In Morganton, veterinarian Don Hemstreet remembered once taking Don Pancho strawberry picking: "He was just in heaven. He picked about ten gallons of strawberries, [my daughter] and I had two! But he picked the weeds among the plants of medicinal things, he was so happy to go home with his bag of plants for María, and for weeks afterwards he would always want to know if we were going to pick strawberries again."[50]

For many migrants, the rhythms of subsistence agriculture are traded for a consumer-oriented world in the United States. Francisco Mejía Chávez, who had worked at Case Farms before returning to Guatemala on a family visit in 1998, cited three major differences in his life in America: he discovered the meaning of the "weekend," he took out a bank account, and television became a part of his daily routine. Francisco noted one other important difference in the two societies. Though beer and other forms of alcohol were prevalent on both sides of the immigrant's journey, drinking had different consequences "over there." "I [no longer] drink," he said. "Those who drink don't show up at work on Mondays and lose their papers. . . . There, you get a check at the end of the week, here there is no paycheck."[51] That Francisco might have experienced all of these "American" changes if he had moved to Guatemala City rather than North Carolina emphasizes the extent to which "globalization" serves as the cutting edge of contemporary capitalist development, uprooting the remnants of peasant economies, imposing a new labor discipline, and creating a world "where all that is solid melts into air" just as it has done, with or without transnational labor migration, for several centuries.[52]

In the end, however, the changes and innovations in the migrant worker's world are not simply a matter of "Americanization," let alone the imposition of universal world capitalistic norms. As those who have made the case for "transnational" identities recognize, the "border country" of the immigrant worker is also the seat of a new, "hybrid" cultural space as distinct from the culture of destination as from the culture of origin. One marker of the new ground is language: ironically, it is in the United States that the Mayan immigrant becomes more fully "Hispanicized." In stores and streets, at school, as well as at the workplace, the majority English-speaking population tends to lump the Guatemalans with Mexicans and other Latin Americans as one indistinguishable "Hispanic" mass. Such grouping is not merely "laid on" by ignorant North American natives but becomes a functional aspect of the immigrant's socialization process. Given the segmentation of the labor, housing, and ultimately even education "markets" by ethnicity as well as class, Spanish becomes the obvious language of daily exchange. As a daughter of Q'anjob'al Don Pancho emphasized, "The only way [I] can communicate with the Aguacatecos is to speak Spanish." A Q'anjob'al worker in Morganton thus can make do for years with the most rudimentary of English-language knowledge so long as he or she has mastered Spanish and can thus fit comfortably—at work, in the neighborhood, at church, and so forth—in the "second" language. Hispanicization, moreover, encompasses more than language use; it is also a cultural process. The local Maya attend Spanish Mass or Hispanic evangelical churches, regularly patronize small Mexican-owned *tiendas* (shops), join all-Hispanic soccer leagues, and respond to special events like the "Feria de las Carolinas" (featuring "*payasos* [clowns], carnival rides, *comida* [food]") sponsored by local employers, including Case Farms and Broyhill Furniture. Even access to mass entertainment has a Hispanic filter, thanks to Univision, which arrived in Morganton in 1996, when Case Farms sponsored the first five-year cable contract, some say, as a political alternative to a community-based Spanish news program directed by Mexican-born schoolteacher-minister Daniel Gutiérrez.[53]

The only question about Mayan Hispanicization in a small town like Morganton was how long it would last. Clearly, it had a wide appeal for the immigrant generation, which, through the late 1990s, was regularly augmented by new arrivals. For the second generation, which came of age in more socially mixed and English-dominated surroundings, the pattern was less clear. With an elder son in community college, for example, Andrés Pascual reported: "In Guatemala we don't speak Spanish, we only speak in dialect. Almost never Spanish [in San Miguel Acatán]. In the U.S. we speak Spanish and a little English. My children speak English, a little Spanish, but we all speak Q'anjob'al. Outside of the house [the children] speak English."[54] Universally, Mayan parents expressed a will to preserve their own language. But the task was not always easy. Married with children herself, Ana José saw her baby brother and sister growing up in an English-language world that was separating them from their parents. "They speak

English in the house, and my parents feel bad about that because they don't speak any English. My mother can't communicate with them." Even the older children, while still comfortable in Q'anjob'al, had largely moved over to an English-language lifestyle. When renting movies at their parents' home, they normally got English-language "family or comedy" films. Although the parents, Don Pancho and María, could not follow the dialogue, "they watch the picture and laugh."[55]

The immigration experience also affected group religious practice. Although the pluralism of faiths in Guatemala was readily replicated in the diasporic communities of the United States, some subtle differences were apparent. Among the Catholic majority of the Mayan population in Morganton, one dramatic change saw the rise of small communities of prayer associated with the Catholic Charismatic Renewal movement.[56] In Morganton and surrounding parishes, the Charismatics, centered on the new Latino immigrants, exploded in numbers during the 1990s. Generally a congeries of small groups who met in church or at homes virtually "every day" of the week, their numbers at regional gatherings had reached nearly five hundred participants by 2001 compared with regular diocesan gatherings of less than one hundred souls.

Such lay-centered faith circles posed a dilemma for a church hierarchy already worried by decades of Pentecostal evangelism among its Latino flock. On the one hand, Catholic Church leaders criticized charismatic practice as being but a halfway house to Protestantism—generating an otherworldly emotionalism with little connection either to theological doctrine or the church's teachings on social justice issues. On the other hand, these lay enthusiasts were often the most pious members of the parish, attending Mass regularly and making themselves available for the church's many volunteer activities. There was no denying the movement's "participatory" appeal to Guatemalan women, in particular, a development replicated in other Latino immigrant communities as well.[57] As Ana José said of her own charismatic involvement, "It helps us in our faith, we clap and sing, it changes our lives."[58] The Charlotte-based diocese to which St. Charles Church belongs originally tried, to no avail, to combat the charismatic tendency by sending to Morganton a nun with training in the "liberation theology" associated with the "small base communities" of Latin America in the 1980s. Father Ken Whittington, despite his own reservations about a growing regimentation in their ranks—the Morganton charismatic group dropped Mayan dialects in favor of services in Spanish, switched from traje and informal wear to dresses and shirts and ties, approved only certain "leaders" as speakers in their services, and generally diminished the leadership role of women—attempted to make them feel "safe" and "comfortable within the Church." Though the Charismatics generally disdained political activism, Whittington took pride in having persuaded the group to "pray a rosary" in front of Case Farms during one union protest rally.[59]

Like the Charismatics, the local ranks of evangelical Protestantism grew with the new Latino migration. By 2000 Morganton counted five Spanish-speaking churches: one Assembly of God, two Church of God (including one primarily Aguacateco, the other K'iche'), one Pentecostal Independent, and one Baptist congregation. Daniel Gutiérrez served as pastor of the Whole New Life Church of God and was something of a "senior citizen" to the new evangelical community, which he estimated was about half Guatemalan.

The religious communities, Gutiérrez observed, were contributing to the larger merger process within the Hispanic population. Originally, as he saw it, the separate national and ethnic groups clung closely to each other. "Aguacatecos [went] with Aguacatecos, K'iche's with K'iche's," he said, "[but] they realize that that won't work, eventually they need to give it up. Especially the ones that come at a very early age. You can see right now a mixing going on in international marriages. I'm beginning to see Guatemalans marrying Mexicans. Now you can be Guatemalan Awaka-teko, Mexican, Evangelical, or Catholic and still live together." Yet, even as he witnessed an internal melting around the edges of ethnic and even denominational identity within the communities of faith, Gutiérrez found relatively little crossover between Hispanic and Anglo practitioners. As much as language, a difference in basic attitudes toward the role of faith, according to Gutiérrez, separated the new immigrants from the native white congregations he had observed. Although the church—Protestant or Catholic—was often the center of immigrant-Hispanic life (Gutiérrez himself lived in an apartment complex where thirteen out of sixteen units housed fellow Evangelicals), North Americans, in Gutiérrez's view, tended toward a less intense form of religious communion. "You write 'I' with a capital letter," he told his Anglo interviewer. "You know that English is the only language in the world that does [that]?"[60]

Gutiérrez's emphasis on the development of a Pan-Latino identity in Morganton was shared by others. Daniel and Angelino Rodríguez Her-nández, two brothers who returned from Morganton in 2000 to visit their ailing father in Aguacatán, told ethnographer Paul Kobrak: "There [in Morganton], everybody drinks to everyone. We're all 'Hispanics' and 'Latinos.' . . . your culture doesn't matter. There, there are no *indígenas*. There's no difference between us." For the Rodríguez brothers, moreover, membership in the Latino–North American working class—however insulated from middle-class Anglo society—offered a welcome egalitarian status crossing ethnic and educational lines: "If you are enemies here, there you're going to be friends. If you're a teacher here, there you're treated the same as someone who never went to school. We're equal [there] with the Ladino, with the Mexican. The Americans treat us the same."[61]

The concentration of women among the churchgoing community points to the larger transformation of gender roles as perhaps the most dramatic life adjustment effected by the transnational cultural sphere. Due as much to the relative scarcity of women in the diasporic community as to inherent differences of expectations within "American culture," the single, male-centered immigrant enclave put pressure on both sexes—in both the host and the sender community. Estimated by observers at 80 percent of the Morganton Guatemalan population, the male workers, most in their twenties and thirties, of necessity assumed a self-sufficiency unknown at home.[62] As one Aguacateco complained, "I hope to stay in North Carolina some three or four years, but you get tired having to make dinner, fix lunch, and work in order to send money home."[63] The male renters typically cooked for themselves, though they might occasionally pick up a sandwich for lunch or buy tortillas and other dishes to eat at home. On weekends, many workers treated themselves to McDonalds, Burger King, or KFC, and occasionally even North Carolina barbecue.[64]

In some cases the move toward domestic labor by the men required a prior "tutorial" from wives or mothers anxious about the future health and economic welfare of their male loved ones. In Aguacatán, for instance, Mam-speaking Letitia Hernández was proud of the cooking skills of her Awakateko husband, Víctor, who had lived in Morganton since 1995. "I have seen him cooking, making tortillas. I told him he needs to cook for himself, because if he pays someone, that's less money for the family." Víctor first took over the kitchen and the wash while still at home, when his wife became ill. "He's a hard worker, active, and intelligent in these matters," Letitia added.[65]

While left to their own devices in the kitchen, the men in Morganton discovered that tight living spaces encourage a form of cooperative housekeeping. In his house, Francisco Mejía reported, the two men assigned the weekly "house duty" on a rotating basis were in charge of a "total" cleanup. "Over there [in Morganton] two men each week do the cleaning, while

Changing Places

here [in Aguacatán], since there are women, [the women] do it all day."[66] Similarly, the six to seven men in the Morganton house of José Samuel Solís López divided up in twos or threes each weekend to clean house. It was "typical," said José Samuel, for one man to be "in charge" of a house and to assume responsibility for assigning necessary tasks to the others.[67]

Just as immigrant men, of necessity, assumed new tasks in the host community, Mayan women took on some of the previous roles of their fathers and brothers in the sender communities. In Aguacatán, for example, each *cantón* (neighborhood district) required—on penalty of a fine—attendance at community meetings and/or participation in designated community projects. Once women found themselves the heads of household, they took on an enhanced role in local affairs and even formed new women-only committees to do so.[68] In the cantón Aguacatán (a district lying just outside the town center), Letitia Hernández wielded the vote of her husband Víctor in village meetings. For Letitia, at least, the new responsibility felt more like a burden than a reward. At times, it meant attending three evening meetings a week on top of her work in the family fields, cooking school meals, and parenting two young children.[69] Despite the "draft" of women into community meetings, Letitia reported, women still did not sit on the cantón's executive *comité*. Other sources indicated that when the men did return from abroad, they generally insisted on their traditional prerogatives in regard to both the division of household labor and familial authority. "They [the male emigrants] go away," commented Aguacatán mayor, Pablo Escobar Méndez, "and they have to learn to *tortear* [narrowly, "make tortillas" or perhaps more generally "handle the kitchen"], but they come home as 'kings.'"[70]

More destructive than the realignment of roles within marriages was the direct threat that migration posed to those relationships. Over and over, interview respondents both in Guatemala and North Carolina referred to cases (usually unnamed) where a migrating husband had "abandoned" his family or even begun a "new life" with a "new woman." Less often fears were invoked of women at home who had not remained "loyal" to their husbands. Father Ken acknowledged that it was not uncommon for Guatemalan men to confess such acts, "sins" that he considered "part of the wretched lure of materialism."[71] To illustrate, Toribia Gamas in Aguacatán mourned the "disappearance" of her brother, Narciso, in Morganton. For the first five years (Narciso left for the United States in 1993), he sent letters and occasionally money to his wife and two children in Cobán as well as to his ailing parents in Aguacatán. But Narciso then suffered periods of unemployment and developed a drinking problem. Since 1998—beginning with his failure to return for the funeral of his mother-in-law—he stopped communicating altogether with his Guatemalan family, suspending payments to his wife and never repaying his father for his passage to the United States. The family was greatly distressed. When a U.S. Army helicopter landed in Cobán to help with Hurricane Mitch relief, Narciso's children cried for their father to emerge from the cockpit. In 1999 Toribia's parents sent an older sister to visit Narciso, but to no avail. "It's my life," he told her. His family pleaded with him to return to Guatemala. "Even with nothing, no money," said Toribia. "It doesn't matter. Just to recover his perspective."[72]

Undoubtedly, the fear of abandonment exceeded the reality. In Morganton, at least, most of the young Guatemalan male workers were "trapped" in a single-sex social world with few chances for significant relationships with females. To be sure, there were reports of prostitution in the Guatemalan and Mexican trailer parks around Morganton. But the more common response of the young men in North Carolina was sexual forbearance. Not that the male workers ignored female arrivals in town. One set of roommates in 1999 half jokingly kept a running total of "Awakatekas" in town, and, when questioned closely, further counted twenty-two "puras Awakatekas" and four "Chalchitekas"![73]

Apart from the question of marital fidelity, the separation of couples imposed both physical and emotional costs. Even where devotion remained steadfast, financial support reliable, and communication uninterrupted, the worry never ceased. Letitia Hernández had been waiting for her husband Víctor's return since 1995. Shortly after he left, she was forced to move out of a debt-ridden house with the couple's two young children, Fabiola and Kenny Alexander ("I like English names," said Víctor). To make ends meet, Letitia sold tortillas and tamales, and in 2000 she secured a job cooking breakfast and lunch at her children's school. Initially, she could find nothing to rent:

Víctor told me, "Keep looking! Pray to the Mercy of God!" Finally, a woman in town lent me a little money to construct a home. When Víctor was working, I paid the woman back. But we have suffered much, and we keep suffering, we're so poor. . . . Before he left, Víctor told me: "You must fight for our children, you've got to take care of them. The same thing with me over there, I'm going to fight." "It's ok," I told him, "I'll do it, I'll do it." [Letitia received letters from Víctor every two or three weeks and money every few months. Phone calls, because of the cost, were infrequent.] Víctor tells me, "Many come here [to the United States] expecting to make a lot of money, but it's not like that, life here is hard. He who doesn't work, doesn't eat. . . . We're slaves over here." When he left, I told him we had a commitment with God, we're married. I know there are women out there who aren't clean, I've heard of this sickness, AIDS. I don't want him to be unfaithful. I begged him to take care, to take care of his health, because for that, there is no cure. [Buoyed by reports that Víctor was more regular than ever before in his church attendance, Letitia beamed.] He knows Father Ken well.

The plan was for Víctor to return with enough money to get the family out of debt and provide for the children's education. "I don't know when that will be," sighed Letitia. "Only God knows when."[74]

The Mayan community continued to hold women chiefly accountable for maintaining a sense of continuity with the past. But whereas the *huipil*, the tortilla pan, and the *pila* once symbolized the world of their ancestors, the web of globalization posed new challenges to communal norms. For those who venerated the old ways, none of the "modern" changes—and least of all migration—affecting the Mayan family pointed to moral progress. On the one hand, the migrant community was dangerously out of balance in its sex ratio. On the other hand, the fact that young daughters and even single adult women had begun to journey northward only enhanced fears of a loss of control, of a sacred society spinning rapidly out of joint.

Despite concerns of some Guatemalans to the contrary, however, women remained a stabilizing and conservatizing force in the diaspora community. Indeed, an internalized set of expectations regarding family and the community placed constraints on immigrant women's freedom of action in Morganton. It was no coincidence that so few Guatemalan women joined the men on the line at Case Farms or that the three who became members of the union organizing committee were unmarried, Ladina, and in one case lesbian. As "Marga," a young working mother, explained, "I am not for the union—what I say is that I need to work . . . and I'm not 'legal,' I'm scared of that."[75] Many Guatemalan women experienced difficulty even entering the labor force. "Here [at Case Farms]," said Marga, "a woman has to get used to working like a man." Work schedules usually meant a reshuffling of family roles. Sonia Rincon-Hevlin, a Colombian-born social worker who coordinated outreach efforts to the Spanish-speaking community in Morganton, observed, "They [the women] want to work and are extremely good workers, but then the dilemma of the children—who is going to take care of the children and how expensive is it going to get?" Rincon-Hevlin spoke of the initial resistance she encountered in enrolling Mayan children in the state's preschool Smart Start program. "Many mothers don't want to send a two or three year old to school. 'He's too young, he doesn't need to be going to school.' You've seen some of the Mayan-Q'anjob'al folks—it's a concept that's not in their culture. It's something you've got to learn when you come to the United States, where you think, 'My child is three. He better go to school; he has to learn to read and get ready.' When you come from the mountains and the highlands you never had to go to school, so to tell a mom that her child maybe should go to school, [the response is] 'why?'" A male codirector of the Consejo Maya project similarly expressed frustration that the program had drawn few Guatemalan women to its English-language classes or other offerings. "I haven't known a Guatemalan woman to take a social justice [i.e., activist] role—that's something I've tried to figure out, I want to know the main cause of this."[76]

The pressures imposed by immigration affected the sender communities as well. Paulino López's daughter, Katarina, related one story from Aguacatán: "When my father left, my brothers often got sick. My mother felt as if she had become a widow because our father was not around. My dad was over there [in the United States] for four years without returning one time, when my second-oldest brother also left and then died [in Florida]. That's when my dad returned for the first time. . . . It was hard in those years. We had to adapt ourselves to his absence, and then, when he would return, get used to him again. It affected us a lot."[77]

The silver lining in the migration process for the remaining López family women lay in their own creative adaptation to a period of stress. Katarina continued:

My mom has kept working, because she is the one who supported the studies of my sister and me. The only ones whose schooling my father supported were the sons . . . they didn't much care that we went to school since we are women. The majority of women aren't sent to school [i.e., beyond grade 6] because they think that as women we are going to marry and leave the house. But we're not all the same. . . . My mom starts crying sometimes when she thinks that we can't make it, because she is rather ill. For that reason I have to work to help my sister through school. We're going to help each other. Paulino wants to live over there and we can't make him live here. He has already changed a lot. He is helping [with the family] now more than he used to. Before, from

Changing Places

what my mom tells me, he was bad, bad, bad. He hit my mom, he was bad. Not anymore. My mom is now the owner [master] of the house. She takes the responsibility.[78]

But neither does the entire burden of familial adaptation fall on the women. Marcelino López—Aguacatán's famous first political exile—had been living in Thunder Bay, Ontario, since 1986, physically distant from both his brother Paulino in North Carolina and his six sisters, who remained in their native town. Over the years, he assumed the major financial responsibility for an ailing mother. After a time, however, neither his remittances from a laboring job, his regular contact by telephone, nor his occasional visits satisfied his need for connection and moral sense of obligation to his family. At the same time, he did not wish to disturb the relatively secure life he had built for his children in Canada. Ingeniously, in the past few years, he devised a halfway measure. Every few months Marcelino purchased a used Blue Bird school bus in Tennessee and drove it, solo, to Guatemala to sell it and visit with family.[79]

Among transplanted couples, affection as well as necessity stirred behavioral change. Because of their Morganton work schedules, Awakatekos Marga (who worked the night shift at Case Farms) and her husband Manuel made mutual adjustments. "My husband helps out with the kids a lot," said Marga. "I drop them off in the morning and he picks them up at night, he also helps around the house, he even cooks. He can cook anything I cook, my daughter cooks too. This is different than in Guatemala, because over there, they [men] don't help. He didn't cook when he was in Guatemala. Here they learn how to help because we're both working." Marga's friend "Demetria," a Mexicana married to an Awakateko, added: "I notice that Marga's husband realizes when she comes home tired she's tired, because he's tired too when he gets home. It really depends on the personal relationship between two people whether or not the husband helps out around the house."[80]

The brief tenure of the Guatemalans in Morganton at the time of this writing—together with its demographic concentration of migrant males—prevents extensive study of generational change, the classic site of historical analysis of cultural transformation within immigrant groups. Still, it is worth taking stock of second-generation behavior, at least at an impressionistic level. Daniel Gutiérrez, for one, worried that the "troubled kids" he was often called on to help in the Latino community had taken too large a bite of the apple of Americanization, a fruit apparently all the more tempting as an ethno-racial hybrid:

> The children are going all the way . . . to [such an] extent that they want to be Anglo-Saxon. They say, "I only speak English. I don't even like your culture; I don't even like your food." Eventually some become completely American, they adopt the black way. You know, they start wearing the pants underneath [their] bottoms. They start walking like this [and wear] earrings and tattoos. So you see this interesting phenomenon from being 100 percent Guatemalan to the other extreme. . . . The kids in jail—they are dropouts, English-only [types], with a strong crisis in their life. . . . They're trying to belong somehow and they feel like a frog—they can't breathe underwater. They're Hispanic by name, by culture, by skin color, but by their acting, their thinking, they're American. They land in jail because they want to have everything, and they want it the easy way.[81]

As a brand-new graduate of Morganton's Freedom High School in July 2000, Teofilo Pedro, who was born in the Q'anjob'al-speaking region of Huehuetenango in 1982 and moved with his family from California to Morganton in 1996, did not fit into Daniel Gutiérrez's category of troubled kids. Yet Teo's continuing, if still evolving, relationship to his Mayan roots indirectly reinforced Gutiérrez's point. Active in the charismatic youth group at St. Charles Catholic Church, Teo was determined to get ahead in his adopted home. With his naturalization application out of the way and acceptance into a nearby community college virtually assured, he happily anticipated a period of work or possibly military service in the United States. Like the handful of other Mayan students in his graduating class, Teo had entered a peculiarly U.S.-defined "Hispanic" world. Spanish, for example, which he could not speak when he entered first grade in the United States, had become his primary communications channel—"It's the only thing I use here with my friends; I have to think first in Spanish and then in English." Likewise, his Mayan classmates "don't think of themselves as Q'anjob'al, they think they're Hispanic, they just forget about the Q'anjob'al." In high school, Teo found both prejudice and friendship in his host community. Despite open hostility from "rednecks outside Burke County," there were plenty of peers to hang out with in Morganton, including a white girlfriend and two close African American pals. Yet, eventually, Teo intended to return to Guatemala on a personal errand. "Over here there's a lot of great people, but one of my goals is to get married over there. I don't know why, but it just is. . . . One thing I'm proud of is being part of the Mayan family."[82]

Back in Guatemala, the impact of mass emigration on the sender communities was a source of lively—if contradictory—judgments. First, nearly everyone acknowledged both the practical necessity (given existing economic conditions in the country) and the individual material gains derived from the process. At the local level, such statistics took on a tangible form. In Q'anjob'al San Rafael, mention was made of *casas agringadas* or new homes based on returning Yankee dollars. Such houses, unlike the adobe and thatch constructions that predominate in rural villages, are distinguishable by their solid concrete block walls and foundations.[83] There was also talk of cars, satellite dishes, and other luxury items facilitated by jobs in El Norte. In Aguacatán, new vehicles on the roads already swamped the capacity of the one gas station in town, and many car owners drove the forty-five minutes to the departmental capital in Huehuetenango to fill up. Texas leather boots and longer North American male hairstyles reportedly penetrated the most remote mountain pastures in Aguacatán; even the *morral* (traditional handwoven male shoulder bag) now sometimes reflected a distant North American destination as well as its hometown insignia.[84] Among indigenous women as well, change was apparent. In the Aguacatán town center, the sight of young native women in jeans was no longer extraordinary. As one Chalchiteka explained to her interviewer, "Better that you learn to use both forms, traje and *pantalón*."[85] Even the traditional huipil felt the impact of the new world economy. Sparkling acetate ribbon, imported from the north, had in the past few years insinuated itself into brocaded designs otherwise passed down over generations.

Nationally, "remittance" income (dollars regularly sent home by immigrants to family members), estimated in 1999 at $3 million per day, ranked just below coffee exports as the largest source of foreign currency for the Guatemalan economy.[86] In Aguacatán, two private mail services reported that they regularly received 100 to 150 letters a week from townspeople living in the United States. Each letter normally contained a monetary insert of at least $100, sometimes considerably more.[87] When such figures are compared to the 20 quetzal (less than $3) average daily wage in a village like Aguacatán, the significance of the outside income is readily apparent.[88]

To be sure, the economic "lift" per family from emigration was generally a modest one. No one returned fabulously wealthy from a laboring job in

Casa agringada or new home construction based on "Yankee" remission dollars under way in Aguacatán, 2000.

New morral showing emigrant influence on native Aguacatán crafts.

America. According to local informants, it cost up to $3,000 to travel (over land, including payment to the *coyote*) from Aguacatán to the United States. To get the money, many families resorted to pawning their most valuable possessions or borrowing with their land as collateral. Even after a good three years of work, estimated Nicolas Perez López, the Intercapitales (a private mail service) manager in Aguacatán, a person was lucky to return with a $10,000 surplus, or a little less than what it cost to buy one well-irrigated cuerda of land in Aguacatán.[89] Despite initial expectations that they would find a "pot of gold" in the United States, most emigrants returned, according to Neyda López (wife of a local newspaper editor and no relation to Nicolas), "only a little better off, [they] remain in the same basic economic niche that they left." At best, said Neyda, those who returned after several years away were able not only to acquire land but also to transform themselves into "administrators," hiring others as farm laborers.[90]

For thoughtful observers like Nicolas and Neyda, transnational migration was simply the latest historical challenge that the Maya were confronting and taking in stride. For these global pragmatists, moreover, migration was less a loss than an extension of the home community. Emiliano Rodríguez, longtime bilingual educator, recent two-time candidate for mayor of Aguacatán, and father-in-law of Morganton's Felipe López, found solace in placing recent events in a longer time sequence:

First only a very few people actually left the country, because here it's very common for people to emigrate to the coffee and coastal cotton plantations, since agricultural production is so poor. . . . Then the young people started to reconsider, "Why go to the plantations? Let's find other means, other places," and a few left for the United States. When [these first] returned people saw that it was good. . . . It was different at that time, to go to the U.S. was like going to the moon. But they came back with good money, they bought land, houses, cars, everything. After the violence [of the early 1980s] the situation in the country became very grave, there was no work, and many more people left for over there. Now, it's like [going to] the coast. Some twenty to thirty leave together. We even have our own coyotes in Aguacatán who take people directly to the States to find work. . . . It's an opportunity for Aguacatán and for any other people in Guatemala to work. Over there one gets on a little better, finds a good job, and, if the man is a fighter, goes with one goal, a determination to make something for his family, to achieve something. But the positive thing for the people who go is that they are able to help their family, [and through this] economic development achieve certain things, such as giving a better education to their children and returning, to buy some land [here].

Emiliano soberly weighed the scales of the migration process. "There are advantages, and there are disadvantages. Everything depends on the person."[91]

Whatever its material rewards, the new economic opportunity also extracted a certain social price. It was common, for instance, to hear deprecating talk of a "new materialism" and "individualism" affecting the community. More tangibly, noted more than one Aguacatán observer, remittance income opened a new social division in Mayan communities—splitting families who had access to dollars from those who did not.[92] Aguacatán campesino organizer Pedro Solís Sales pointed to the minority of families with dollar incomes who could quickly access expensive health care in emergencies.[93] And one scholar commented on the "meals at Pollo Campero [Guatemala's version of KFC fast-food chicken] in Huehuetenango that are almost obligatory on the days that money orders are filled."[94] Of course, not all who left Guatemala ever tasted the fruits of economic "luxury." Within the spectrum of emigrants, admitted Emiliano Rodríguez, were those who get lost and "fall into vice." These were the ones who lost their money and returned with nothing, or "worse than nothing, return only with Miller Light or Coors Light by the six-pack."[95] Speaking generally of the impact of remittance income, Marilyn Moors refers to a "facade of prosperity [that] covers the underlying poverty of the still land-poor Guatemalan Maya."[96]

For some commentators, the negatives of migration bespoke a darker, nearly apocalyptic threat to traditional community structure and a catastrophic "breakdown" of Mayan culture. The Spanish United Nations observer in Huehuetenango, Jésus Acevedo, called attention to an internal conflict "which the communities [in Huehuetenango] do not have the instruments to resolve."[97] Even the gains of migration, by some accounts, carried long-term destabilizing consequences. Many migrants, recounted one Aguacateco, never really "return" to Guatemala, "they just visit." Unable to readjust to old agrarian ways and a lesser living standard, coming home became a "vacation" before the next North American fix.[98] In Quetzaltenango, trade union leader Osvaldo Saqvich claimed that the flight to the United States led to a loss of identity. "They stop wearing *ropa típica* [traditional dress] and don't know our language or our music any longer," he said, indicating a general decline of "moral principles" and "religious alienation." Obsessed with economic ambition, arriving with "boom boxes, jeans, and tennis shoes," they often "abandon their families and stop "relating to their neighbors."[99] Aguacatán's Padre Gabriel referred equally darkly to an ongoing "disintegration" of the traditional Mayan family and community structure as more and more young men leave the country for economic reasons. Having visited his extended parishioners in Morganton among other U.S. stops, Gabriel professed alarm at what one commentator called the "social remittances" of immigration. The emigrant, according to the priest, adopts a different "vision of the world." Preoccupied with material enrichment, he shows more concern for his own house than the community's welfare. In particular, Gabriel cited the arrival of gangs and delinquency, drugs, and AIDS, as well as the rising rates of divorce and estranged marriages as concomitants of the immigration process and other North American influences. Finally, there is the threat of a loss of faith—a threat manifest to Gabriel not only in the outer assaults of secularism and Protestantism but also in the stealth attack of the charismatic movement within the Catholic Church itself. Though he knew that some of the returning emigrants had "fallen" for the charismatic tendency, Padre Gabriel, unlike Father Ken in Morganton, offered them no official recognition. Indeed, Padre Gabriel told Father Ken that while ministering to the Q'anjob'al district in the late 1970s, he had charismatic leader Rafael Ramírez "thrown out" of his church. "Things are quiet," Gabriel insisted from Aguacatán in 1998. "There's not room here for their clapping and shouting."[100]

Although the threats attending migration from both internal economic privation and external family dispersal were serious ones, there was another way to read the "social declension talk" taken up by Mayan representatives and their allies. The very preoccupation with the *problem* of the decline of the Mayan community also reflected its opposite—a revitalization movement affecting numerous actors within both the home and diaspora communities. For Guatemalanists, one of the most remarkable developments of the late civil war and postwar years was the steady rise of indigenous organization and identity across the countryside. As one anthology on Mayan cultural activism put it: "One would hardly have expected Maya self-determination to be the rallying cry to rise out of the ashes of Guatemala's holocaust . . . and yet that is exactly the case. Maya from all over Guatemala are uniting around a variety of causes."[101]

Manifestations of the new Mayan self-organization abounded. Politically, the insistent testimony of the K'iche'-speaking Rigoberta Menchú— for which she won the Nobel Peace Prize in 1992—brought global attention to the plight of Guatemalan Indians at the hands of an oppressive state regime. Even as the guerrilla movement to which Menchú originally paid allegiance lost strength and credibility as an opposition force, the pressure of indigenous peoples' mobilization in public life did not abate. In the national elections of fall 1999, the two dominant center-right parties made extensive appeals to Indian constituencies (even as the nation's third force, the left-leaning Alianza Nueva Nación [ANN] slated an indígena for vice president), and, in an unprecedented move, the winning FRG (the party of Ríos Montt) appointed an indigenous man, Demetrio Cojtí, as vice minister of education and an indigenous woman, Otilia Lux, as minister of culture.[102] Even more striking than events at the national level was the success enjoyed by explicitly indigenous comités cívicos at the municipal level. Beginning with the mayoralty of the city of Quetzaltenango and then spreading into many municipios of the Mayan highlands, these comités offered a dramatic sign of a changing mass political and cultural consciousness. In Aguacatán, a municipal election in spring 1998 left the Comité Cívico just a few votes shy of the national governing PAN's total for the mayoral seat. A little over a year and a half later, new mandated elections witnessed *two* indigenous comités placing first and second for the same office. With international sanction both from specific United Nations mandates and continuing multilateral pressure on the Guatemalan government to comply with indigenous rights commitments contained in the Peace Accords of 1996 as well as the national constitution of 1985, Indian rights may have become the best-protected aspect of Guatemala's always-fragile democratic structures.

Nor is political power per se the clearest sign of the Mayan revival. Beginning in the 1940s under the revolutionary governments of Juan José Arévalo and Jacobo Arbenz Guzmán, and continuing intermittently ever since, the political-economic development of indigenous communities was closely intertwined with the symbolic politics of cultural representation and language survival. In reaction to repression and violence in the political sphere, a younger Mayan elite pushed all the harder on the cultural front. A new phase of such indigenous cultural work was reflected in the activities of the Academia de las Lenguas Mayas (ALM), formed in 1986 to apply a unified Mayan alphabet in bilingual education and publicity projects throughout the country.[103] Educated, fluent in Spanish, and economically mobile, these "organic intellectuals" of the Pan-Mayan movement rejected the path of Ladino assimilation in favor of a multicultural (or "pluricultural," as one heard more often in Guatemala) future.[104]

Given the momentum behind the indigenous peoples' movement in Guatemala, it should surprise no one that the same sentiments were reflected in the Mayan diaspora population in the United States. In 1990, for the first time, the U.S. census listed "Latin American Indian" as a population category alongside "Caucasian," "African American," "Hispanic," and others. And during the 1990s, an estimated 35,000 to 40,000 Latin American Indians (mostly Maya) arrived annually in the United States.[105] As a 1998 headline in Guatemala's leading daily put it, "Immigrants: Thousands of Mayas in Florida Seek to Maintain Their Identity." Assessing the situation of an estimated 15,000 (likely an underestimate) indigenous Guatemalans in Florida, the report painted a picture of a tightly knit, self-sustaining community as equally intent on cultural preservation as on economic survival.[106] CORN-Maya, an advocacy group established by Q'anjob'al refugees in Florida, offered an early example of revitalization sentiment within the diaspora settlement: "We are an Indian Nation in Exile. Dynamic cultural conservation is a key issue for us to continue and practice our way of life in order to live here with dignity and self-sufficiency as we survive the culture shock of a new society. Let's work together and build the survival of a people who are in danger: the Maya."[107]

Such a message—initially formulated at a major crossroads of new Guatemalan immigration—echoed even in a relatively distant laboring outpost like Morganton through the efforts of Justo Lux and his wife Tránsita Gutiérrez. Born in 1962 in a remote village near Santa María Chiquimula (roughly three hours on foot from the departmental capital of Totonicapán), Justo received little formal education but a wealth of schooling in community organization. As he grew up in an old CUC (Campesino Unity Committee) stronghold, he explained, "Rigoberta Menchú was a very important person where I lived."[108] Engaged as a staff worker for ADESCO (Association for Community Development), established under the civilian Cerezo government (1985–86), Justo was constantly working at the edge of what was possible in a militarized but also highly politically conscious K'iche' countryside. Forced to flee the country after a coworker was abducted and executed in 1988, Justo regularly "disappeared" back into Guatemala to commune with Maya-K'iche' activists, such as Juan León, a leader in the early 1990s of Defensoría Maya and future candidate for vice president on the left-leaning FDNG (Democratic Front for a New Guatemala) ticket. After a generally dispiriting sojourn in Indiantown and Miami, Florida, including disaffection from the factionalized ranks of the CORN-Maya project, Justo followed a friend to Morganton and Case Farms, where he participated in the first mass walkout in 1993. In and out of the community several times in the mid-1990s, he ultimately established a close friendship with Father Ken Whittington at St. Charles (even though he chose not to attend Mass). While fully supportive of the workers' struggle at Case Farms—and clearly possessed of considerable gifts of both political articulation and analysis—Justo oriented himself less to the union than to other forms of community mobilization in Morganton, eventuating in the local Maya Council for Community Development.[109]

While invoking what he called the *cosmovisión de los indígenas* (worldview of the Indian peoples), Justo neatly reconciled the Mayan heritage with contemporary social ends. For instance, of the performances of the Consejo's music group, he noted, "It is not our objective to create a fiesta as in Guatemala where the people get drunk . . . rather that they realize how the music can be shared to unite the people." Democratic self-government, he insisted, had ancient Mayan roots; *somos todos iguales* (we are all equal). "We have lost much of the knowledge and consciousness of our ancestors," he lamented. Similarly, while complaining about the traditionalism of domestic and church roles that made it difficult to attract Guatemalan women to Consejo activities, Justo maintained that things were once different. "There were no differences [male or female] among the ancient gods, and, unlike [in] the [Catholic] church, women can still be *sacerdotes mayas* [Mayan priests]."[110]

Perhaps not surprisingly, the first publication of the local Consejo Maya was a copy of the Mayan calendar with the following message attached: "This is the beginning of the struggle for the recuperation of the culture of the Maya peoples. Since the European invasion of our continent, they tried hard to make the Maya culture self-destruct. The Maya calendar is useful not only as a daily guide, like any other almanac, but the most important thing is that each day of the Maya calendar holds an important meaning in the life of human beings." Combining old and new resources, cultural workers like Justo fought for the future of the Mayan community. As he tried to explain the Consejo's efforts, "There is a phrase in our sacred book, the Popol Vuh, that says, 'No one will stay behind, not one, not two, [but] all will rise together and walk together.'"[111]

Together, Justo and Tránsita were a study in creative adaptation. A former schoolteacher, Tránsita regularly wore traje and nursed a dream to one day possess a huipil from every pueblo in Guatemala. The great-grandson of a sacerdote maya and self-consciously identifying with the great K'iche' warrior Atanasio Tzul (whose rebellion against the Spanish authorities near Totonicapán in the 1820s helped spur Guatemalan independence), Justo regularly invoked the memory and beliefs of his ancestors to shed light on current-day problems.[112] At the same time, he was well wired into the global marketplace. Equipped with computer and internet access, he kept up weekly with the news and friends from Guatemala as well as other Mayan diaspora groups in the United States. Struggling to support both his immediate and extended family, moreover, Justo had also learned something of the ways of the marketplace in which he was himself adrift. He and Tránsita sold discounted Sprint telephone cards to their Guatemalan neighbors. Subsequently, he advanced from salesman to acting manager and co-owner of a neighborhood Amoco station and convenience store that he renamed "Abarroteria Zaculeu" (after the Mayan ruin in Huehuetenango) and stocked with a variety of Guatemalan and Mexican products as well as offering a private fast mail service.

Part of the extended trial of the Mayan peoples has been their inability to unite discrete communities around a common path of action. Even in Morganton, within the small core of indigenous community activists, one sensed the difficulty of getting everyone aboard the same train. Perhaps the biggest obstacle encountered by the Consejo Maya, for example, was the weak response from the town's biggest Mayan population group, the Aguacatecos. Of this group, neither Felipe López nor José Samuel had connected to the K'iche'-led Consejo. While Felipe pleaded lack of time due to union duties, José Samuel acknowledged both a personal and a group reluctance to join Pan-Mayan configurations. "Our identity is Aguacateco," he explained, confessing that the people of his valley had always feared being swallowed up by the more numerous K'iche' or Mam populations around them. It was hard enough to concentrate on Aguacateco matters in adverse circumstances, he suggested, let alone larger Mayan unity projects.[113]

The differences of perspective between Justo Lux, José Samuel, and Felipe López only partially reflected their places of origin—the difference, that is, between the expansive, self-confident identity of the populous K'iche's from Justo's native Totonicapán versus the defensiveness of the comparatively tiny community of Aguacatecos. They also demonstrated classic, strategic variations within any population of oppressed minority peoples. There was, for example, the split between dreamers on the one hand and pragmatists on the other. Thus, even as Justo presented the face of abstract, lofty ideals, José Samuel emphasized the immediate tasks at hand. As one of the plant's longest-serving employees, he explained, "I want to finish this business, this struggle." After that, he contemplated a return to Guatemala City and the beginning of a new life. "That's my vision," he said simply. "We need to keep helping each other, to defend ourselves and unite."[114] More mercurial in mood, Justo alternately expressed great hope or despair for the future, transcendence or destruction for his people. Yet both men brought a wisdom and resiliency born of prior experience and a specifically Guatemala Mayan orientation to present-day challenges.

Felipe López offered a "third way" of Mayan assimilation into North American "working-class" institutions. A former Guatemala City law student who had fled his native country for political reasons in 1991 and returned after the Peace Accords to frustrating unemployment, he arrived in Morganton in the summer of 1997 anxious to put his talents, both as a lawyer and as a community organizer, to new use. Felipe combined the pragmatic approach of his cousin José Samuel with the longer-range vision of Justo—but in his case it was a vision focused less on the Mayan than the North American future. Having adjusted quickly to a new political as well as linguistic terrain, Felipe (in addition to minding the day-to-day affairs of the Morganton union local) emerged as a valuable representative for LIUNA in union campaigns around the country. Coming from a family with a love of politics (and a gift for reconciling the irreconcilable), Felipe might well have run for office in Aguacatán if things had worked out differently. When asked in Morganton if he could ever imagine renewing his political quest in his adopted country, he replied matter-of-factly: "Yes, I like politics. I think I would join the Democratic Party."[115]

A union, a burial society, a community council, perhaps even a convenience store—in the end, such constructive efforts by the Maya in places like Morganton may well point to a historic reconstruction as well as a destruction of ancient community standards. A study of the transplantation of settlers from rural Totonicapán to Houston, Texas, suggested that "the Maya have developed extensive community-based networks while maintaining strong cultural and economic ties with the home community in Guatemala. . . . These well-developed organizational forms not only regulate migratory flows but also explain the successful Maya settlement experience."[116] Among transplanted indigenous communities, Morganton was likely an exceptional situation in the predominance of a single employment magnet as well as in the accompanying preponderance of young men over family units within the immigrant population. Yet, while seizing on different institutional bases from those in Houston (where initial economic mobility beckoned through the ranks of an upscale, and reportedly solicitous, grocery chain), the Maya of Morganton appeared to be facing an uncertain future in the United States with similar energy and resolve.[117]

The pattern in the diaspora may well reinforce the trends apparent in the home country. At the Recuperation of Historical Memory (REMHI) project, sponsored by the Catholic Church's Human Rights Office, lay worker Edgar Hernández, who in 1997 oversaw a team of twenty-five social workers spread out in indigenous communities, offered a surprising commentary on the effects of the Guatemalan civil strife: "When we have asked the people [about] this war, this violence, all this suffering, what has it given you, the answer is generally positive. 'Thanks to the war [they say] we have promoters of health among us, we have agricultural agents, we have organizations.' You are going to discover a transformation of the Maya culture of survival."[118]

Some Maya long contemplated the progressive uses of their "little communities." In *A Mayan Life* (1966), purportedly the first novel by a Mayan writer, Q'anjob'al author Gaspar Pedro González ends a sad tale of poverty, strife, and oppression in the fictive Cuchumatanes hamlet of Jolomk'u with a projection of hope by the heroic character Lwin:

"What shall we do, Lwin?" they asked.

"What we should do, friends, is start right here and now. We can't wait for people to come from the outside to bring us a shirt that doesn't fit. Let's weave our own shirts with our own threads, our own strength and our own designs, our own colors, to our own tastes. Shirts made to order for other people will never fit us."

"Yes," everyone said. "Let's work, but how?"

"Let's go back," said Lwin. "Let's start with the very first problem, and go over the long list hanging on the wall in this room. Let's see which is first and which follows. What are the problems that affect us the most and how do they affect us? From the child to the senior, we all have a role to play here," he told them. . . .

They formed committees, organized the community, assigned responsibility and tasks. . . . As their eyes began to open, as their consciousness began to clear, they were finding their way to God, from whom they had become estranged. They nailed images of dark-skinned Christs with Mayan features on their grandparents' crosses. . . . Then came the white-haired elders and carried Lwin's spirit to the starry heavens to contemplate from the dwelling of God and the sacred days the future of his people.[119]

Pedro González's vision of a people organized at once for the daily task of survival and for the preparation of a brighter future would likely appeal to many immigrant Maya in North Carolina, as well as to indigenous readers in late-twentieth-century Guatemala. It is a vision that in its balance of respect for the past and accommodation of the future was amplified in the declaration of the First Maya Congress in North America in 1999: "Loyalty to our roots must not become an obstacle to the study of the wondrous advances of these developed nations, of their science, of their technology, of their outstanding characteristics; because all that joined with the richness of our cosmovision and ancient culture will enable us to recover from our suffering in order to contribute to the advancement and solidarity of our brothers who remain on Guatemalan soil and to establish brotherly ties much more effectively with the nations which inhabit Mother Earth."[120] We might wonder if such a dream could serve other audiences, as well, especially those trying to salvage a workaday sense of community in a globalized working world.

7

Sticking Together

A priority on "sticking together," we are reminded by a commentary on post–World War II steelworkers, fundamentally separates working-class or "blue-collar" values from the more individualistically driven ambitions of "professional middle-class" Americans.[1] Yet, who sticks with whom and under what conditions poses one of the classic questions of labor history as well as a continuing challenge to organizers on the ground. The record of U.S. labor struggles, in particular, is replete with extended periods of "fragmentation" punctuated by relatively brief moments of "solidarity."[2]

While adding another chapter, however modest, to the history of labor solidarity in the United States, the Morganton story offers provocative and perhaps instructive leads on several fronts. As we have seen, against considerable odds—and not without some defections—a community of immigrant laborers displayed a powerful capacity to rely on each other. In explaining the stubborn persistence of the Case Farms union, several factors come to the fore. Among them, the workers' leaders—indigenous Guatemalans supplemented by longer-established Mexicans—convinced a larger community of workers to give the union a chance as a defender of their rights and an advocate of their longer-term welfare. This alliance, initially sealed in the immediate aftermath of the 1995 strike, remained viable despite subsequent frustration and punishing setbacks. Even as the company stonewalled a contract, even as the workforce experienced wholesale turnover, even as the most stalwart local leader was felled by illness, indeed, even as the national union itself lost confidence in the Case Farms campaign, the core strength of organization, including continuing displays of day-to-day power in the workplace, endured as late as the summer of 2002.

Within the majority Guatemalan community itself, several allied forms of group action helped to sustain the union cause. The Aguacateco burial society, the ministrations of Father Ken and Padre Gabriel to their parishioners, as well as the Pan-Mayan radicalism of the Consejo Maya all lent support to a defense of worker rights and collective action. The result, it is not exaggerating to say, was a "pocket" of union strength within an otherwise union-averse political culture. One anecdote is revealing here. Efraín Sebastién Martín, one of the pioneer K'anjob'al workers who left Case Farms following the 1991 protest, went to work in one of the area's large furniture factories. Given what he had seen, he would like to have had a union at his new workplace. But the chances for organizing, he estimated in 1998, were minimal: "They're almost all Americans here, just blacks and whites."[3]

Aside from the dynamic among the immigrant workers themselves, the Morganton poultry workers' struggle owed much to organizational skills and investment at both local and national levels. Whatever doubts and strategic weaknesses led LIUNA to abandon its larger foray into the food-processing industry (and whatever real regret its leaders may have felt for having waded into the Case Farms effort in the first place), the international union provided a crucial infrastructure for the continuation of the organizing campaign. By garrisoning its local union outpost—serviced by legal assistant Felipe López and occasional visits by national organizer Yanira Merino—LIUNA kept its word to local leaders and, in turn, maintained *their* legitimacy in the eyes of their peers. Moreover, at great financial expense the union scrupulously contested each legal bend in the road, never allowing Case Farms to shake itself entirely free of the influence of its employees.

However important the monetary and organizational investment from union headquarters in Washington, D.C., proved, an effective organization in Morganton required a network of local support. Crucial communication with the national headquarters was conducted via the local legal offices of attorney Phyllis Palmieri—a link further solidified by the presence of Felipe López. Especially following the illness and forced retirement of Nacho, the local organizing committee looked to Felipe—even though he never worked in the plant himself—for strategic and tactical guidance. Apart from continually pressing the legal issues against Case Farms, Palmieri's office also served the union cause indirectly. Scores of Case Farms workers as well as others in Morganton looked to her for assistance with their immigration-related problems: when aid to immigrant workers on and off the job emanated from the same union-identified center, it could not help but solidify union loyalty within the worker community.[4] If Palmieri's law office constituted a semi-official headquarters of the local workers' movement, other allies also played important roles. Father Ken Whittington and the welcoming arms of St. Charles Borromeo Catholic Church were the most obvious forces, but the Evangelical Daniel Gutiérrez also maintained supportive links to Case Farms workers.

The organizing example of the Case Farms workers, moreover, counters a common stereotype about new immigrant and especially undocumented workers as a "threat" to American labor standards. The restructuring of U.S. industry after 1980—including the flight of capital abroad and a general emphasis on a flexible labor force at home—risked a renewal of nativist fears.[5] Even the AFL-CIO bounced back and forth on the issue of immigration. Long an advocate of restricting immigration, the labor federation initially supported the limited-amnesty-plus-employer-sanctions principles of the 1986 Immigration Reform and Control Act in an attempt to stem the flow of (largely Mexican) illegals. The very porousness of that act, however, made it more an instrument of labor, rather than employer, sanctions, since in practice the law allowed employers to turn a blind eye to workers' credentials on hiring while still holding the whip handle of subsequent INS exposure over their heads. Indeed, after the INS announced a new policy of "interior enforcement" in 1997 (enforcing the immigration law away from the borders), several unionizing and contract campaigns were chilled by INS raids, indicating again the vulnerability of the new workers to employer coercion.[6] Only a general amnesty for the undocumented, concluded the AFL-CIO national convention in Los Angeles in October 1999 (the federation was less clear on what to do about entry at the borders), would allow immigrant workers to claim their rights and join with other workers to defend their welfare at the workplace.[7]

It was no accident that U.S. labor's reappraisal of the immigration issue was confirmed in a Los Angeles setting. For a decade, that city's new immigrant Latino and Asian workforce had spurred the most sustained and successful union-organizing work in the country. Beginning with SEIU's Justice for Janitors campaign at the Century City luxury office complex in 1990, sustained by the extended New Otani drive by Local 11 (Hotel and Restaurant Employees) and fueled by *drywalleros*, house framers, county workers, tortilla makers, and even bus rider unionists, the new Angelenos have effectively made their city "the major R&D [research and development] center for 21st century trade unionism."[8] While the spirit of Cesar Chavez and the *huelgas* of the 1960s and 1970s among Mexican American farmworkers has certainly been one influence within the recent rising, Central Americans have also played a crucial part. The slogan of the marching janitors in downtown Los Angeles and Beverly Hills—"This is war!"— echoed of real-life experience. Moreover, it was not the marchers themselves, who, according to a local reporter, had previously "faced down terror in Salvador and Guatemala," but a legion of community activists who came to the workers' aid.[9] As Mike Davis notes, "immigrant rights groups, liberationist clergy, Latino college students, and other communities of color" lent their talents to the new wave of social movement unionism. "The 'best and brightest' of the second generation," he suggests, "want to be organizers and teachers, not MBAs."[10]

Although two sites could hardly be more different in political geography than Los Angeles and Morganton, the basic logic of the Case Farms campaign echoed many of the themes documented by Hector Delgado in a study of a successful fourteen-month unionizing struggle during the mid-1980s among undocumented Hispanic workers at a Los Angeles "Camagua" water bed factory. Among the important factors in the Camagua outcome, Delgado cites poor treatment from supervisors, the stirring of group emotion and passion by union organizers, and events that created "opportunities for collective action." Finally, writes Delgado, "the union provided experience, legal assistance, contacts, telephones, transportation, and other organizational capabilities so vital to the success of any organizing campaign."[11]

Each of these factors was operative at Case Farms. In poultry processing, as in the secondary labor market more generally, employers take little time or effort to win workers' loyalties. At Case Farms, as at Camagua, paternalism or a personalistic approach to the employees (which had once been a factor at Breeden's Poultry and Egg, Inc.) had disappeared with company expansion and given way to a brusque hire-and-fire approach to a new workforce. Especially for workers steeped in a personalistic relationship to authority—as is classically the case in the Latin American countryside—the cold expediency of U.S. industrial relations invited alternative if not outright oppositional forms of loyalty. It was a situation, in particular, where the speed of production regularly inflamed relations between workers and supervisors. As at Camagua, moreover, the logic of solidarity appeared to depend less on individual calculation of costs and benefits than on a wave of emotion cemented by the allegiance of workplace protest leaders for the union option. Similarly, only the outside resources of the international union could turn an act of protest, a moment of rebellion, into an enduring struggle.

Delgado makes a final claim that bears provocatively on the events in Morganton. Undocumented workers, he concludes, "seem to be neither more nor less organizable because of their citizenship status than other workers in the secondary sector."[12] At Camagua, as Delgado discovered, workers had largely lost fear of both INS reprisals (raids were few and far between) and employer threats (similar jobs were plentiful and only the immigrants were willing to take them). The Camagua union, he asserts, allayed workers' apprehensions by assuring them that they were protected—"and technically they were and have remained so"—by the NLRB. Even though Delgado gathered his evidence before the 1986 Immigration Reform and Control Act and its formal threat to crack down on illegal immigrants, his argument appears to hold for the subsequent period as well. To be sure, undocumented workers at Case Farms generally dared not take on official "leadership" roles that might attract public attention to their noncitizenship status. Yet, in Morganton, the decline of official protection inherent in work permits based on asylum applications did *not* in itself appear to trigger a loss of support for the union. As in Los Angeles, the bogeyman of INS raids was largely countered both by the practical scarcity of the federal presence and by the union's continuing assurances to the workers that the INS would not intervene in the midst of a labor dispute.[13] Again, both the Camagua and Case Farms examples suggest that organizing low-wage immigrant workers may require "exorbitant amounts of financial and other resources" before a union victory is won. However, as Delgado concludes, "given the shift away from heavy manufacturing and toward the services and light manufacturing, especially marked in regions and cities around the country, organized labor may be left with few, if any, alternatives."[14]

Indeed, the rising new-immigrant composition of the low-wage labor force presented not only U.S. labor leaders but also the nation itself with a stark set of alternatives. In one scenario, America's "uninvited guest workers" would become frozen as a permanent, apartheidlike lower caste, largely cut off from the benefits of a larger culture, itself increasingly riveted by unbridgable class distinctions. By another scenario, these workers would rise up in a mighty social movement to claim both political rights and an enhanced economic future. The latter image conjures up the memory of the last great immigrant worker upsurge in U.S. history—namely, the rise of the CIO in the 1930s and 1940s—when the previous denizens of the turn-of-the-century industrial "jungle" established significant workplace leverage and a powerful foothold within the Democratic Party. In turn, one might

Union organization across borders—as measured on the back of a T-shirt in the town square of Aguacatán, summer 1999.

further imagine two different "tracks" toward such an advance. One would take the form of a Latino (or better yet, African American/Asian/Latino) coalition to claim full rights of participation in a renewed American democracy. The other path would follow a more "global labor rights" trajectory, connecting the struggles of low-wage and undocumented workers in the United States to those of sweatshops (*maquiladoras*) and unemployed persons the world over. In the end, the fate of immigrant poultry workers in the United States will likely be linked both to the political dynamic in the host country and its elaboration in a world marketplace, with or without protections for its humblest producers.

In addition to confirming the political potential of a new immigrant labor force, the Morganton example carries a conceptual lesson for scholarly observers. In particular, the communal focus of the Mayan union cadre at Case Farms poses a challenge to the conventional juxtaposition of "traditional" versus "modern" social actions. Until relatively recently, political theory of both a liberal and Marxist variety contrasted the "unconscious reflex" of traditionalism with the "conscious and purposeful" action associated with modernity. "Progress" (whether as liberal economic development or revolutionary liberation, based on one's political preference) depended on rational revolt against inherited custom and the tyranny of tradition.[15]

Sticking Together

"The tradition of the dead generations" scoffed Karl Marx, "weighs like a nightmare on the minds of the living."[16] Similarly, Thomas Jefferson proclaimed to John Adams, "I like the dreams of the future better than the history of the past—so, good night!"[17] When invoked at all within the classic paradigm of political thought, the organic community was associated with conservative tradition, not revolutionary or reformist transformation. Within this framework, it is not surprising that both liberal and Marxist political traditions tended to scorn the seemingly backward and benighted collectivity of the peasantry, that most "organic" of social formations.[18]

Moreover, even those who have turned a more positive light on the peasantry have rarely imagined how this class might directly contribute to the political and cultural enrichment of its urban-industrial counterparts. On the one hand, certain conservative romantics celebrated peasant culture for its "backward-looking reactions against contemporary society."[19] On the other hand, left-wing, late 1960s "dependency theory"—which attacked the dualism of prior models by insisting that peasants had long served as the most exploited (and, hence, most potentially revolutionary) victims of global capitalism—tended to see little worth preserving in the peasant's world.[20]

Altogether, these were interpretive assumptions with a long reach. One case from U.S. historiography is illustrative. In an influential 1970 interpretation of the early Puritans, Kenneth Lockridge drew on Eric Wolf's Mayan-centered community criteria for the premodern peasantry to label seventeenth-century Dedham, Massachusetts, "a Christian Utopian Closed Corporate Community."[21] What is relevant for our purposes is less the accuracy of Lockridge's formulation of early New England society (for it was soon criticized for neglecting the ties of the Puritans to a larger Atlantic commercial world) than the negative connotations both he and his critics attached to the concept. More obviously than did Wolf, for example, Lockridge stressed the reactionary nature of the peasant community. A vestige of Old World pessimism, Christian corporatism—in Lockridge's characteristically North American view—would give way to an optimistic "opportunity" society characterized by liberty, individualism, and cultural pluralism. Communalism, in short, was regarded as inherently conservative and backward-looking, whereas, modern American individualism—reflected in "the America of Jefferson, Jackson, and de Tocqueville"—was progressive and liberating.[22] The tether of the older community, to the extent that it remained an influence, cast a dark, even insidious shadow over the country's otherwise bright and expansive prospects: "On this conservative foundation a large part of the history of our nation has been constructed. In the depths of the American experience lies a craving for peace, unity, and order within the confines of a simple society. Though it is not a la mode to say so, next to it lies a willingness to exclude whatever men and to ignore whatever events threaten the fulfillment of that hunger."[23] In short, read the older conventional wisdom, only when the superstitious fetters of communal allegiance were shed could a liberal, modern-day society emerge.

To be sure, the example of a more "simple society" was not always seen in a negative light. Disillusioned by the limits of "technocratic" or "corporate" forms of social organization and impressed by the power of new social movements that invoked a "community"-based mobilization model, social historians rediscovered genuine expressions of popular democracy and radical upheaval within the trappings of previously discarded traditions and social formations. A common point of reference in the new works was E. P. Thompson's 1963 reconstruction of the political resistance of late-eighteenth- and early-nineteenth-century artisans in the *The Making of the English Working Class*. With Thompsonian insight, certain social formations that had once been seen as archaic and backward-looking were given a new lease on life. Indeed, the reevaluation of the political capacity of traditional community grew well beyond Thompson's own attempt to connect the pre-industrial artisan world with that of the modern-day labor and socialist movement. Craig Calhoun, for instance, turned the valuation of modern and traditional historical actors on its head in his 1983 invocation of the "radicalism of tradition" and those he called "reactionary radicals." In this reckoning the traditional community, or more accurately its self-defense under outside attack, becomes the very motor of revolutionary advance:

> Community constitutes the preexisting organization capable of securing the participation of individuals in collective action. Communities provide a social organizational foundation for mobilization, as networks of kinship, friendship, shared crafts, or recreations offer lines of communication and allegiance. People who live in well-integrated communities do not need elaborate formal organization in order to mount a protest. They know, moreover, whom to trust and whom not to. Communal relations are themselves important resources to be "mobilized" for any insurgency. . . . Traditional communities . . . give their members the social strength with which to wage protracted battles, the "selective inducements" with which to ensure full collective participation, and a sense of what to fight for that is at once shared and radical. This sets traditional communities apart from the modern working class.[24]

In the United States, in particular, where the "politicized working class" (one equipped with a powerful trade union apparatus and self-conscious political party) has been mostly absent, the community-based model of social movement analysis proved a welcome analytic brace for a new generation of labor and social historians.[25] Perhaps nowhere was this phenomenon of community or place-based struggle more intense than among the immigrants and their children who dominated industrial America's rank and file from the 1880s through the 1930s. Victor Greene's classic account of Slavic immigrant participation in the 1887–88 Pennsylvania anthracite strike is illustrative. Typically, Greene's subjects constituted a community new to industrial disputes. But once the fight was on, strike loyalty, according to Greene, "approached fanaticism . . . the English-speaking miners, whether labor leaders or only followers, seemed less unified, more individualistic, less provident, and perhaps less determined."[26]

As developed in the literature, moreover, community—more than a residual or unchanging category—carried a dynamic shape and genealogy of its own. Like a union or other political institution, community identity takes shape over time and carries an ideological and even strategic compass of its own. In their study of the immigrant cigar-making community of Ybor City, Florida, Gary Mormino and George E. Pozzetta offer compelling evidence that for immigrant workers, social change might occur "in a complementary fashion . . . on both sides of the Atlantic." In this particular case, 1890s emigrants from the Sicilian village of Sante Stefano carried with them the lessons of agrarian agitation headed by a local intellectual-activist named Lorenzo Panepinto. Even after the *fasci* (workers' league) movement was violently repressed and officially disbanded in 1893, Panepinto carried on a transnational peasant organizing campaign—at once inspiring labor-organizing activity in Tampa and, in turn, receiving emigrant support for his agricultural union in Italy.[27] The Sante Stefano story connects to the Morganton story as a graphic illustration of how, in another time and place, community mobilization at opposite ends of the immigration process might affect political institution building. What is more, the fact that Marc Panepinto, the first LIUNA organizer in Morganton, is most likely a distant relative of Lorenzo Panepinto, suggests that the layering of immigrant community struggles typical of U.S. labor history may leave an inheritance unknown even to its beneficiaries.[28]

In general terms, therefore, the Maya of Morganton offer a modern-day example of the "radicalism of tradition" thesis proposed for the early nineteenth century and subsequently sustained, at least by reference to outlying immigrant communities, through the early twentieth century. Today's global-age democrats, it would seem, have much to learn from the carriers of a still comparatively closed corporate community. Like the hand-loom weavers who turned once-conservative ties to family, friends, and craft toward insurrectionary ends in response to an outside threat, the Morganton Maya drew on a similar communal repository to wage a several-year fight for a union contract.

Yet, if we are to valorize the continuing power of local community in a globalized marketplace, we must do so in qualified and flexible ways. For the Aguacatecos in Morganton, for instance, it is important to recognize that a shifting relationship of local and global socioeconomic factors under-lay their existence. The same forces that were "breaking up" the home com-munity (causing much consternation among religious and secular leaders in Aguacatán) were also "creating" new centers of cooperation abroad. Moreover, compared to other Mayan groups, the Aguacatecos came from a place relatively divorced from ancient Mayan traditions. Thus, the tradi-tional cargo system of interlinked civil and religious offices that John M. Watanabe observed in the Mam-speaking community of Santiago Chimal-tenango at late as 1980 seemed nowhere in evidence in modern-day Agua-catán, where the combined cultural effect of economic development and religious pluralization added up, as we have seen, to a "revolt against the dead."[29] It may even be that the Aguacatecos functioned more cohesively in Morganton than their Q'anjob'al counterparts precisely because their home culture gave them a foretaste of the social diversity and need for flexibility that they would encounter abroad. "Closed" and "corporate," at the very least, are relative terms. Rather than something monolithic and determi-nant, therefore, community itself should be approached as a strategic and evanescent institution, something less than the sum of its parts. Paraphras-ing anthropologist Watanabe, we might call communal culture "[our] own conceptual shorthand for those interactions that [convey] the meaningful-ness of individual experience against a common background of time, place, and circumstance."[30]

While stressing the power of community in the Morganton story, we should not discount the "globalizing" effects of change on the home com-munities of the workers themselves. The combination of poverty, milita-rization, and migration (both within and beyond Guatemala's borders) over the last quarter of the twentieth century broke down much of the traditional structure of a pre-industrial society. Moreover, the two locales most closely associated with "progressive" political organization among the Morganton Maya—Aguacatán, which gave birth to the union, and Totonicapán, which engaged the Consejo Maya—were both more economically and socially differentiated than much of the surrounding countryside. In Aguacatán's case, proximity to the regional capital benefited commercial agriculture as well as educational institutions. Totonicapán, as a long-established craft and cultural center of the populous K'iche' region, likewise always prized a certain worldliness from its indigenous leaders. The recent globalizing shake-up of these Mayan regions was symbolized by a hole-in-the-wall grocery near the city of Totonicapán with a sign affixed above the window reading "Kmart."[31] In short, the "traditionality" of the Mayan community—whether in Guatemala or in the U.S. diaspora—is a matter of degree.

The leaders of Morganton's diasporic community clearly drew sustenance from both traditional and modern wells. On the one hand, the homeland with its commitment to the ancient inheritance of family plots and veneration of the souls of the dead inspired Paulino López to organize his fellow Aguacatecos abroad. Similarly, in the face of repression at home and a competitive jungle in the land of exile, Justo Lux appealed to a Pan-Mayan consciousness of an egalitarian society based on reconciliation with nature. On the other hand, immigrant leaders like Felipe López relied on professional-level education, even if uncertified, to serve their community, and Mayan hackers like Justo connected to the faith of the ancestors via internet linkages and conferences facilitated by rapid, affordable transportation. Moreover, as "organic intellectuals" or self-conscious representatives and interpreters for the larger indigenous community around them, these leaders readily adopt the political tools available—be it United Nations–sanctioned human rights discourse, U.S.-made labor law and union rights, or immigration reform policy—to advance and defend the welfare of the larger group. For them, "sticking together" necessarily implied adhering to an expanding, and previously unknown, menu of political choices.

Another kind of sticking together was much on the minds of American political and social commentators at the end of the century. National identity—its sense of common civic principles—announced Arthur M. Schlesinger Jr. in 1991, was threatened by a "cult of ethnicity."[32] Whether derived from the new social movements, multicultural and ethnic educational projects, or postmodernist relativism, a new "identity politics" based on attachment to race, ethnic, or other "cultural" affinities, in the critics' eyes, was upsetting the very basis for a liberal, progressive polity. Even former

1960s activist-turned-sociologist Todd Gitlin spoke anxiously of what he called "the twilight of common dreams."[33] In short, the critics warned, a revitalization of intimate group ties might undo the larger knot that held a diverse nation together.

It is common to classify the "identity" issue as a peculiarly, even quintessentially, American problem. After all, a diverse settler and immigrant society like the United States has no common past or blood line to fall back on; rather, it must depend on an identity with the core political values of a representative democracy for national unity. The fraying of that identity—however temporary or exaggerated—inevitably sends a chill through the guardians of America's public culture. With the murderous examples of Bosnia and Rwanda lending an eerie backdrop to the rhetorical heat of our own group-centered politics, the forces of contemporary globalization—including mass migrations—may seem to threaten cultural fragmentation. As Schlesinger worried: "What happens when people of different ethnic origins, speaking different languages and professing different religions, settle in the same geographical locality and live under the same political sovereignty? Unless a common purpose binds them together, tribal antagonisms will drive them apart. In the century darkly ahead, civilization faces a critical question: *What is it that holds a nation together?*"[34]

Yet, the dominant position of the United States in the world economic system will surely save it from cultural implosion. Among the immigrant peoples who continued to find permanent or even temporary refuge in this country, there was ready allegiance and admiration for the American economic and political system. Should they have the good fortune—which alas, immigration law as of 2002 prevented—to remain in the United States as permanent residents and ultimately as citizens, many of the Morganton Maya would no doubt follow in the footsteps of the millions of immigrant Americans who preceded them. Most likely their own contemporary ethnic identity would at once equip them to defend their group interests in a pluralistic society while also adapting to the overwhelming force of a nationalizing consumer culture. Rather than posing a threat to the social fabric, Maya Americans, one might predict, within three generations would prove as American as any constituency within the larger Latino melting pot.

In the course of research for this book, a rich example of conflict over identity politics did present itself within the population under study. It was not in Morganton, however, that ethnic differences became increasingly politically pronounced during the late 1990s but rather in the Guatemalan town of Aguacatán. In many respects, the challenge of sticking together versus pulling apart—so basic to labor union battles in the United States—was every bit as relevant in the agricultural communities "back home." Just what Mayan identity meant for social and political organization was tested across Guatemala, perhaps nowhere in more intricate fashion than in Aguacatán.

Initially, one might find it amusing that in Aguacatán's public life, the "big" issues circa 2000 had nothing to do with postwar reconciliation, the return of former dictator Ríos Montt's party to power, nor even local economic problems such as the lack of roads or a reliable water system. Rather, after the Peace Accords of 1996, a reassertion of indigenous political power and identity—evident in the support of *comités cívicos* at the expense of the national political parties—was the most dramatic development in local civic life.[35] Even that involved an uncommon complexity, as attested to by a photo-finish election of the *alcalde* in the fall of 1999. The election reflected a high-water mark of support for the Comité Cívico Union Aguacateca—better known locally by its visual symbol, *tinajas* (earthenware jars for carrying water)—which, with open encouragement from Padre Gabriel, had drawn increasing support over several years in the town center and selective adjoining aldeas. But in 1999 Tinajas lost by eighteen votes to the La Balanza (Scales of Justice) ticket of Comité Cívico de mi Pueblo, a brand-new formation headed by anthropologist-turned-politician Pablo Escobar Méndez.[36] Balanza's appeal centered on a collective reassertion of ethnic identity and sense of justice denied among local Chalchitekos.

In a spring 2000 interview, Mayor Pablo Escobar (who joked about being mistaken for the Columbian druglord of the same name) offered an extensive and passionate account of the new turn in his native Aguacatán. Like many of his generation, in 1985, at age twenty-eight, he had fled his country's violence for refuge in Mexico and did not return until a full decade later. In the meantime he enrolled at the Escuela Nacional de Antropologia e Historia and, after research in the borderlands of Chiapas and Campeche, wrote a thesis on the identity of Guatemalan refugees in exile. On reentering Guatemala in 1995, Escobar worked on a Danish-run development project in Quetzaltenango, regularly returning on weekends to his native Aguacatán. Soon he was pulled back into local issues that drew directly on his skills as an ethnohistorian. "Aguacatán," he explained, "was considered a town inhabited by Awakatekos, this was the story in which we were inculcated. . . . But with the Peace Accords, especially the agreement signed between the government and the guerrillas over the identity and rights of indigenous peoples, we saw that there was an element that the official story didn't take into account." The last straw for Escobar came in 1996, when, in accordance with a general movement toward bilingualism (acceptance of indigenous languages in schools and other government projects began in 1988), local bilingual promoters linked to the national Academy of Maya Languages began distributing pamphlets and schoolbooks across the district written in a newly formalized "Awakateko" script. But many Chalchitekos balked. Not only were individual vocabulary differences between Chalchiteko and Awakateko forms settled in favor of the latter, but the new phonetic spelling replaced an older script (originally composed by Evangelicals Harry and Lucille McArthur while they lived on the Chalchiteko side of town) with a new orthography that appeared strange and occasionally tilted toward Awakateko preferences. As Escobar recalled, many older people approached him and complained, "What is happening, why have they changed our language?"[37] In response, he and some friends began an intensive study of the "real" history of Aguacatán. "I remember," he said, "once in Mexico a Guatemalan friend asked me, 'Are you Chalchiteko or Awakateko?' I had never thought about it. . . . Our grandparents had told us we were Chalchiteko but that was the end of it."[38]

In short order, the message with which Escobar and friends returned to their community was one of a people betrayed by history and subordinated by their Awakateko neighbors. The "descent" of the Chalchitekos, in this reckoning, began with the dark day of February 27, 1891, when once-proud Chalchitán, a township of nearly three hundred families, was consolidated into Aguacatán, a previously separate settlement of about fifty families. Escobar insisted that the two groups reflected two historically distinct peoples with distinct cultures; his own research, admittedly yet to be confirmed, suggested that the Chalchitekos were the more "ancient" of the two groups. More provocatively still, he suspected that the Awakatekos emigrated from Mexico behind the Spanish Conquistadores, a "fact" that in some sense makes them double expropriators of Chalchitán's legacy. Such historical claims, however, fueled more recent grievances, of which the language changes were only the most prominent. According to Escobar and his followers, the Chalchiteko majority (estimated by Escobar to number 25,000) were regularly snubbed in decision-making authority by the Awakateko minority (estimated at 10,000, with the remaining 8,000 "others" mainly K'iche' but also including Mam and Ladinos). He pointed not only to the makeup of the local Academia de Lenguas Mayas but also to the staffing of international aid projects like "Christian

Chalchiteko community protest meeting in local football stadium on
July 25, 1998. Photo courtesy of Pablo Escobar Méndez.

Children" and the "Agricultural Association." In all such venues, as in the
Comité Cívico Tinajas, key positions went to Awakatekos, while Chalchitekos participated only as "*amigos*," a word Escobar pronounced in a manner that might best translate as "Uncle Toms."

There is no question that the issues Escobar articulated touched a nerve
in the community. In the late 1990s there were reports of angry quarrels
and physical confrontations in the streets over the language issue and the
symbolic "boundaries" of the two ancient settlements. The first stage of
Chalchiteko unrest crested on July 25, 1998, in a mass rally at the local
football stadium, where several thousand Chalchitekos demanded recognition of their language. Their immediate target was the local director of the
Academia de Lenguas Mayas, Simon Rodríguez, who earlier that day, as
quoted in a national press article, denied the existence of a discrete Chalchiteko people and language. That Simon was the brother of Padre Gabriel,
himself a man of wide-ranging social and political influence, lent a further
tint of conspiracy to apparent Awakateko "control" of the municipio. According to Escobar, only the calming hand of community leaders prevented
the roused Chalchiteko crowd from doing violence to Simon Rodríguez
and his family. Following mass mobilization, Escobar's election to the mayoralty represented a second, institutional response to local inequalities. In

May 2000, while still assembling the municipal administration and program, the Escobar forces established an alternative language center from whence they would continue to defend their cultural "rights." With official, national recognition, they hoped to supply distinct Chalchiteko grammar books to schools, modify spelling in local signage, and receive state support for their own bilingual *promotores* (language instructors).[39]

From the testimony of Mayor Escobar, migration appeared not only as a source of cultural dispersion and dilution but also as the springboard of the new ethnic consciousness. The entire inner circle of the Chalchiteko movement consisted of men in their thirties and forties who, for political or economic reasons, were forced to leave their native village for a period of exile. They had come of age at a time of fear and isolation. "We indigenous people closed our mouths, we had to remain in the middle, neither on one side or the other, just surviving here in the *municipio*. We saw the massacres and the terror which infested our communities and made impossible the work of local government, voluntary organizations, the *comités*. People were forced into the army or the civil patrols. You couldn't tell who was on one side or the other, because nobody could say. Some of our people were with the guerrillas but never openly. This was the way we managed not to be killed." Yet, whether they went to "the capital" (Guatemala City), to Mexico, or to the United States, the exiles from Aguacatán never forgot their native ties. "We have to return to where we were born," explained Escobar. "You carry it in your blood, in your heart. Even though we were gone for five or ten years, we had to come back to our *pueblo*." Displacement, then, with its accompanying sense of longing and search for *lost* roots, in an important sense served Escobar and cohorts as the impetus for cultural rebirth. Though he and his close friends had no direct contact with Morganton, for instance, they were convinced that today's emigrant generation would support them. There had been talk of sending a delegation to Morganton to "reach out to our *compañeros*," but so far it was only a pipe dream.[40]

Back in Morganton, there was also an almost universal longing among immigrants to reconnect with their native Aguacatán. Yet, by and large, news of the Chalchiteko revival both puzzled and disturbed the diaspora community. Víctor Hernández, the Awakateko who shared a rented house with three Chalchitekos, happily posed in front of an Escobar-for-alcalde campaign poster on his living room wall. Though well aware of growing hometown conflicts, he saw little manifestation of such divisions within the immigrant community. "The people here generally identify themselves

Sticking Together

COMITE CIVICO DE MI PUEBLO

Por un gobierno municipal representativo

PLANILLA

ALCALDE — Lic. Pablo Escobar Méndez

PRIMER CONSEJAL — Gaspar Ortiz Aícón

SEGUNDO CONSEJAL — Téc. Sal. Samon Brígido Rodríguez Aícón

Political poster for Aguacatán mayoral candidate Pablo Escobar Méndez
hanging on the Morganton living room wall of Víctor Hernández, 1999.

at the level of 'Aguacateco,' there's not much difference between Chalchitekos and Awakatekos like there is in Aguacatán." Whether in residential
patterns, work friendships, or church and choir participation, "we're equal,"
he said. "The majority are Chalchitekos but we don't take into account such
differences." In his own house, though the occupants spoke in their native
tongue, "sometimes a word will come out [that's different between the two
communities], we'll start to laugh, but we don't take such differences seriously."[41]

For their part, Morganton labor activists, Case Farms worker José Samuel
Solís López and his cousin Felipe López, eyed the Chalchiteko movement
with greater concern. Not that they were entirely unsympathetic toward
the distant insurgency. Felipe acknowledged a "monopolization" of power
and influence by Padre Gabriel's family and a heavy-handed politicization
of the church dating to a Christian Democratic Party mayoral candidate
in 1988. He also generally supported the move toward nonpartisan comités cívicos in municipal affairs. The people were tired of the corrupt national parties, he suggested.[42] Yet, both Felipe and José Samuel suspected
that the new movement was mostly a power grab by an alternative set of
"professionals." "I can't make sense of this form of thinking [distinctions

between Awakatekos and Chalchitekos]," said José Samuel, "because we are one people." "However, there are people who want to be leaders—educated people, lawyers, doctors—who have initiated this conflict. It pains me when I hear such a person trying to divide the people."[43]

In the minds of Morganton *directiva* members, the issue of ethnic division combined in February 2000 with the most unsavory of intracommunal conflicts. Francisco Fuentes, long outcast from community leadership, challenged the legitimacy of the current directiva and on his own called a community meeting. After an emergency session, the directiva decided to bring its own forces to the meeting. Fuentes and about ten followers not only charged the directiva with misappropriation of funds but also openly played the ethnic card by calling for a separate Chalchiteko organization. In response, representatives of the directiva documented their past activities and future plans. "When work is done well you don't have to be afraid of anybody. We have always made a commitment that our work must be clean, must be on the side of the community." According to José Samuel:

Then, one guy from Chalchitán got up, and said, "Why should we divide ourselves, we are one people. If they [Fuentes's people] want to separate off, let them. But we don't want to divide ourselves." We decided to put things to a vote. What happened? The community said, "We have our leaders, we recognize our leaders, and you [Fuentes] have no business here." And Sr. Fuentes left, it was a complete defeat for him. The fact is we are all equal here. No one is more than anyone else. In fact, I believe that there are more Chalchitekos on the directiva than from the other side [Awakatekos]. We're proud that we're working here together. For us, unity is the most important thing.[44]

On both ends of the migratory stream, the boundaries of community were, clearly, still being negotiated. Padre Gabriel returned for a second time to Morganton in October 2000. In addition to celebrating Mass with Father Ken, he visited privately with some of his distant parishioners from Aguacatán. When I asked Father Ken the essence of Gabriel's public message, delivered in Spanish, Father Ken and Spanish-speaking parishioner Maureen Dougher recalled the theme of "unity," that all Catholics are one people. But Víctor Hernández, who heard the priest speak in both Spanish and Awakateko, remembered a different emphasis in his hometown priest's talk. "He spoke of 'unity'—the unity of the Maya. 'You are not 'hispanos,' he told us, 'you are *indígenas*.'"[45] Meanwhile, by one on-site account in the spring of 2002, Mayor Escobar's municipal regime had run into trouble at home. Former teacher Emiliano Rodríguez reported that frustration was everywhere in the municipio—"They have not fulfilled any of their promises and the people have lost faith." Rodríguez went so far as to suggest that the honeymoon with the local cultural identity project was over. "[The people] want jobs, roads, and water," he said.[46]

Even as Aguacatecos in Morganton tried valiantly to stick together, their efforts proved insufficient for the unionizing campaign at Case Farms. The fact is, stories of contemporary U.S. industrial relations produce few fairy-tale endings. By summer 2001—despite the second court-ordered round of negotiations—the six-year standoff between Case Farms and its unionized workers had moved less to resolution than exhaustion—an irresolution that served the employer and its lawyers much better than the union. In mid-July company and union stopped talking after a series of fruitless exchanges. The LIUNA bargainers, anxious and even desperate to relieve themselves of an organizationally dysfunctional and costly operation, found nary a crumb offered to them at the negotiating table. Not only did the company withdraw the token raise it had offered in the 1999 negotiating round, but also it now attached severe new conditions to any contract settlement. Before a modest increase of 40 cents per hour would be considered, the company demanded a 20 percent increase in production rates; even more punitively, management reportedly proposed to withhold 30 cents per hour from workers' paychecks until the end of the contract year for deposit into an "insurance fund" to cover the cost of potential work stoppages.[47] For perhaps the first time in history, a company was asking workers to subsidize its own strike fund! Under such terms, the union would serve less as an advocate for worker welfare than an enforcer of managerial discipline. LIUNA associate general counsel Michael Barrett, who flew into Morganton for the negotiating sessions and who had personally supervised about three dozen other contract talks, was astounded by the company's intransigence. "It goes beyond economics," noted Barrett. "It must be either personal or ideological [on Robert Shelton' part]."[48] "I could never recommend [the proposed contract] to anybody," concluded Yanira Merino. "[The workers] are better off without a contract."[49]

Once again, the union had its back to the wall, but this time its strategic cupboard was bare. With nothing to show from the negotiations, Case Farms workers—ordered by the NLRB not to disrupt production during the talks—were growing restless and increasingly unresponsive to union discipline. On July 17—while union representative Felipe López was in Miami on another LIUNA campaign—paros [quickie strikes] broke out among some two hundred "whole-bird" and "front-half" workers. The trigger was an old one at Case Farms: Supervisors had cut back bathroom breaks to rein in workers from extending the breaks to include a smoke or a soda in the cafeteria. In defiance of union orders, even in-plant leader Francisco Aguirre had "gone out" (actually, workers massed in the cafeteria until management promised to make adjustments): "You have to join with the people," he explained.[50] Such activity only exacerbated tensions with national union officials. "A single department will stop work for two hours at lunchtime," Merino complained, "then return [after the grievance is settled] and work until 8 [instead of the usual 6:00 P.M. quitting time]. . . . "That's not a real strike." To Merino and other LIUNA representatives, the Morganton workers appeared to have lost the discipline to sustain a winning campaign. Local leader Felipe López sympathized as much with the frustrations of the Washington LIUNA office as those in the workplace. Miffed at the poor attendance at meetings, Felipe attributed a "lack of patience," a "loss of hope," and a general decline of "union consciousness" to the poultry workers and variously singled out a "decline of abuses" in the factory (the company was smarter than previously), accumulation of debts to *coyotes*, and simple "ignorance" of new workers unacquainted with the long struggle at the plant as explanations for the union's inability either to rally—or quiet—rank-and-file members at times of its choosing.[51]

Local union leaders might have mentioned another factor in workers' disinclination to publicly rally around the union. From an extraordinarily low unemployment rate of 2.2 percent as late as spring 2000, the Catawba Valley manufacturing belt had suddenly fallen on hard times. Indeed, a register of 7.2 percent unemployment in the Hickory metropolitan area (which includes Morganton) in September 2001 represented "the nation's highest increase in joblessness over the past year" and the worst for the state of North Carolina since 1993. Among other things, the employment turnabout generally transformed power relations between workers and their bosses. Area employers quickly noticed the difference on the shop floor. "Instead of employees being in the driver's seat, now we're in the drivers' seat," summarized a manager of one of the big Hickory furniture factories.[52] In such circumstances, even if poultry employment did not slacken, the discipline of a depressed job market—combined with a severe tightening of U.S. border patrols following the terrorist attacks of September 11— undoubtedly affected the willingness of workers to put their own jobs in jeopardy.

Faced with a company that would not budge and workers it could not control, LIUNA played its last card in Morganton. In December 2001—following a lapse of nearly five months of any general membership meeting—the union officially decided to withdraw from the Case Farms campaign, but also to leave the community with some resources for continuing self-organization. The latter would take the form of a Workers Center to be administered by the National Interfaith Committee for Worker Justice, the Chicago-based organization that had cut its organizational teeth on an earlier phase of the Case Farms campaign. Committing thirty thousand dollars per year to an area center for a minimum of two years, LIUNA hoped, in Merino's words, to "give [the workers] the respect they deserve." Even Yanira Merino, however, could not conceal the sense of defeat, if not surrender, implicit in the union's decision. As she knew full well, once the union officially announced its withdrawal, the original recognition election of 1995 would lose all legal standing. To forestall that outcome, LIUNA representatives had approached their old UFCW competitors to try to "hand off" the local, but they received no encouragement from this or any other union alternative. "It's sad," Merino admitted. "Basically you've got no protection under the NLRB, no tools within the law that we can use to push companies like Case Farms."[53]

At its best, the Workers Center was the most attractive alternative available to low-wage workers unable to draw the full-scale attentions of the major American unions. With numerous versions of the concept having appeared after the prototype Workplace Project (Centro de Derechos Laborales) was established in Hempstead, Long Island, in 1992, the centers typically took on several interrelated functions. Out-and-out workplace organizing, community education, worker-owned cooperatives, leadership training, legal and social service support, English-language courses, and even pastoral counseling defined the tasks of the fledgling centers. Typically, workers centers form on the basis of work sectors (such as housekeeper and day laborer programs at the Long Island Workplace Project) or to serve specific ethnic communities (such as the Los Angeles Korean Immigrant Worker Association, which actually serves both Korean and Latino workers in Koreatown, and the Minneapolis Latino Worker Center). They also established an important international presence in *maquila* (export-processing) zones in Mexico, Central America, and Southeast Asia. Although a product of the weakness—and often the downright invisibility—of the union presence among low-wage workers, the worker center provided an alternative organizing capacity through the development of "worker associations," which in turn might ultimately reconnect with union recognition and contract drives.[54]

Between 2000 and 2002, NICWJ alone established centers in Las Vegas and Boston and had plans for another in Chicago. Interfaith Committee director Kim Bobo likened the new institution to the Catholic labor schools of the 1930s and 1940s where religious activists and union organizers collaborated from church basements, as well as the "farmworker service centers" that grew up around the United Farmworker Organizing Committee and boycott movement of the late 1960s. Hoping to tap into regional clusters of poultry and industrial plants dominated by immigrant workers, NICWJ in July 2002 named Francisco Risso, previously a leader of the local Catholic Worker House and the Consejo Maya, as director of a new Western Carolina Worker Center to be located in Morganton. The Case Farms workers, Bobo insisted, would constitute a prime constituency for the new project: "Those people deserve the medal of honor for their struggle."[55]

In the end, the Case Farms campaign appeared to be a dramatic but by no means singular "case" where union resources could not cope with the obstacles arrayed against them. That is not to say, however, that the workers had given up their own struggle for dignity at the workplace. Having faced multiple setbacks and delays—and despite having been written off by most of those who had once shown them interest—the immigrant workers at Case Farms continued to act as if they had the right to a voice and just treatment at work. José Samuel, for example, was in no mood to quit. The company, he stated, had made things "very hard" at the plant, and if the union now withdrew from town, it would be both "catastrophic" [for the workers] and "very sad for me." Yet, with or without outside assistance, José Samuel insisted, workers would continue to support the in-plant organizing committee: "That's the only way we can keep a little respect." And of the Aguacateco core to which he owed his primary allegiance, he asserted, "we remain united."[56]

All the evidence suggests that the workers at Case Farms are still "ready." They are prepared to defend their "rights" and to act on behalf of their common interests. But is the United States—as represented by employers, government, and formally sanctioned labor unions—ready for them? Will the major economic and political institutions of American life accommodate the most basic needs of a new immigrant labor force?

To do so, a few things will have to change in this country. Low-wage food-processing firms will need to recognize union representation—just as cutthroat urban garment manufacturers did in the early twentieth century—as a potential source of order and stability as well as social justice in the industry. The way it is now, companies like Case Farms evade both the spirit and the letter of the nation's labor laws. Not only do they keep wages low and the work high-speed—negatively affecting workers' physical health and welfare—but by selectively threatening to "bring in the INS" they also interrupt positive community building among the newest "American" immigrant groups.[57]

The federal government needs to restore the "right to organize" by strengthening penalties for infringement of the labor law; it also must bring immigrant workers out of the shadow of intimidation through a massive amnesty for the undocumented. Current U.S. policy attracts foreign workers but stifles them once they have arrived. The American free trade agenda disrupts the world's older, less-efficient agricultural systems, while state-of-the-art communication and transportation systems—both official and unofficial—broadcast employment possibilities in El Norte. Corporate giants—in agriculture, meatpacking, poultry, and other industries—regularly gain a low-wage if illegal labor force at little penalty to themselves. Yet, if the new workers complain, if in consort with native-born workers and their unions, they demand rights to representation, they risk their very livelihood. In the *Hoffman* decision of March 27, 2002, the U.S. Supreme Court ruled that an illegal immigrant worker does not have the protection of the "backpay" provision of U.S. labor laws (inadequate as they are) when fired for union activity.[58] Another check on the replanting of a new workplace "Jungle" was thus removed.

In the longer run, Americans will need to make a principled—and practical—choice among three immigration policy alternatives: build walls and close borders, open borders to workers who can—over time—become citizens, or create a guest worker policy that does not entrap participants as powerless pawns of their employers. Finally, unions themselves will have to significantly modify their normal method of operation. Instead of making "contract unionism" its overwhelming focus, the labor movement needs to embrace independent worker organization in whatever percentage it is found in order to act as the "conscience of the American economy."[59] If such had been the case, the steadfast union core in Morganton need never have feared abandonment.

There are many ways, in short, whereby the nation's institutions might better accommodate their hardest-working "hands." Workers themselves, to be sure, are at the heart of this struggle, but to succeed they will need to join with members of an aroused, and established, citizenry. It is common to talk about immigrants and the American Dream as if the latter were something that U.S. citizens already possess and others have to strive for. Yet, when it comes to the prospects for American democracy at the dawn of a new century, the welfare of new immigrant labor forces will likely tell us as much about our own dreams as about theirs.

Notes

Note on Interview Method

Although the nature of my (and my assistants') contacts with the subjects of this book varied somewhat with the person, there was a certain method to our operations. Once we had established the respondent's basic connection to the story's main events, we tried first to elicit a thread of life history, dipping back in time to understand the rudiments of family background, education, migration, and prior work experience. Then, we zeroed in as much as possible on the migration, labor, and political experience (where applicable) in Morganton and across borders. Interviewing contacts mounted with the "snowball" method—that is, newspaper stories as well as union and church officials gave us our first contacts, who led to our next set, and so on. Formal interviews (including several by telephone) were almost always recorded, although brief follow-ups (often by telephone) were not. Interviews with individuals with Hispanic names, except for Rosa Benfield, Daniel Gutiérrez, and Yanira Merino, were conducted in Spanish and subsequently translated by Alvis Dunn or myself. This pattern broke down with two frequent contacts—Felipe López and Juan Ignacio "Nacho" Montes— whose English over the course of this project improved faster than my Spanish, a situation that prompted sometimes unplanned excursions in both tongues. Unless otherwise noted, the interviews listed below were conducted in Morganton, North Carolina. The names of those interviewed (except where clearly noted) are provided with the interviewee's explicit permission. Most of the interviews were recorded and are stored—again with the interviewee's permission—with the Southern Oral History Program in the Southern Historical Manuscripts Department, Wilson Library, UNC–Chapel Hill.

Interviews

Acevedo, Jésus, July 2, 1997 (United Nations compound, Huehuetenango)
Aguirre, Francisco, July 31, 2001
André, Jean-Claude, June 8, 2002 (telephone)
Barlowe, Ray, July 9, 1997

Barrett, Michael, July 20, 2001 (telephone)

Barrondo, Eduardo (with wife Neyda López), June 29, 1999 (Aguacatán)

Beck, Richard, February 1, 2000 (telephone)

Beecher, Norman, June 23, July 7, 1998 (both telephone)

Benfield, Rosa, January 18, 1998

Bobo, Kim, July 9, 1998, October 31, 2001 (both telephone)

Bourg-Williams, Gisela, January 20, 1999 (telephone)

Café conversation, July 1, 1997 (San Rafaél la Independencia)

Case Farms ex-manager (anonymous by request), July 19, 1998 (telephone)

Castro, Gaspar Méndez, June 18, 1998 (Aguacatán)

Castro, Marcelino Pérez (nephew of Paulino López), May 21, 1998 (Aguacatán)

Castro, Walter, July 5, 1999 (Quetzaltenango)

Chávez, Francisco Mejía, May 22, 1998 (Aguacatán)

Cohen, Mel, July 9, 1997

Currie, David, January 16, 2000

Diego de Diego, May 24, 1998 (Lajcholaj)

Dougher, Maureen (with Father Ken Whittington), May 17, 1997, October 14, 2000

Ervin, Jean Conyers, July 31, 2001

Ervin, Robert L., June 30, 1998 (telephone)

Escobar Méndez, Pablo, May 21, 2000 (Aguacatán)

Fondriest, Stephen, May 21, 1998 (Aguacatán)

Francisco, Gaspar, February 20, March 1, 2000

Fuentes, Francisco, April 19, 1998 (with son Max); July 19, 2000; March 30, 2001 (with son Max and wife María)

Gálvez, Marta Olivia, June 1, August 28, 1997; August 15, 1999

Gamas, Narciso (with Víctor Hernández), November 9, 1997, June 5, 1999

Gamas, Toribia, May 21, 1998, July 1, 1999, May 22, 2000 (with husband Francisco Cruz Ortiz) (Aguacatán)

Garcia, Carlos, July 3, 1999 (Totonicapán)

Gold, Lawrence, July 2, 1999 (Washington, D.C.)

González, Luís Alberto "Beto," February 27, 2000

González, Marcos Miguel, May 23, 1998 (San Miguel Acatán)

Gutiérrez, Daniel, July 9, 1997, July 19, 2000

Harbison, Katherine, October 12, 1997

Hastings, Joel, June 11, 1997

Hemstreet, Donald and Joy, October 5, 1997

Hernández, Edgar, July 17, 1997 (Huehuetenango)

Hernández, Letitia Paulina Hernández (wife of Víctor Hernández) May 21, 1998, July 1, 1999, May 22, 2000 (all in Aguacatán)

Hernández, Maximo (with Juan Ignacio "Nacho" Montes), January 16, 2000

Hernández, Víctor, November 9, 1997 (with Narciso Gamas), June 20, 1998, June 5, 1999; April 29, June 18, 2000

Hughes, Denny, November 9, 1997

Inscoe, Harriet and Linwood (with Elizabeth Ervin), July 31, 2001

Inscoe, John C., June 24, 2001 (telephone)

Jordan, John, June 29, 1998 (telephone)

José, Ana Sebastién, Petrona, and Isabel (daughters of Francisco "Don Pancho" José), March 13, 2000; Ana José, March 14, 2000 (telephone)

José, Francisco "Don Pancho," May 17, June 1, 1997; January 23, 1999

Lee, Seng and Xai, June 18, 2000

López, Felipe, June 29, 1997 (Aguacatán); August 28, 1997; April 11, 1998 (with Paulino López); December 6, 1998, March 24, 1999 (both telephone); February 13, March 14, June 18, 2000; June 27, 2000 (telephone); July 14, 2000, May 20, July 31, 2001

López, José Samuel Solís, May 25, 1997 (with Mario Ailón); June 1, August 17, 1997; January 18, March 11, 29, April 22, 1998; April 17, 1999 (telephone); June 18, 2000; May 20, September 1, 2001 (both telephone)

López, Katarina (with her mother), May 21, 1998 (Aguacatán)

López, Neyda (with husband Eduardo Barrondo), June 29, 1999 (Aguacatán)

López, Paulino, August 10, 1997; April 11, 1998 (with Felipe López)

López Castro, Marcelino, May 21, 2000 (Aguacatán)

Lux, Justo German Castro, June 6, 19–20, 1998; June 5, October 24, 1999; February 20, March 13–14, October 14, 2000

Lux, Tránsita Gutiérrez Solís, March 13, 2000, July 31, 2001

"Marga" (with "Demetria"), July 11, 1998 (names changed to protect identities)

Martín, Efraín Sebastién, July 5, 1998

Martínez, Dora, July 11, 1998 (with Julia Luna)

Martínez, María E., May 19, 2002 (New Haven, Conn.)

Mascioli, William, May 18, 2001 (telephone)

Matejka, Michael, July 6, 1998 (telephone)

McArthur, Harry and Lucille, July 2, 1999 (Huehuetenango)

McHaffey, David, February 23, 1999 (telephone)

McIntosh, Rev. W. Flemon, Jr., July 31, 2001

Mendoza, Camilo and Franco, May 21, 1998 (Aguacatán)

Mendoza, Gaspar Mejía, July 1, 1999 (Aguacatán)

Merino, Yanira, October 30, 1997; October 17, 2001 (telephone)

Michaelis, Mark, July 5, 1998

Miguel, Félix, January 23, 1999

Montes, Juan Ignacio "Nacho," September 7, 1997; January 16, 2000 (with Maximo Hernández); February 12, 18, 27, March 6, 2000; January 19, September 29, 2001 (both telephone)

Okun, Michael, October 2, 2000 (telephone)

Okun, Will, October 2, 2000 (telephone)

Pallacios, Guillermino Herrero, May 20, 2000 (Aguacatán)

Palmieri, Phyllis, February 24, March 8, August 10, 17, 1997; February 21, 1998 (telephone); March 11, December 16, 1998; July 24, 1999; April 29, July 30, 2000

Panepinto, Marc, December 2, 1998 (telephone)

Pascual, Ana and Eulalia (with Petrona Tomás), May 24, 1998 (Lajcholaj)

Pascual, Andrés and Juana, May 17, October 5, 1997; November 17 (Juana) and November 18 (Andrés), 2001 (telephone)

Pascual, Gaspar (with Juan Sebastién), May 24, 1998 (Lacholaj)
Pascual, Jiménez, June 30, 1997 (Huehuetenango)
Pedro, Teofilo, July 19, 2000
Pérez López, Nicolas (with Max [last name unknown], a high school teacher), May 21, 2000 (Aguacatán)
Poteat, William, July 9, 1998 (telephone)
Ramsey, Charles, July 10, 1998 (telephone)
Rincon-Hevlin, Sonia, March 14, 2000
Risso, Francisco, March 13, 2000; July 22, 2002 (telephone)
Rodríguez, Emiliano Castro, May 22, 1998, June 30, 1999 (both Aguacatán); December 14, 2001, and March 24, 2002 (telephone)
Rodríguez, Félix (aka Roberto Mendoza), April 11, 1998
Rodríguez, Rev. Gabriel Yol L'un ("Padre Gabriel"), June 28, 1997 (Aguacatán); July 15, 1998; July 1, 1999, and May 21, 2000 (Aguacatán)
Rubén Raymundo Raymundo, Víctoriano, May 20, 1998 (Aguacatán)
Sales, Pedro Solís, June 30, 1999 (Aguacatán)
Salido, Carlos Alberto, October 12, 1997
Saquich, Oswaldo, May 13, 1998 (Quetzaltenango)
Sebastién, Juan (with Gaspar Pascual), May 24, 1998 (Lajcholaj)
Stillwell, Duane, March 1, 2000 (telephone)
Tomás, Matías, September 14, 1997; June 20, 1998; February 6, 18, 1999 (telephone); June 18, 2000
Vail, John, January 6, 1999 (telephone)
Velásquez, Marcelino Mendoza, June 29, 1997 (Aguacatán)
Wanless, John, January 20, 1999 (telephone)
Whittington, Rev. Kenneth J., March 8, 1997; May 17, 1997 (with Maureen Dougher); September 14, 1997; April 11, November 20, December 10, 1998; January 13, 1999, March 11, 2000 (both telephone); March 13, April 29, 2000; June 30, 2000 (telephone); July 30, 2000; October 14, 2000 (with Maureen Dougher); March 30, July 31, 2001; October 31, 2001 (telephone)

Introduction

1 "Hispanics in Iowa Meatpacking," *Rural Migration News*, October 1995, <http://migration.ucdavis.edu>. See also Deborah Fink, *Cutting into the Meatpacking Line: Workers and Change in the Rural Midwest* (Chapel Hill: University of North Carolina Press, 1998), 57–60; Stephen J. Hedges and Dana Hawkins with Penny Loeb, "The New Jungle," *U.S. News and World Report*, September 23, 1996, 34–45; and William Greider, "The Last Farm Crisis," *Nation*, November 20, 2000, <http://www.thenation.com>.

2 "Hearing Officer's Report and Recommendations on Objections," NLRB, Region 11, Case No. 11-RC-6089, September 12, 1995; Raymond Mohl, "Latinization in the Heart of Dixie: Hispanics in Late-Twentieth-Century Alabama," *Alabama Review* 55 (October 2002, forthcoming).

3 For a more extensive report on name switching among migrant poultry

workers, see "Workers Answer to Multiple Names," *Washington Post*, November 30, 1999.

Chapter One

1   Marion H. Lieberman, *Morganton on My Mind* (Morganton, N.C.: News Herald Press, 1974), 3–4.

2   John C. Inscoe, *Mountain Masters, Slavery, and the Sectional Crisis in Western North Carolina* (Knoxville: University of Tennessee Press, 1989), 27, 61–63, 116, 169.

3   Edward W. Phifer Jr., *Burke County: A Brief History* (Raleigh: North Carolina Department of Cultural Resources, 1979), 31, 43–44, 46.

4   Jean Conyers Ervin interview.

5   David Griffith, "Consequences of Immigration Reform for Low-Wage Workers in the Southeastern U.S.: The Case of the Poultry Industry" (paper presented at the Eighty-eighth Annual American Anthropological Association Meeting, Washington, D.C., November 17, 1989), 4.

6   John C. Inscoe and Gordon B. McKinney, *The Heart of Confederate Appalachia: Western North Carolina in the Civil War* (Chapel Hill: University of North Carolina Press, 2000), 249–50; John C. Inscoe interview; U.S. Bureau of the Census, General Population Characteristics, 1990, <www.census.gov/prod/cen1990/cp1>. On North Carolina's characteristically drawn-out response to school desegregation, see William Henry Chafe, *Civilities and Civil Rights: Greensboro, North Carolina, and the Black Struggle for Freedom* (New York: Oxford University Press, 1980). Integration of the school system did spur a protest, and a subsequent losing lawsuit, by black teachers squeezed out of the consolidated "Freedom High School." See Harriet and Linwood Inscoe interview.

7   Rev. W. Flemon McIntosh Jr. interview.

8   U.S. Bureau of the Census, General Population Characteristics, 1990, <www.census.gov/prod/cen1990/cp1>.

9   McIntosh interview.

10 Morganton Chamber of Commerce, *Morganton: A Special Report* (Morganton, N.C.: Artcraft Press, 1975). The balance of the material is drawn from Eunice Worth Ervin, "Burke County and Morganton, Her County Seat," in H. Russel Treibert, ed., *The Heritage of Burke County* (Winston-Salem, N.C.: Hunter Publishing Co., 1981), 8–20; "Brief History of Burke County as Given by W. C. Ervin," in *Charlotte Observer*, Burke County Special Ed., [1894?]; J. Randall Cotton, *Historic Burke: An Architectural Inventory of Burke County, North Carolina* (Asheville, N.C.: Biltmore Press, 1987); North Carolina Department of Commerce, statistics from "Burke County Profile," <http://cmedis.commerce.statenc.us/cmedis/outlook/PROFILES.HTM>; Ines M. Miyares, *The Hmong Refugee Experience in the United States: Crossing the River* (New York: Garland Publishing, 1998), 22–41; and U.S. Department of Commerce, *1990 Census of the Population, General Population Statis-*

tics, table 54, pp. 142–43, and table 5, p. 18. A further indication of how quickly Morganton, with its two new immigrant groups, had emerged as a bellwether of state population change lay in the fact that of the total student enrollment in North Carolina's Limited English Proficiency classes, 60 percent were Spanish speaking; the next largest group (less than 8 percent) consisted of Hmong immigrants. Federation for American Immigration Reform (FAIR) state profiles, April 26, 2001, <www.fairus.org>.

11 John Vail interview.

12 Daniel Gutiérrez interview, July 9, 1997.

13 Eric Schlosser, *Fast Food Nation: The Dark Side of the All-American Meal* (Boston: Houghton Mifflin, 2001), 23, 140.

14 Ibid., 139; Roger Horowitz and Mark J. Miller, "Immigrants in the Delmarva Poultry Processing Industry: The Changing Face of Georgetown, Delaware, and Environs" (paper presented at the Changing Face of Delmarva Conference, University of Delaware, September 11–13, 1997; copy courtesy of Roger Horowitz); R. Hetrick, "Why Did Employment Expand in Poultry Processing Plants?" *Monthly Labor Review* 117 (June 1994): 31–34. Though dominated by large processors, the poultry industry pales as an oligopoly compared to meatpacking, where four giant firms slaughter 84 percent of the cattle. See Schlosser, *Fast Food Nation*, 137–38.

15 Horowitz and Miller, "Immigrants"; David Griffith, "*Hay Trabajo*: Poultry Processing, Rural Industrialization, and the Latinization of Low-Wage Labor," in Donald D. Stull, Michael J. Broadway, and Griffith, eds., *Any Way You Cut It: Meat Processing and Small-Town America* (Lawrence: University Press of Kansas, 1995), 129–52. In 1990 the five biggest biggest poultry producers by state (in rank order) were Arkansas, Georgia, Alabama, North Carolina, and Texas (p. 130). On the industry's competitive pricing structure and the resulting pressures on wage rates, see esp. Steve Bjerklie, "On the Horns of a Dilemma: The U.S. Meat and Poultry Industry," in *Any Way You Cut It*, 41–60. The gender division at Case Farms was peculiarly and disproportionately male for an industry that nationally has been nearly evenly split (49 percent female) between men and women employees. See Horowitz and Miller, "Immigrants."

16 Katherine Harbison interview.

17 Charles Ramsey interview.

18 *Washington News*, November 26, 1996.

19 "Profiles: Case Foods," *Broiler Industry*, January 1996, 28.

20 *Washington Post*, November 28, 1999.

21 Mark Michaelis interview.

22 Griffith, "*Hay Trabajo*," 135; Juan Ignacio "Nacho" Montes interview, February 12, 2000; Michaelis interview.

23 Denny Hughes interview.

24 Sarah Anderson, "OSHA under Siege," *Progressive*, December 1995, 26–28. As late as February 1998, a Labor Department study of the nation's poultry plants "found that more than 60 percent . . . violated overtime laws" and "also found widespread safety problems, among them frequent back injuries that

usually occurred when workers slipped on wet and greasy floors." *New York Times*, February 10, 1998; *Washington Post*, November 28, 1999.

25 Harbison interview. Cf. the graphic description of poultry-processing work in an eastern North Carolina plant found in Carol Stack, *Call To Home: African Americans Reclaim the Rural South* (New York: Basic Books, 1996), 72–78.

26 Harriet and Linwood Inscoe interview.

27 Norman Beecher interview. Attorney John Vail first learned of Beecher's recruiting enterprise indirectly: "I got a call one day from some nuns who ran an assistance center in Immokalee, Fla. Immokalee is a cut-and-flash town; it's a hard place. It's kind of the capital of the sugar cane fields, and it's where you can go if you don't have an identity and don't speak the language. If you have nothing, you can be handed a machete and make a little money chopping sugar cane. Then nuns wanted to know whether there was a labor dispute going on at the chicken plant, because they had a fellow named Norman Beecher down there with a van offering jobs if they'd come up to Morganton. My response was, 'There may not be a labor dispute, but it might not be a much better place to work than Immokalee.'" John Vail interview.

28 Beecher interview; U.S. Department of Commerce, *1990 Census of the Population, General Population Statistics*, table 6, p. 47, and table 79, p. 511. Several Morganton interviewees mentioned a $50/recruit incentive from the company. Even this small trace evident in 1990 represented a dramatic change from preceding years. Maureen Dougher, who returned to Morganton in 1985 after seven years of marriage and residency in Bolivia as Maureen Ríos, remembered searching the local telephone directories and finding "only one or two" other Hispanic surnames. Dougher interview.

29 *Raleigh News and Observer*, November 30, 1996; Hughes interview. David Griffith, *Jones's Minimal: Low-Wage Labor in the United States* (Albany: SUNY Press, 1993), cites a general employer perception of Hispanics "as having a work ethic superior to most American workers, Black or White" (p. 171).

30 On the politicization of asylum cases, see, e.g., Nora Hamilton and Norma Stoltz Chinchilla, *Seeking Community in a Global City: Guatemalans and Salvadorans in Los Angeles* (Philadelphia: Temple University Press, 2001), 135.

31 Karen Musalo, Jennifer Moore, and Richard A. Boswell, *Refugee Law and Policy: Cases and Materials* (Durham, N.C.: Carolina Academic Press, 1997), 88–89, 267. On the implementation of IRCA among Guatemalan refugees, see Nora Hamilton and Norma Stoltz Chinchilla, "Central American Migration: A Framework for Analysis," *Latin American Research Review* 26 (1991): 100; Griffith ("Consequences of Immigration Reform," 16, 20) notes that through new immigrant "network" recruiting, the poultry owners have not only met their supply needs, they "have been able to transfer the burden of assuring legal status from their own shoulders to workers' shoulders, since the flow of information between the plant and the immigrant community is such that workers know they need documents, whether false or not, well before coming to the plants."

32 Stanley Mailman and Stephen Yale-Loehr, "Amnesty for Central Americans," reprint from *New York Law Journal* (September 5, 1997), <http://www.twm

law.com/resources/general4cont.htm>; "The INS 'Gets Tough' on Immigrants: New Law Threatens Guatemalans in the U.S.," *Report on Guatemala* 18 (Summer 1997): 6–7, 11–13.

33 U.S. Department of Justice, Executive Office for Immigration Review, <www.usdoj.gov/eoir>.

34 On the political struggles behind changing U.S. immigration policies, see Hamilton and Chinchilla, *Seeking Community*, 134–51.

35 Beecher interview. Case Farms had, in fact, hired a few Mexicans in the year prior to the Guatemalan experiment. Maximo Hernández, brother-in-law of future Case Farms union leader Nacho Montes, transferred to the night shift at the poultry plant along with a brother, a cousin, and a couple of other countrymen who had all been working on a Christmas tree farm in nearby Boone, N.C. Maximo Hernández interview.

36 William Poteat interview.

37 Dougher interview, October 14, 2000.

38 Raymond Mohl, "Latinization in the Heart of Dixie: Hispanics in Late-Twentieth-Century Alabama" (paper in author's possession, 2001). Prior to the official census reports, local estimates of Hispanics in the Catawba Valley area had varied wildly from 2,000 to 10,000 people.

39 State Hispanic leaders, moreover, suspect that the official figures represent an undercount of at least one-third of the actual resident population. *Raleigh News and Observer*, March 30, 2001; *Morganton News-Herald*, March 28, 2001.

40 *New York Times*, August 4, 2001. The other states were Tennessee, Utah, and Virginia.

41 Robert L. Ervin interview.

42 Joel Hastings interview. In fact, the mass of Guatemalan Mayan émigrés came from high mountain plains (not jungles) that were dry much of the year.

43 Ibid.

44 Mel Cohen interview.

45 Ray Barlowe interview. In a survey of the poultry and other low-wage food-processing industries, David Griffith (*Jones's Minimal*, 195) concludes: "While the Hispanic workers cannot be said to be carriers of the South's anti-union sentiments, they possess qualities, as new immigrants, that feed the continued weak positions of labor relative to capital. As long as new immigrants and undocumented workers permeate their networks, there are few incentives to organize, join labor unions, or resist plant authority in any capacity besides leaving the plant's sphere of control altogether."

46 Barlowe interview.

47 *Morganton News-Herald*, June 14, 1994.

48 Katie Hyde and Jeffrey Leiter, "Overcoming Ethnic Intolerance," *Journal of Common Sense* 5 (Winter 2000): 14.

49 *Morganton News-Herald*, November 21, 1999.

50 *Morganton News-Herald*, October 9, 2000.

51 Seng and Xai Lee interview.

52 Gutiérrez interview, July 9, 1997.

53 Gisela Bourg-Williams interview.

54 *Morganton News-Herald*, March 18, 1994.

55 John Wanless interview.

56 Bourg-Williams interview.

57 Vail interview.

58 *Official Catholic Directory*, 1999 (New Providence, N.J.: P. J. Kenedy and Sons, 1999), 204.

59 Father Ken Whittington interview, March 8, 1997; Dougher interview. I have no idea how common was the practice of "made-up" names, though my guess is that this was the exception. For my respondents' protection, I have used here the names that people have given me as an interviewer without probing their authenticity.

60 Whittington interviews, March 8, 1997, January 13, 1999.

61 Whittington interview, September 14, 1997.

62 Hughes interview.

63 Ibid.; Whittington interview, March 8, 1997.

64 Bourg-Williams interview; Donald and Joy Hemstreet interview.

65 *I, Rigoberta Menchú: An Indian Woman in Guatemala*, introduction and translation by Elizabeth Burgos-Debray (New York: Verso, 1984), xii.

66 David Currie interview.

67 See, e.g., Robert M. Crunden, *Ministers of Reform: The Progressives' Achievement in American Civilization, 1889–1920* (New York: Basic Books, 1982); Andrew Feffer, *The Chicago Pragmatists and American Progressivism* (Ithaca, N.Y.: Cornell University Press, 1993); and Leon Fink, *Progressive Intellectuals and the Dilemmas of Democratic Commitment* (Cambridge: Harvard University Press, 1997), esp. 13–51.

68 Susan Graham Erwin, *The Village That Disappeared* (Charlotte: Laney-Smith, Inc., 1996), v.

Chapter Two

1 Rosa Benfield interview.

2 Ibid.; Phyllis Palmieri interview, August 10, 1997.

3 Benfield interview.

4 Terence Kaufman, *Projecto de alfabetos y ortografías para hablar las lenguas mayances* (Guatemala: Proyecto Lingüístico Francisco Marroquín, Editorial José de Pineda Ibarra, 1976); Dirección General de Estadística, *Censo nacional de población y de habitación, Departamento de Huehuetenango*, 1994 (Guatemala City, August 1996), 30. More technically, the people from San Miguel Acatán speak Akateko, which belongs to the larger Q'anjob'al ethno-linguistic family that also includes Jacalteko, Motozintleko, Tuzanteko, Tojolabal, and Chuj.

5 Francisco Aguirre interview; Juan Ignacio "Nacho" Montes interview, January 16, 2000.

6 W. George Lovell ("Surviving Conquest: The Maya of Guatemala in Historical Perspective," *Latin American Research Review* 23 [1988]: 25–51) identifies Mayan cultural survival across three devastating cycles of conquest: "by

imperial Spain . . . by local and international capitalism . . . and conquest by state terror" (p. 27). Ladinos, a term preferred in Guatemala over *mestizos*, are people of mixed Spanish and Indian blood—or, for that matter, even full-blooded Indians—who identify culturally with Hispanic rather than indigenous culture.

7 On the long-term economic and state-sanctioned repression of the Mayan countryside, esp. the effects of the late-nineteenth- and early-twentieth-century "liberal" economic policies of Justo Rufino BarRíos, Manuel Estrada Cabrera, and Jorge Ubico, see David McCreery, *Rural Guatemala, 1760–1940* (Stanford, Calif.: Stanford University Press, 1994). See also Stephen Connely Benz, *Guatemalan Journey* (Austin: University of Texas Press, 1996). Even the "ten years of spring" under the politically progressive administrations of Juan José Arévalo and Jacobo Arbenz Guzmán—though witness to scattered efforts by the Mayan population to mobilize—had little lasting effect on the general repression of the indigenous population at the hands of whites and mestizos and saw little modification of traditional survival strategies. Jim Handy, *Revolution in the Countryside: Rural Conflict and Agrarian Reform in Guatemala, 1944–1954* (Chapel Hill: University of North Carolina Press, 1994), 45–76, 191–207. See also Shelton H. Davis, "The Social Roots of Political Violence in Guatemala," *Cultural Survival Quarterly* 7 (Spring 1983): 32–35.

8 On the evolving balance of power in the Mayan highlands, see esp. Greg Grandin, *The Blood of Guatemala: A History of Race and Nation* (Durham, N.C.: Duke University Press, 2000).

9 See, e.g., Andrew R. Morrison and Rachel A. May, "Escape from Terror: Violence and Migration in Post-Revolutionary Guatemala," *Latin American Research Review* 29 (1994): 111–32.

10 Report of the CEH as cited in *New York Times* and *Prensa Libre*, February 26, 1999.

11 Lovell, "Surviving Conquest," 47.

12 Rosalva Aída Hernández Castillo, "Mecanismos de producción social y cultural de los indígenas Q'anjob'ales refugiados en Chiapas" (Ph.D. diss., Escuela Nacional de Antropología e Historia, Mexico City, 1988), 1–4, 43. Already by 1986, there were an estimated 40,000 to 100,000 Guatemalan refugees living in Mexico. Dirección Géneral de Estadística, *Censos nacionales*, 9 *Población*, 1981 (Guatemala City, 1984), 330–31.

13 Hernández Castillo, "Mecanismos de Producción," 42.

14 Shelton H. Davis and Julie Hodson, *Witnesses to Political Violence in Guatemala: The Suppression of a Rural Development Movement* (Boston: Oxfam America, 1983). *Guatemala Nunca Más*, the report of the Project for the Recuperation of Historical Memory sponsored by the Human Rights Office of the Archbishop of Guatemala (whose effective director, Monseñor Juan José Gerardi Conedera, was assassinated on April 26, 1998, two days after officially presenting a summary of the report to the Guatemalan public), attributes eight of the nine attacks mentioned above to the army or the state-backed Armed Civilian Patrols and one to the Guerrilla Army of the Poor. *Guatemala*

Nunca Más: Summary Version (republished by Prensa Libre, June 6, 1998), 35, 58.

15 Davis and Hodson, *Witnesses to Political Violence*, 51; Anonymous interview in Lajcholaj with an Alabama poultry worker returning to visit his family, May 2, 1998.

16 CEH, *Guatemala: Memory of Silence*, app. 1, vol. 1, case 84, <http://hrdata. aaas.org>.

17 On the internal complexities and continuing uncertainties associated with the peace accords, see Susanne Jonas, *Of Centaurs and Doves: Guatemala's Peace Process* (Boulder, Colo.: Westview, 2000).

18 Hernández Castillo, "Mecanismos de Producción," 4. To be sure, the Q'anjob'al have a history—predating even the guerrilla war—of migrating to Mexico in search of work and markets.

19 Allan F. Burns, *Maya in Exile: Guatemalans in Florida* (Philadelphia: Temple University Press, 1993).

20 Allan Burns writes that Q'anjob'al began arriving in Indiantown in late 1982, "when a Mexican-American crew boss brought several refugees from Arizona to Florida. As with many refugees, the only jobs available to them were as migrant laborers. Soon, family members were contacted on the west coast of the United States and in Guatemala. Indiantown offered a 'safe haven' from both the violence of Guatemala and *anomie* of the large American cities of Los Angeles and Phoenix." Burns, "Internal and External Identity among Q'anjob'al Mayan Refugees in Florida," in Nancie L. González and Carolyn S. McCommon, *Conflict, Migration, and the Expression of Ethnicity* (Boulder, Colo.: Westview Press, 1989), 46–59 (quotation, p. 49).

21 Andrés and Juana Pascual interview, October 5, 1997.

22 Matías Tomás interview, September 14, 1997.

23 Ibid.

24 Matías Tomás interview, September 14, 1997; Víctor Perera, *Unfinished Conquest: The Guatemalan Tragedy* (Berkeley: University of California Press, 1993), 130.

25 Tomás interview, September 14, 1997.

26 Efraín Sebastién Martín interview.

27 Herbert Gutman, *Work, Culture, and Society in Industrializing America: Essays in American Working-Class and Social History* (New York: Knopf, 1976), 3–78 (quotation, p. 13).

28 Manning Nash, *Machine Age Maya: The Industrialization of a Guatemalan Community* (Glencoe, Ill.: Free Press, 1979), esp. 13, 17, 26, 31.

29 Among the Q'anjob'al in Morganton, for example, Andrés Pascual, Don Pancho, and Efraín Martín had all worked coffee; Matías Tomás had also worked in sugar plantations on the coast. Andrés Pascual interview, November 18, 2001.

30 Philip Berryman, *The Religious Roots of Rebellion: Christians in Central American Revolutions* (Maryknoll, N.Y.: Orbis Books, 1984), 186. The miners' leader was assassinated within a year of the demonstration (p. 191).

31 Palmieri interview, March 8, 1997.

32 Don Pancho interview, January 23, 1999.

33 Ana, Petrona, and Isabel José interview.

34 Martín interview.

35 Stoll cited in Marc Zimmerman, *Literature and Resistance in Guatemala: Textual Modes and Cultural Politics from El Señor Presidente to Rigoberta Menchú* (Athens: Ohio University Center for International Studies, 1995), 1:44. For a contrasting view on indigenous sympathies, see, e.g., Ricardo Falla, *Massacres in the Jungle: Ixcan, Guatemala, 1975–1982* (Boulder, Colo.: Westview Press, 1994), 5–8.

36 Challenging the veracity of the personal testimony of Guatemala's leading human rights figure and Nobel Prize winner, Rigoberta Menchú, Stoll argues that for reasons of guerrilla propaganda, Menchú turned a story of complicated local land conflicts into a morality tale of *indios* versus persecuting government authority. Stoll, *Rigoberta Menchú and the Story of All Poor Guatemalans* (Boulder, Colo.: Westview Press, 1999). For a searching historiographical discussion and critique of Stoll's argument, see Arturo Arias, ed., *The Rigoberta Menchú Controversy* (Minneapolis: University of Minnesota Press, 2001).

37 Piero Gleijeses, "Grappling with Guatemala's Horror," *Latin American Research Review* 32 (1997): 229.

38 Jacqueline María Hagan, *Deciding to Be Legal: A Maya Community in Houston* (Philadelphia: Temple University Press, 1995), 9–10; Burns, *Maya in Exile*, 21–23, 90–91.

39 Palmieri interviews, March 8, August 10, 1997; David McHaffey interview. McHaffey was asylum/detention attorney for Boston's Political Asylum/Immigration Representation project.

40 Palmieri interview, July 24, 1999.

41 Palmieri interview, March 8, 1997. As Burns (*Maya in Exile*, p. 91) confirms, "More recent asylum seekers, who tend to have less sound cases, have switched from applying through recognized assistance programs to using notary publics in Miami who fill out asylum papers for whatever price they can get."

42 Tomás interview, September 14, 1997.

43 Daniel Conde, "Indiantown, Florida," in Alain Breton and Jacques Arnaud, eds., *Mayas* (Paris: Autrement, 1991), 260; David Stoll, *Is Latin America Turning Protestant?: The Politics of Evangelical Growth* (Berkeley: University of California Press, 1990), 9, 12, 180.

44 David Stoll, "'Jesus Is Lord of Guatemala': Evangelical Reform in a Death-Squad State," in Martin E. Marty and R. Scott Appleby, *Accounting for Fundamentalisms: The Dynamic Character of Movements* (Chicago: University of Chicago Press, 1994), 99–123; Douglas E. Brintnall, *Revolt against the Dead: The Modernization of a Mayan Community in the Highlands of Guatemala* (New York: Gordon and Breach, 1979), 117–48. On Pentecostalism more generally, see Anna L. Peterson, Manuel A. Vásquez, and Philip J. Williams, eds., *Christianity, Social Change, and Globalizaton in the Americas* (New Brunswick, N.J.: Rutgers University Press, 2001).

45 Tomás interview, September 14, 1997; Martín interview.

46 Diego de Diego interview.

47 Donald and Joy Hemstreet interview.

48 Andrés Pascual interview, May 17, 1997.

49 Kay B. Warren, *Indigenous Movements and Their Critics: Pan-Maya Activism in Guatemala* (Princeton, N.J.: Princeton University Press, 1998), 92–93.

50 Jeffrey L. Gould, "Revolutionary Nationalism and Local Memories in El Salvador," in Gilbert M. Joseph, ed., *Reclaiming the Political in Latin American History: Essays from the North* (Durham, N.C.: Duke University Press, 2001), 138–71 (quotation, p. 161).

51 Andrés Pascual interview, May 17, 1997; Tomás interview, February 18, 1999.

52 Tomás interview, September 14, 1997.

53 Norman Beecher interview, July 7, 1998.

54 Beecher interview, June 23, 1998.

Chapter Three

1 John Jordan interview, June 29, 1998.

2 Phyllis Palmieri interview, August 10, 1997.

3 *Morganton News-Herald*, July 19, August 30, 1994; Félix Miguel interview.

4 *Morganton News-Herald*, July 17, August 30, 1994.

5 Palmieri interview, August 10, 1997.

6 Strike information compiled from *Charlotte Observer* (May 15, 1995), *Morganton News-Herald* (May 15–18, 1995), and interviews with Palmieri (August 10, 1997), Daniel Gutiérrez (July 9, 1997), and Carlos Alberto Salido. The "trés muchachos" were Francisco Vicente (age 19), Juan Mendoza (22), and Víctoriano López (21). José Samuel Solís López interview, August 17, 1997.

7 Salido interview. That the Case Farms strikes beginning in 1993 were not, in fact, limited to the Aguacatecos and Mexicans is suggested by the arrest in the first strike of Félix Miguel, a native of San Miguel Acatán. On the advice of an in-law, Miguel had moved to Morganton from Los Angeles following the Rodney King riots (which shut down the garment factory where he worked) in 1992. Félix Miguel interview.

8 Union organizer Yanira Merino, who arrived at the tail end of the 1995 strike, remembered a workers' committee that was led by Aguacatecos but also included Marta Gálves from Guatemala City, one man of K'iche' origin, and one Q'anjob'al. Yanira Merino interview, October 30, 1997.

9 In this chain the Q'anjob'al came first, followed by Aguacatecos, and more recently by people from the departments of Totonicapán and San Marcos.

10 José Samuel López interview, April 17, 1999. José Samuel maintained the local written "census" of the Aguacatán community.

11 Marta Olivia Gálves (interview, August 28, 1997), for example, a Ladina from Guatemala City and a Case Farms worker since 1993, observed that Aguacatecos were simply "more civilized" and "more clever" than other indigenous

groups. By contrast, the "San Miguelenses" (or Q'anjob'al), who had "suffered more" from the guerrilla wars, to her eyes appeared "ignorant" and "illiterate" and "don't understand well" the world around them. To Carlos Salido (interview), the Guatemalans as a whole seemed fearful, ignorant, and largely unprepared for the challenges facing them in a new land. But among these seemingly confused refugees, in Salido's opinion, the Aguacatecos stood out as the "most progressive" and "united" grouping.

12 José Samuel López interview, May 25, 1997.

13 Instituto Nacional de Estadística, *Censo nacional de población y de habitación, Departamento de Huehuetenango* (Guatemala, 1996), 30–31. Francisco Aguirre (interview), a native of San Miguel Acatán and perhaps the only Morganton immigrant familiar with both Q'anjob'al areas and Aguacatán (which he had visited in the 1970s), emphasized the greater access to Spanish-language education and "urban" influence of the regional capital of Huehuetenango on Aguacatán.

14 By the mid-1990s Aguacatán, unlike other pueblos in the Cuchumatanes, witnessed no appreciable seasonal migration of labor. FUNCEDE, *Diagnóstico del municipio de Aguacatán* (Guatemala City, 1996), 9, 12. Literacy, according to the national census of 1981, encompassed 35 percent of the population in Aguacatán compared to 22 percent in San Miguel Acatán. Dirección General de Estadística, Censos Nacionales, 9 Población, 1981 (Guatemala City, 1984), 331, 344.

15 Paul Hans Robert Kobrak, "Village Troubles: The Civil Patrols in Aguacatán, Guatemala" (Ph.D. diss., University of Michigan, 1997), 76–77, 88. Connecting to factors in Guatemala City, Aguacatecan garlic regularly competed in markets across Central America and, at least according to local legend, sometimes reached as far as the United States, Europe, and Japan. Emiliano Castro Rodríguez interview, December 14, 2001.

16 Kobrak, "Village Troubles," table 1, p. viii. Kobrak's figures were based on unpublished statistics from the Guatemalan National Institute of Statistics together with estimates supplied by *alcaldes auxiliares* (elected village leaders). E-mail from Kobrak to author, December 22, 2000. For clarity's sake, I use the spelling "Aguacateco" to refer generally to the residents of the municipio of Aguacatán. In keeping with current preferred spellings, I use "Awakateko" and "Chalchiteko" to refer to the specific ethno-linguistic groups.

17 Douglas E. Brintnall, *Revolt against the Dead: The Modernization of a Mayan Community in the Highlands of Guatemala* (New York: Gordon and Breach, 1979), 2–5, 24, 50, 102, 111. The Ladino population estimate was drawn from Instituto Nacional de Estadística, *Censo nacional de población*, 31. The old pueblo of Chalchitán, which had grown up on the site of a pre-Columbian ruin (now a national archaeological monument) was officially incorporated into the municipio of Aguacatán on February 21, 1891. FUNCEDE, *Diagnóstico del municipio de Aguacatán*, 7. When asked to name a linguistic difference between the Awakatekos and Chalchitekos, locals most commonly cited the words for "dog"—*chuip* in Chalchiteko versus *tchep* in Awakateko. Yet, as retired bilingual schoolteacher Emiliano Rodríguez explained, the difference

is even finer than that: the Chalchitekos call a *chiquitillo* (small dog) "chuip" and a *grande* (large dog) "tchep," whereas Awakatekos call all canines "tchep." Rodríguez interview, June 30, 1999. According to several local informants, approximately fifty vocabulary words separate the two groups.

18 Brintnall, *Revolt against the Dead*, 84–85.

19 Ibid., 89–94.

20 Ibid., 92.

21 Ibid., 94–104. The first Indian alcalde in Aguacatán was not elected until 1970. Kobrak, "Village Troubles," 90–92. As late as 1965, the resident priest, José Nerino, identified only 1,600 "true Catholics" among Aguacatán's population of 16,000. *Guia de la iglesia en Guatemala* (Santa Isabel: Guatemala City, 1968), 186.

22 Brintnall, *Revolt against the Dead*, 117–48.

23 Ibid., 155–83.

24 The McArthurs moved to Guatemala from Mexico, where Wycliffe Bible translators had, in the 1930s, settled among the Tzeltal-Maya of Chiapas. For the Wycliffe movement and "ethnotheology," see David Stoll, *Is Latin America Turning Protestant?: The Politics of Evangelical Growth* (Berkeley: University of California Press, 1990), 83–91.

25 Harry and Lucille McArthur interview, July 2, 1999. Shortly after the McArthurs moved to the Solomon Islands, Harry developed cataracts, and they were compelled to return to Guatemala. Although they continued to spend time in Aguacatán until 1989, they made their permanent residence in the departmental capital of Huehuetenango.

26 Jésus García Ruiz, "Eglise . . . Eglises," in Alain Breton and Jacques Arnaud, eds., *Mayas* (Autrement: Paris, 1991), 260–61.

27 Harry and Lucille McArthur interview.

28 Kobrak, "Village Troubles," 11, 99–102.

29 Emiliano Rodríguez interview, May 22, 1998.

30 Interviews with Paulino López, April 11, 1998; José Samuel López, August 17, 1997; Felipe López, June 29, 1997; and Padre Gabriel Rodríguez, June 28, 1997.

31 Víctor Hernández interview, November 9, 1997.

32 Unlike the case of many K'iche' and Q'anjob'al exiled communities, FUNCEDE, *Diagnóstico del municipio de Aguacatán* (p. 13) found no "repatriated" population in Aguacatán.

33 David McCreery, *Rural Guatemala, 1760-1940* (Stanford, Calif.: Stanford University Press, 1994), 64; Jim Handy, *Revolution in the Countryside: Rural Conflict and Agrarian Reform in Guatemala, 1944-1954* (Chapel Hill: University of North Carolina Press, 1994), 157–58.

34 On the destructive role of *envidia* in Mayan communities, see Kay B. Warren, *Indigenous Movements and Their Critics: Pan-Maya Activism in Guatemala* (Princeton, N.J.: Princeton University Press, 1998), 99, 108–9, 175.

35 Padre Gabriel interview, June 28, 1997. More generally, on the role of the war in spiking mistrust based on "personal differences" and "envy," see Warren, *Indigenous Movements*, 99, 108–9, 175.

36 Kobrak, "Village Troubles," 145, 179.

37 Marcelino López Castro interview; Felipe López interviews, August 28, 1997, March 24, 1999. Marcelino's son, Felipe, recalled that the distinguished Guatemalan jurist (and future president), Ramiro de León Carpio, a cousin of assassinated journalist-politician Jorge Carpio, personally urged Marcelino to take advantage of his "one chance" to leave the country. Felipe López interview, July 14, 2000.

38 FUNCEDE, *Diagnóstico del municipio de Aguacatán*, 13.

39 Stephen Fondriest interview. Fondriest, a U.S. Peace Corps agronomist, noted that the alleged problem of crop yields had received no scientific confirmation, that it might in local minds have been confused with the undisputed decline in the price of garlic, and that the "worm" infestation that local campesinos feared was probably a fungus.

40 Paul Hans Kobrak, "Las relaciones interétnicas en Aguacatán, Huehuetenango" (manuscript, 2001, courtesy of the author), 34.

41 As late as 1999, of an estimated 300–350 Aguacatecos in Morganton, there were only 50–75 women. José Samuel López interview, April 17, 1999.

42 Paulino López interview, August 10, 1997; Felipe López interview, August 28, 1997; Pedro Solís Sales interview.

43 For a full discussion of the padrone in North American labor recruitment, see Gunther Peck, *Reinventing Free Labor: Padrone and Immigrant Workers in the North American West, 1880–1930* (New York: Cambridge University Press, 1980).

44 Francisco Fuentes interview, March 30, 2001.

45 Gutiérrez interview, July 19, 2000. Anecdotal evidence suggests that a $50/worker recruiting fee was common in the industry. See, e.g., Greig Guthey, "Mexican Places in Southern Spaces: Globalization, Work, and Daily Life in and around the North Georgia Poultry Industry," in Arthur D. Murphy et al., *Latino Workers in the Contemporary South* (Athens: University of Georgia Press, 2001), 64.

46 José Samuel López interview, August 17, 1997.

47 Francisco Fuentes interview, April 19, 1998.

48 On the struggles of the Coca Cola workers, see Deborah Levenson-Estrada, *Trade Unionists against Terror: Guatemala City, 1945–1985* (Chapel Hill: University of North Carolina Press, 1994).

49 On patron-client relations in Latin American historiography, see, e.g., Eric R. Wolfe and Edward C. Hansen, *The Human Condition in Latin America* (New York: Oxford University Press, 1972), and Steffen W. Schmidt et al., eds., *Friends, Followers, and Factions: A Reader in Political Clientelism* (Berkeley: University of California Press, 1977).

50 Paulino López interview, April 11, 1998. To be sure, Paulino may have invented something of a "golden past" here. Or perhaps his own experience simply did not accord with that of the reported 10,000 persons reportedly assassinated under the Méndez Montenegro regime (1966–70), which had initially painted itself in revolutionary colors as "a genuine alternative to the regimes of tyranny and subjugation." Nonetheless, there did exist a legal/con-

stitutional framework of labor law in Guatemala that might indeed have conditioned the rights claims of sojourning laborers. The country's Labor Code of 1961, strengthened by new constitutional protections in 1986, provided a broad arc of worker rights to be enforced by the General Inspectorate of Labor (IGT), which was given broad powers to inspect any workplace in the country, typically on the complaint of a worker, union, or employer. Though the IGT has long been notoriously understaffed and underfunded, perhaps its presence did make a difference at certain times and places. Moreover, the fact that the Guatemala constitution "grants to international human rights agreements [including forty International Labor Organization conventions] preeminence over domestic law" likely further accounts for the salience of "human rights" consciousness on the part of Guatemalan workers. James A. Goldston, *Shattered Hope: Guatemalan Workers and the Promise of Democracy* (Boulder, Colo.: Westview Press, 1989), 9, 19, 147–59.

51 Richard Newbold Adams, *Crucifixion by Power: Essays on Guatemalan National Social Structure, 1944–1966* (Austin: University of Texas Press, 1970), esp. "Access to Law: Labor and Justice," 422–37.

52 The one request José Samuel made of his two Chapel Hill interviewers was that they procure for him a book of philosophy in Spanish.

53 José Samuel López interview, June 1, 1997.

54 López Castro interview.

55 Ríos Montt's three promises remain pictorially represented to this day in the three-fingered symbol of the FRG (Frente Republicano Guatemalteco) Party, which in 1999 elected Alfonso Portillo president and General Ríos Montt head of the congress.

56 José Samuel López interview, June 1, 1997. In his first electoral battle of 1974, Ríos Montt, running on a progressive social and economic platform, was denied a clear victory in the election by government chicanery. Montt then took a position as military attaché to Spain, returned to Guatemala in 1977 a born-again Evangelical, and assumed direction of the Verbo missionary church until he was summoned to office as part of a military junta following a March 1982 coup d'état. Quickly gathering the power of the state unto himself and declaring war on corruption and subversion, Montt ruled with a *mano dura* (hard hand) until he was deposed by a countercoup in August 1983. "Ríos Montt," *Current Biography Yearbook* (New York: H. H. Wilson Co., 1983), 321–25.

57 José Samuel López interview, June 1, 1997.

58 Paulino López interview, April 11, 1998.

59 Marcelino Pérez Castro interview.

60 W. George Lovell, *A Beauty That Hurts: Life and Death in Guatemala* (Toronto, Canada: Between the Lines, 1995), 97. Use of the gendered pronoun here is intentional, as schooling for girls in rural Guatemala was, according to Lovell, "often basic or non-existent, with only one girl in eight advancing beyond sixth grade."

61 In fact, it was the official policy of the early-nineteenth-century Republic of Guatemala to "extinguish the languages of the Indians." Julia Becker Richards

and Michael Richards, "Maya Education: A Historical and Contemporary Analysis of Mayan Language Education Policy," in Edward F. Fischer and R. McKenna Brown, *Maya Cultural Activism in Guatemala* (Austin: University of Texas, 1996), 210.

62 During the worst of the war years in the early 1980s, bilingual education projects came under intense suspicion by the army for breeding guerrilla sympathizers. Three of the four leaders of the National Project for Bilingual Education (1981–84) and scores of teachers, both from the project and the general public school system, were murdered by the army. Richards and Richards, "Maya Education," 212–13. With aid from a Norwegian foundation, the Instituto moved into an impressive new building in 1993.

63 Víctoriano Rubén interview.

64 Félix Rodríguez interview, April 11, 1998.

65 Ibid.

66 John M. Watanabe, *Maya Saints and Souls in a Changing World* (Austin: University of Texas Press, 1992), 253; CEH, *Guatemala: Memory of Silence*, chap. 3, "Rupture of the Social Fabric," para. 263, <www.hrdata.aaas.org/ceh/mds>; Víctor Hernández interview, November 9, 1997. A *cuerda* (drawn from the word "rope" or from the "length of a rope") is a basic unit of land measurement constituting approximately one-tenth of an acre but varying a bit by local custom. The La Salle school is now called "Santiago-Miller."

67 Víctor Hernández interview, November 9, 1997.

68 Gálves interviews, June 1, 1997, August 15, 1999.

69 Norita Vlach, *The Quetzal in Flight: Guatemalan Refugee Families in the United States* (Westport, Conn.: Praeger Publishers, 1992), 21.

70 Gálves interview, June 1, 1997. On practical political knowledge, see James C. Scott, *Seeing Like a State: How Certain Schemes to Improve the Human Condition Have Failed* (New Haven: Yale University Press, 1998).

71 Nora Hamilton and Norma Stoltz Chincilla, *Seeking Community in a Global City* (Philadelphia: Temple University Press, 2001), e.g., count up to one hundred "hometown associations" formed by Salvadorans and Guatemalans in the Los Angeles area during the 1990s, many of which (especially among the Guatemalans) originated, as in Morganton, as burial societies. Unlike in Morganton, in the larger city such associations evolved to concentrate on investment projects in the hometown communities (see p. 208).

72 Paulino López interview, August 10, 1997. A directiva appeal from Morganton in January 1998, e.g., netted monetary responses from the following places (as listed in the current treasurer's book): Ohio, Arizona, Alabama, Georgia, Kansas City, Bonita Springs and Indiantown (Fla.), Washington State, Delaware, Southern Pines (N.C.), Chattanooga (Tenn.), Elizabeth (Ill.), and Canada. José Samuel López interview, January 18, 1998. Felipe López (interview, February 13, 2000) supplied the additional grisly detail that Remigio actually committed suicide using his car following a stroke and extended illness.

73 Aguacatán Libro de actas (courtesy of José Samuel López); Paulino López interview, August 10, 1997.

74 Marcelino Mendoza Velásquez interview.

75 Paulino López interview, August 10, 1997. López's view of the Chalchitekos corresponds to the traditional ethnic stereotypes that Douglas Brintnall (*Revolt against the Dead*) found in the pueblo in the 1970s; the inverse prejudice harbored among the proudly independent Chalchitekos was that the "Westerners" (or puros Awakatekos) were "weak, dependent, and servilely submissive to their leaders" (p. 72).

76 José Samuel López interviews, May 25, June 1, August 17, 1997. Paulino's son (and José Samuel's cousin), Felipe López, who arrived in Morganton in late summer 1997 and immediately put his Guatemalan legal training to use as an assistant on immigration cases, explained the intermixing of Awakatekos and Chalchitekos in Morganton in only slightly different terms: "They are not in their country so they have to stick together. They are all together [in Morganton]. But they know who's who." Felipe López interview, August 28, 1997.

77 Felipe López interview, June 29, 1997.

78 Yanira Merino interview, October 30, 1997.

79 Sidney Webb and Beatrice Webb, *Industrial Democracy* (1897; reprint, London: Longmans, Green, 1914), 152–54. "In a certain sense," they observed, "it would not be difficult to regard all the activities of Trade Unionism as forms of Mutual Insurance" (p. 152). Given the high accident and mortality rates in mining, death benefits emerged early in mineworker unionism in Britain and the United States. "The largest funeral processions ever witnessed in Butte, or for that matter, in all Montana," a newspaper reported in 1896, "are those formed by the Butte Miners' Union." Quoted in Alan Derickson, *Workers' Health, Workers' Democracy: The Western Miners' Struggle, 1891–1925* (Ithaca, N.Y.: Cornell University Press, 1988), 76.

80 A recent sociological study of a diaspora community of Dominicans in Boston finds a similar practice of sending bodies home for burial. Peggy Levitt, "Local-Level Global Religion: The Case of U.S.-Dominican Migration," *Journal for the Scientific Study of Religion* 37 (1998): 74–89; Dino Cinel, *From Italy to San Francisco: The Immigrant Experience* (Stanford, Calif.: Stanford University Press, 1982), 204. See also Donna Gabaccia, *Militants and Migrants: Rural Sicilians Become American Workers* (New Brunswick, N.J.: Rutgers University Press, 1988), 137–38.

81 Gary R. Mormino and George E. Pozzetta, *The Immigrant World of Ybor City: Italians and Their Latin Neighbors in Tampa, 1885–1985* (Urbana: University of Illinois, 1987), 178.

82 Moses Rischin, *The Promised City: New York's Jews, 1870–1914* (Cambridge: Harvard University Press, 1962), 104. One important difference between the Guatemalan settlement in North Carolina and the Jewish Lower East Side is that, as Rischin notes, the cross-class society that supported the lansmanshafts might at times obstruct rather than promote trade unionism (pp. 182–83). Near the turn of the century, the Jewish socialist labor movement drew on the self-help features of the lansmanshafts to create the powerful Arbeiter Ring (Workmen's Circle) which by 1910 was paying out $20,000 in death

benefits to nearly 39,000 members. Irving Howe, *World of Our Fathers* (New York: Harcourt Brace Jovanovich, 1976), 357–59.

83 Margaret Eleanor Rose, "Women in the United Farm Workers: A Study of Chicana and Mexicana Participation in a Labor Union, 1950 to 1980" (Ph.D. diss., University of California at Los Angeles, 1988), p. 300 (n. 14).

84 Among "perhaps 100 hometown associations formed by Salvadorans and Guatemalans in the Los Angeles area," e.g., Nora Hamilton and Norma Stoltz Chincilla (*Seeking Community*, 208) find that "some Guatemalan associations . . . originated earlier as burial societies to assist families in sending the bodies of deceased Guatemalans back to Guatemala for burial and to provide assistance to the families. Several of the associations continue to maintain an emergency fund for the cost of funerals or the transport of caskets of the deceased."

Chapter Four

1 Marc Panepinto interview. Cf. local newspaper reports, which more conservatively estimated that three hundred people demonstrated outside the plant. See, e.g., *Morganton News-Herald*, May 18, 1995.

2 Panepinto interview.

3 *Charlotte Observer*, May 13, 1995 (quotations); Luís Alberto "Beto" González interview.

4 Case Farms memo, May 18, 1995, Phyllis Palmieri office files.

5 Palmieri interview, August 10, 1997.

6 Ibid.

7 Palmieri interview, July 24, 1999.

8 Case Farms memo, May 18, 1995, Palmieri office files. In likely her first contact with many of these Guatemalan workers, Palmieri (or her assistant) inevitably misspelled a few names—e.g., "Marta Gartez," "Enrique Fuentes," and "Samuel Juan."

9 LIUNA organizer Yanira Merino (interview, October 17, 2001) remembered Francisco "gearing up" and encouraging others to strike, then, at the last moment, deciding to go to work. Teacher/translator Daniel Gutiérrez (interview, July 19, 2000), who was sympathetic to the workers' plight but never got close to the union, offered as impartial a perspective on Francisco's actions as can be found in Morganton. Gutiérrez "never saw [Francisco] at a [strike] meeting" but did recall that he sent his three vans to transport workers to meetings during the strike.

10 Francisco Fuentes interview, April 19, 1998.

11 Palmieri interview, August 10, 1997.

12 Francisco Fuentes interview, March 30, 2001.

13 Francisco Fuentes interview, April 19, 1998.

14 Carlos Alberto Salido, José Samuel Solís López (August 17, 1997), and Paulino López (August 10, 1997) interviews. "He [Francisco] was a *caudillo* [political boss]," recalled Yanira Merino. After his "turning" Fuentes was in-

volved in repeated conflicts with his compañeros, including protests over allegedly exorbitant rents in buildings he owned and a dispute over a widow's insurance money that he allegedly attempted to pocket for his own use.

15 Félix Rodríguez interview.

16 Complaints against Francisco Fuentes in Burke County criminal court for "communicating threats" and "simple assault" resulted in a $160 fine and the provision that he not appear "on the premises of the prosecuting witness or any member of his family." Record 071395, August 14, 1995, Clerk of Court, Criminal Division, Burke County.

17 *Catarina Méndez Mendoza v. Case Farms of North Carolina Inc., Francisco Fuentes Castro, and Royal Maccabees Life Insurance Company*, 98 CVS 1863, complaint filed November 11, 1998. Fuentes was ultimately fined $46,000, although the court would likely have had trouble collecting the principal, since Fuentes (interview, March 30, 2001) had redistributed his assets (viz., four houses) in the names of other family members.

18 Max Fuentes interview, April 19, 1998.

19 Francisco and Max Fuentes interview, April 19, 1998.

20 E-mail from Jill Cashen, Communications Dept., UFCW, May 11, 2001. LIUNA's closest local to Morganton was in eastern Virginia.

21 Palmieri interview, August 10, 1997.

22 Panepinto interview.

23 *Morganton News-Herald*, May 18, 1995, August 18, 1996.

24 Merino interview, October 30, 1997.

25 Ibid.; *Wall Street Journal*, October 23, 1995.

26 Merino interview, October 30, 1997.

27 Ibid.

28 Ibid.; Gutiérrez interview, July 19, 2000.

29 According to the official NLRB report on the election, of 514 eligible voters, there were 421 valid votes counted, while 24 challenged ballots were ultimately set aside, since they would not, in any case, have determined the results of the election. "Decision and Certification of Representative," Case Farms of North Carolina and National Poultry Workers Organizing Committee, Case No. 11-RC-6089, December 12, 1995, 1–2.

30 *Charlotte Observer*, July 14, 1995.

31 Merino interview, October 17, 2001. At the time of the 1995 strike, a reporter quoted two nonstriking North American workers (likely African American by their last names) as somewhat sympathetic but personally distant from the organizing action: "They deserve to be treated like human beings like everybody else," said one. "They [the company] brought them [the foreign workers] here," said another, "but they don't treat them like they deserve. It's not right." *Charlotte Observer*, May 18, 1995.

32 Juan Ignacio "Nacho" Montes interview, September 29, 2001.

33 Marc Panepinto interview.

34 Merino interview, October 17, 2001.

35 Montes interview, September 7, 1997. In early January 1996 a snowstorm delayed the trailers carrying chickens to the plant. The company refused to

pay the workers for the approximate two-hour delay, explaining that an early morning radio announcement was sufficient to notify workers not to report at the usual starting time. Salido interview.

36 Montes interview, September 7, 1997.
37 Ibid.; Barry Yeoman, "Spiritual Union: A Case Study," *Nation*, December 1, 1997, 18.
38 Salido interview.
39 Beto González interview.
40 Ibid.
41 Montes interview, September 7, 1997; Salido interview.
42 Katherine Harbison interview.
43 Ibid.
44 Salido interview. Admittedly, Beto González (interview) was less sanguine about the poststrike social arrangements: "When we were working together at the plant, we were all close. Very strong. But unfortunately [afterward] each went to his own corner. We started to separate, I over here, Fofo over there."
45 Montes interviews, September 7, 1997, February 18, 2000.
46 Palmieri interview, August 17, 1997.
47 Dora Martínez interview.
48 Harbison's earlier work protests are detailed in Chapter 1 above.
49 Harbison interview.
50 Ibid.
51 Mark Michaelis interview.
52 Ibid.

Chapter Five

1 Meany quoted in Harold Myerson, "A Second Chance: The New AFL-CIO and the Prospective Revival of American Labor," in Jo-Ann Mort, *Not Your Father's Union Movement: Inside the AFL-CIO* (New York: Verso, 1998), 3.
2 Myerson, "Second Chance," 2; Juan González, "An Interview with John Sweeney," in Mort, *Not Your Father's Union*, 227–28. To be sure, the Bridgestone-Firestone strike ended with mixed results. See, e.g., Stephen Franklin, *Three Strikes: Labor's Heartland Losses and What They Mean for Working Americans* (New York: Guilford Press, 2001).
3 In 1995 the ACTWU joined with the Garment Workers to form UNITE.
4 Quoted in John F. Goodman, *Working at the Calling*, foreword by Arthur E. Coia (Hopkinton, Mass.: New England Laborers' Labor Management Trust, 1991), 9–10.
5 Here I have used the estimate of former LIUNA staffer John Jordan rather than the union's own "officially" reported figures of 500,000 members in 1990 and upward of 750,000 in 1996, which, for public relations reasons, Jordan (E-mail to author, June 27, 2001) suggested were padded by the inclusion of retirees.

6 "LIUNA's Public Relations Tour de Force," *Union Democracy Review* 107 (June 1996): 5.

7 *Chicago Sun-Times*, July 13, 1997; *New York Times*, October 23, 1997; Coia biographical press release, ca. 1996 (courtesy, LIUNA public relations department).

8 *New York Times*, October 23, 1997; "In the Laborers' Union," *Union Democracy Review* no. 115 (November 1997): 7.

9 Cf. "Pretty much from the day Coia got in there, everything was designed to avoid a government take-over." John Jordan interview. Attorney Lawrence Gold (interview), LIUNA's key legal strategist from 1993 to 1996 (and then associate general counsel to the AFL-CIO), believed that it was "preposterous" to explain LIUNA's organizing effort as an attempt to "stave off the Feds." He pointed to the fact that the "draft complaint from the Justice Department—the first notice that we had that they were embarked on a serious effort to take some kind of drastic action against the international—didn't occur until November 1994, six months plus after the organizing department was started and staffed. We could have had a hundred fantastic programs, and I don't think anything would have deterred the Justice Department from doing what it did." Again, whatever the original intentions of the organizing department, it served a critical public relations role in Coia's self-defense. As congressional sniping continued at the alleged "sweetheart deal" handed the Laborers by the Clinton administration, Coia held up the new organizing campaigns as a badge of authenticity. In a full-page advertisement circulated to leading major dailies in early 1996, LIUNA would ask, "When Did Reform Become a Dirty Word?" "Opponents of change and right-wing extremists," the ad charged, were picking on a "dynamic union" that was speaking up for workers and poor people. *Union Democracy Review* 107 (June 1996): 5.

10 Letter from Arthur A. Coia, May 10, 1995, published in *Union Democracy Review* 103 (September–October 1995): 1–2.

11 Duane Stillwell interview.

12 Coia letter, May 10, 1995.

13 Marc Panepinto interview.

14 Ibid.

15 Ibid.

16 Jordan interview. "Hotshop" organizing referred to the practice, common in the 1970s–80s ACTWU organization among other unions, of responding quickly, and if necessary across geographic and jurisdictional lines, to indications of rank-and-file ferment and self-organizing activity.

17 Panepinto interview.

18 Jordan interview. An old-style construction trades business agent, Wilkinson's son Rocky, who administered one of the union's trust funds, was once overheard saying, "Big Jack loves the Mexicans . . . he has them clean his house once a week."

19 Marc Panepinto interview.

20 Ibid. As a symbol of underlying tensions even after the Case Farms rivalry, when the two unions agreed to conduct a "joint" campaign against the Per-

due company, LIUNA's special projects staffer John Jordan recalled that "Marc Panepinto videotaped [a LIUNA organizer] pissing against the side of the UFCW office." Jordan E-mail to author, July 21, 1998.

21 NLRB decision, Case Farms of North Carolina, Inc., and LIUNA, Case No. 11-RC-6089, May 31, 1995.

22 Mike Matejka interview.

23 Ibid.

24 Ibid.

25 Jordan interview. Shortly after the union vote, Coia publicly singled out Father Ken as a "good friend of this union and a true man of God." Arthur A. Coia, "Yes We Can!," *The Laborer* 49 (July–August 1996): 3.

26 Section 14-b of the 1947 Taft-Hartley amendments to the National Labor Relations Act (1935) permitted states by statute to outlaw the "union shop," whereby all employees were bound by a collective bargaining contract—i.e., in cases where the union had already been designated the legal representative of those employees—to pay union dues. About twenty-one states, mainly in the South, passed such "right-to-work" (what the unions call "work-for-less") laws. The North Carolina comparison is a more speculative estimate based on conversations with statewide labor leaders.

27 Memo from Kate Bronfenbrenner to author, June 28, 1999, based on data compiled in Bronfenbrenner, "Seeds of Resurgence: Successful Union Strategies for Winning Certification Elections and First Contract Campaigns in the 1980's and Beyond" (Ph.D. diss, Cornell University, 1993); "The Effect of Plant Closings and the Threat of Plant Closings on Worker Rights to Organize," *Supplement to Plant Closings and Workers' Rights: A Report to the Council of Ministers by the Secretariat of the Commission for Labor Cooperation* (Dallas, Tex.: Bernan Press, 1997). In 1993–95 the calculated union victory rate for the Southeast in elections involving fifty or more employees, e.g., was 39 percent.

28 *Keesing's Record of World Events*, vol. 141 (London: Longmans, 1995), index.

29 *Reply Brief of Appellant, Case Farms v. NLRB*, Record No. 96-1402 (L), 96-1566 XAP, July 29, 1996, 1–2.

30 In the case of *Zartic, Inc.*, 315 NLRB 495 (1994)—e.g., "The union repeatedly played a tape for employees continuing derogatory remarks by a supervisor about its Hispanic employees. . . . In addition, the Union issued two leaflets linking the Employer to the KKK [Ku Klux Klan]. . . . The [NLRB] found that the Union's circulation of the two leaflets constituted a sustained appeal to the ethnic sensibilities of the Employer's Hispanic employees which was inflammatory, gratuitous, and irrelevant to any bonafide campaign issue." Hearing Officer's Report and Recommendations, NLRB Region 11, Case Farms of North Carolina and National Poultry Workers Organizing Committee, Case No. 11-RC-6089, September 12, 1995, 12.

31 Hearing Officer's Report and Recommendations, NLRB Region 11, September 12, 1995, 3–7.

32 At Smithfield, prior to the NLRB election, the union had issued a bilingual leaflet that included the English phrase "VOTE NO" IS A DANGEROUS

STATEMENT next to the poorly constructed Spanish phrase "VOTAR NO" PEUDO RESULTAR PELIGROSO!"—both in bold type. The employer contended that the Spanish phrase (unlike the English) conveyed the message that "voting no can be dangerous" and was "threatening and coercive" to unsophisticated non-English-speaking Hispanic employees." But Gold argued that the phrase as written must be translated, "Voting No I could be dangerous" and in the context of the leaflet implied not a "danger" of physical threat or bodily harm but that "voting no" "means an employee wants, and will get, no more 'respect,' 'voice,' or 'money.'" On this issue (and all others in the Smithfield case) the hearing officer dismissed the company's objections and upheld the union election. Brief of Petitioner, Virginia and North Carolina Laborers District Court, *Smithfield Packing Co. v. Virginia and North Carolina Laborers' District Council AFL-CIO*, December 20, 1994, 33–36, and Hearing Officer's Report, January 19, 1995, NLRB Region 11, Case No. 11-RC-6050.

33 Lawrence Gold interview.

34 Intervenor's (Union) Brief, *Case Farms v. NLRB*, U.S. Court of Appeals, Fourth Circuit, Case Nos. 96-1402-L, 96-1566, July 11, 1996.

35 Hearing Officer's Report and Recommendations, NLRB Region 11, Case Farms of North Carolina and National Poultry Workers Organizing Committee, Case No. 11-RC-6089, September 12, 1995, 11.

36 Jordan interview.

37 The IUF, located in Geneva, Switzerland, is one of several international trade secretariats—more recently calling themselves "global unions"—that serve as the coordinating office for multinational coalitions of unions by occupational and trade grouping. John Jordan to Kurt Stand, August 18, 1995, Jordan private papers in author's possession.

38 Deborah Levenson-Estrada, *Trade Unionists against Terror: Guatemala City, 1954–1985* (Chapel Hill: University of North Carolina Press, 1994), 3–4, 109–10, 176–230.

39 Jordan to CFCTF, May 14, July 30 (press release), 1996, and Jordan to Duane Stillwell, December 2, 1996, Jordan private papers.

40 Jordan to Arthur A. Coia, February 27, 1996.

41 ACTWU first triumphed with a boycott/publicity-oriented campaign against company directors and shareholders in the Farrah Manufacturing Co. fight of 1974. It initiated a more famous effort (highlighted in the 1979 Hollywood film *Norma Rae*) in 1976 against J. P. Stevens Co. and won its first Stevens contract in 1980.

42 Jordan to CFCTF, February 26, 1996, Jordan private papers.

43 Jordan to Stillwell, February 13, 1996, ibid.

44 *Los Angeles Times*, February 23, 1996.

45 Jordan to Stillwell, February 23, 1996, Jordan private papers.

46 Jordan to CFCTF, April 19, 1996, ibid.

47 Ibid.

48 "Dear Case Farms Customer" letter, July 8, 1996, Jordan private papers.

49 Jordan to Greg Giebel (LIUNA research director), January 22, 1997.

50 Marc Panepinto interview.

51 Kimberley Bobo interview, July 9, 1998.

52 *Raleigh News and Observer*, July 7, 1996. Indeed, about three years after his appearance in Morganton, Rev. Creech was formally stripped of his ministerial position in the United Methodist Church for presiding over gay and lesbian marriages. *New York Times*, November 18, 1999.

53 *Charlotte Observer*, April 25, 1996.

54 *Charlotte Observer* and *Morganton News-Herald*, April 30, 1996.

55 NICWJ, "More Than Grace over Chicken: A Report of the Fact Finding Delegation to the Case Farms' Poultry Processing Plant in Morganton, NC, April 28–29, 1996" (Chicago, 1996), 9.

56 Ibid., 1–5.

57 Richard Beck interview; "Case Farms: Helping Define New Labor" (John Jordan memo), July 1997, Jordan private papers.

58 *Hickory Daily Record*, June 8, 1996.

59 Bobo interview, July 9, 1998.

60 Rev. Kenneth J. Whittington interview, July 31, 2001; Rev. W. Flemon McIntosh Jr. interview.

61 Jim Pierce letter to the editor, *Morganton News-Herald*, July 3, 1996. In a rather tepid response to Pierce, Bennett M. Judkins, a representative from the North Carolina. Council of Churches, insisted that "Churches (whether they be Catholic, Protestant, or otherwise) generally do not get involved until people have arrived, and then they simply function to help immigrants to adjust to their new surroundings." *Morganton News-Herald*, July 26, 1996.

62 Robert Reich (November 27, 1996), quoted in CFCTF mailing, December 18, 1996.

63 *Raleigh News and Observer*, November 30, 1996.

64 "Pressure Needed in Support of Poultry Industry Investigation," *Labor Alerts/Labor News* E-mail, Campaign for Labor Rights, July 2, 1997. Substantial violations—especially of the Fair Labor Standards Act (including the finding that 100 percent of plants investigated did not pay employees for all hours worked)—were reported by Department of Labor surveys of the poultry industry in 1997 and again in 2000. By the time they were announced, however, such findings were no longer linked to an organizing campaign that could take advantage of them. NICWJ, <www.nicwj.org/pages/outreach. DOLpoultry>; *New York Times*, May 10, 2002.

65 Jordan interview.

66 *Morganton News-Herald*, June 27, 1996.

67 *Morganton News-Herald*, June 28, 1996.

68 John Jordan letter to union supporters, July 14, 1996, Jordan private papers.

69 Juan Ignacio "Nacho" Montes interview, September 7, 1997.

70 *Charlotte Observer* and *Morganton News-Herald*, July 23, 1996.

71 Jordan interview.

72 *Charlotte Observer*, August 9, 1996. At the beginning of the strike there were an estimated seventy strikebreakers.

73 *Morganton News-Herald*, August 8, 1996.

74 *N.C. Catholic*, August 23, 1996. Student organizer Jean-Claude André recalled that the union doled out strike funds (representing 30 percent or more of worker wages) from Father Ken's rectory. Jean-Claude André interview.

75 *Morganton News-Herald*, August 8, 9, 13, 18, 1996.

76 *Morganton News-Herald*, August 8, 1996.

77 Ibid. (Panepinto); André interview; Diego de Diego interview. For more on Diego de Diego's account, see Chapter 2.

78 André interview; Montes interview, February 18, 2000.

79 Montes interview, September 7, 1997.

80 JoAnn Wyppijewski, "AFL-CIO Convention," *Labor Notes*, November 1997, 9.

81 "LIUNA Organizers Strike for Week; Return to Work without Resolution," *Daily Labor Report* (Washington, D.C.: Bureau of National Affairs, April 1, 1997); Will Okun interview, February 23, 2000 (Okun, a LIUNA organizing intern at the time, reported that the chief irritant in the dispute was the frequent cancellation of the organizers' "day off" after a 60–70 hour workweek); Jordan and Marc Panepinto interviews.

82 Bobo interview, July 9, 1998.

83 *New York Times*, October 15, 1997.

84 *Raleigh News and Observer*, January 23, 1999.

85 *Wall Street Journal*, December 7, 1999; *New York Times*, January 28, 2000.

86 Gold interview.

87 Beto González interview; Montes interview, January 16, 2000.

88 Beck interview. By contrast, the Tyson Foods plant, in nearby Wilkesboro, offered a starting wage of $8.35/hour. Wage data courtesy of researching anthropologist, Steven Striffler, May 22, 2001.

89 Beck interview; *Morganton News-Herald*, May 30, 1999.

90 Ibid.

91 Felipe López interview, May 20, 2001. The union's discovery of two eyewitnesses to the petition gathering of longtime personnel supervisor Alberto Echeverria constituted the linchpin of the union's—and subsequently the regional NLRB's—demand for redress against the company's suspension of contract negotiations dating to 1999.

92 Phyllis Palmieri interview, July 24, 1999.

93 Ibid.

94 Throughout the negotiating period, the union attempted to collect application cards and signatures for potential dues checkoff. Over the course of the year, the returns on such efforts grew more and more meager. Beck interview.

95 Beto González interview.

96 Montes interview, January 16, 2000.

97 Off-the-record conversation with LIUNA official, 2000.

98 Stillwell interview.

99 Bobo interview, July 9, 1998.

100 Jordan interview.

101 Panepinto interview.

102 *Morganton News-Herald*, November 24, 1999; Whittington interview, May 17, 1997.

103 Montes interview, February 18, 2000.

104 Beto González interview.

105 Gold interview.

106 In 1999, e.g., the private sector rate was 9.6 percent compared to a robust 37.5 percent among public sector employees. Harold Myerson, "Rolling the Union On," *Dissent* (Winter 2000): 49.

107 See, e.g., Martin Jay Levitt, with Terry Conrow, *Confessions of a Union Buster* (New York: Crown Publishers, 1993).

108 Harley Shaiken, "Labor's Decline Pulls Wages Down," *Cleveland Plain Dealer*, March 12, 1998; *Wall Street Journal*, December 1, 1999.

109 Alton W. J. Craig, *The System of Industrial Relations in Canada* (Scarborough, Calif.: Prentice-Hall Canada, 1990), 133–35. Reference courtesy of Michelle McBride.

110 William Mascioli interview.

111 José Samuel Solís López interview, May 20, 2001.

Chapter Six

1 Justo German Castro Lux to author, March 18, 1999.

2 Marcos Miguel González interview. Actually, Marcos misremembered the score as 105–103, a slip familiar to most sports fans. *Raleigh News and Observer*, May 24, 1998. The absence of Guatemala City newspapers in the San Miguel region is confirmed in an Associated Press dispatch by Will Weissert, published in the *Morganton News-Herald*, October 8, 2000.

3 The full name of the council was Consejo Maya Ixmukane para el Desarrollo Humano (Maya Council for Community Development), changed slightly in early 2000 to Consejo Jun R'akan Pueblo Maya e USA. Lux interview, March 13, 2000.

4 Lux to author, March 18, 1999.

5 See report on "Maya Declaration in Florida," December 3–4, 1999 <www. sover.net/~imlusa/congeng.html>.

6 Tojil, Canil, and Ixchel are all characters in the Popul Vuh, the Mayan epic, preserved in the oral tradition of the K'iche'. Another historical and prophetic text committed to print in the colonial era, the Books of Chilam Balam, the "Jaguar Prophet," derive from the Yucatán-Maya.

7 Interview with Ana Sebastién, Petrona, and Isabel José.

8 Stuart Hall shrewdly suggests the advantages of thinking in terms of "identifications" rather than "identities," the former allowing for overlapping multiplicity within the boundaries of the latter. Hall, "Old and New Identities, Old and New Ethnicities," in A. King, ed., *Culture, Globalization, and the World System* (London: Macmillan, 1991), 47.

9 Recent scholarship is at odds on the likelihood that second-generation (as

well as subsequent) "new immigrants" will maintain strong attachments to their families' ancestral homes. Peggy Levitt and Rafael de la Dehesa, "Redefining the Boundaries of Politics: The U.S.–Latin American Experience" (paper presented at Transborder Peoples Workshop, Bloomington, Ind., June 1–2, 2001).

10 Diane M. Nelson, *A Finger in the Wound: Body Politics in Quincentennial Guatemala* (Berkeley: University of California Press, 1999), 249. Nelson writes, "One Maya leader told me, 'The Maya give thanks for food, for air, for the tools that serve us, the office machines, and the computers'" (p. 258).

11 For the classic frameworks on immigration, see, e.g., Oscar Handlin, *The Uprooted* (Boston: Little, Brown, 1973), and John E. Bodnar, *The Transplanted: A History of Immigrants in Urban America* (Bloomington: Indiana University Press, 1985). For a more recent synthesis, see Alejandro Portes and Ruben G. Rumbaut, *Immigrant America: A Portrait* (Berkeley: University of California Press, 1990).

12 Malcolm Waters, *Globalization* (London: Routledge, 1995), 3.

13 See, e.g., Thomas L. Friedman, *The Lexus and the Olive Tree* (New York: Farrar, Straus and Giroux, 1999), and William Greider, *One World, Ready or Not: The Manic Logic of Global Capitalism* (New York: Simon and Schuster, 1997).

14 Arjun Appadurai, *Modernity at Large: Cultural Dimensions of Globalization* (Minneapolis: University of Minnesota Press, 1997), 21–22.

15 Peter L. Berger, "Four Faces of Global Culture," *Public Interest* (Fall 1997): 23–29; Appadurai, *Modernity at Large*, 32.

16 Maurice R. Stein, *The Eclipse of Community: An Interpretation of American Studies* (New York: Harper and Row, 1960), 247–48, 250. Concern about the loss of face-to-face community in the modern city, as Thomas Bender has noted, preoccupied early-twentieth-century progressive intellectuals like Charles Horton Cooley, Jane Addams, Robert Park, and John Dewey. Bender, *Community and Social Change in America* (New Brunswick, N.J.: Rutgers University Press, 1978).

17 Robert D. Putnam, *Bowling Alone: The Collapse and Revival of American Community* (New York: Simon and Schuster, 2000). With a touch of sarcasm, feminist anthropologist Micaela di Leonardo uncovers a renewed efflorescence of "ethnological anti-modernism" in post-1960s anthropology. A reaction, in her view, to "American racism at home and imperialism abroad; the environmental crisis; women's status and aspirations; and the American 'crisis of meaning,'" the contemporary Western imagination yearns "to let primitives teach us their 'tribal wisdom.'" Di Leonardo, *Exotics at Home: Anthropologists, Others, American Modernity* (Chicago: University of Chicago Press, 1998), 32.

18 I am employing the same poetic license here that Putnam does: i.e., he means to emphasize that contemporary U.S. bowlers no longer bowl in organized leagues, as self-constituted groups, not that individuals bowl all by themselves. See Alan Ryan's review of Putnam in *New York Review of Books*, August 10, 2000, 47–50.

19 Sol Tax, "The Municipios of the Midwestern Highlands of Guatemala," *American Anthropologist* 39 (1937): 423–44. See also John M. Watanabe, *Maya Saints and Souls in a Changing World* (Austin: University of Texas Press, 1992), 5–6.

20 *The Little Community* (1955), quotation, p. 3, and *Peasant Society and Culture* (1956) (Chicago: University of Chicago Press, 1967), 3.

21 "Mesoamericanists have long viewed the cargo system as the core of contemporary Maya social structure. Ideally all men in the community participate in a system of rotating administrative and religious offices by holding a succession of ranked positions, or cargoes, during lifelong public careers." Watanabe, *Maya Saints and Souls*, 106.

22 On the Maya as peasants, see Eric R. Wolf, *Peasants* (Englewood Cliffs, N.J.: Prentice-Hall, 1966), 2–4, 86. For a sophisticated summary of recent anthropological views of the Maya, see Watanabe, *Maya Saints and Souls*, esp. 7–11.

23 Carol A. Smith, "Class Position and Class Consciousness in an Indian Community: Totonicapán in the 1970s," in Smith, ed., *Guatemalan Indians and the State, 1540 to 1988* (Austin: University of Texas Press, 1990), 205–29 (quotation, p. 215). See also Watanabe, *Maya Saints and Souls*, 10–11, 17.

24 Douglas E. Brintnall, *Revolt against the Dead: The Modernization of a Mayan Community in the Highlands of Guatemala* (New York: Gordon and Breach, 1979). On modern Mayan community persistence, see also Watanabe, *Maya Saints and Souls*, 106–26, and Robert S. Carlsen, *The War for the Heart and Soul of a Highland Maya Town* (Austin: University of Texas Press, 1997), 151–69.

25 Alison Mountz and Richard A. Wright, "Daily Life in the Transnational Migrant Community of San Agustín, Oaxaca, and Poughkeepsie, New York," *Diaspora* 5 (Fall 1996): 403–28 (quotation, pp. 424–25).

26 John Tomlinson, *Globalization and Culture* (Chicago: University of Chicago Press, 1999), 29–30, 106–49. For an extended treatment exploring transnational identity and organization among Guatemalan and Salvadoran migrants, see Nora Hamilton and Norma Stoltz Chincilla, *Seeking Community in a Global City* (Philadelphia: Temple University Press, 2001), 152–218.

27 Félix Rodríguez interview.

28 Katarina López interview, May 21, 1998.

29 Tránsita Gutiérrez Solís interview, March 13, 2000.

30 Gaspar Pascual interview.

31 "Marga" interview.

32 The term *naturales*, long used in a disparaging way by the Spanish and Ladinos to distance themselves from the indigenous exotics, is sometimes adopted as a nonpejorative signifier by the indigenous themselves.

33 Víctor Hernández interview, April 29, 2000.

34 Félix Rodríguez interview.

35 Kay B. Warren, *The Symbolism of Subordination: Indian Identity in a Guatemalan Town* (Austin: University of Texas), 51.

36 On the function of civil-religious hierarchies in Guatemala, see, e.g., ibid., 51.

37 Gabriel Yol L'un "Padre Gabriel" Rodríguez interview, June 28, 1997.

38 Jésus Acevedo interview.

39 Jim Handy, *Gift of the Devil: A History of Guatemala* (Boston: South End Press, 1984), 20.

40 David Stoll, *Rigoberta Menchú and the Struggle of All Poor Guatemalans* (Boulder, Colo.: Westview Press, 1999), 29–40.

41 Warren, *Symbolism of Subordination*, xi.

42 Diego de Diego interview.

43 Francisco Mejía Chávez interview.

44 Francisco Risso, July 22, 2002 (telephone).

45 Appropriately enough, at the 1999 Fiesta del Pueblo (a recent, annual celebration of the local Latino community) in Chapel Hill, North Carolina, Western Union (no fools they!) sponsored the soccer competition. Neyda López interview.

46 Sonia Rincon-Hevlin (Outreach Coordinator, Smart Start Programs) interview. A similar finding was recorded by Nancy J. Wellmeier, *Ritual, Identity, and the Mayan Diaspora* (New York: Garland Publishing, Inc., 1998), 78.

47 Félix Miguel interview; "Marga" interview.

48 Allan F. Burns, *Maya in Exile: Guatemalans in Florida* (Baltimore: Temple University Press, 1993), 108–10.

49 Domingo Hernández Ixcoy, "A Maya Voice: The Maya of Mexico City," in James Loucky and Marilyn M. Moors, eds., *The Maya Diaspora: Guatemalan Roots, New American Lives* (Philadelphia: Temple University Press, 2000), 113.

50 Donald Hemstreet interview.

51 Chávez interview. In his 1993 study of the Maya in Indiantown, Fla., Allan Burns (*Maya in Exile*, 148–49) placed the problem of heavy drinking in a useful context: "When Oliver La Farge worked in the Q'anjob'al area of Guatemala in the 1920s, he noted that the Q'anjob'al drank heavily. He said, though, that 'one would hesitate to remove the bottle from them until the entire pattern of their lives is changed. They are . . . eternally chafing under the yoke of conquest, and never for a moment forgetting that they are a conquered people. In occasional drunkenness . . . they find a much needed release" [Oliver La Farge, *Santa Eulalia* (Chicago: University of Chicago Press, 1947, 100)]. If local residents or social workers are asked what they see as the principal problem with the Q'anjob'al people today, they will usually say drunkenness. . . . Those Maya who are Seventh-Day Adventists and members of other Protestant denominations do not drink."

52 Karl Marx ("where all that is solid") quoted in Marshall Berman, *All That Is Solid Melts into Air: The Experience of Modernity* (New York: Simon and Schuster, 1982), 21.

53 Daniel Gutiérrez interview, July 9, 1997. According to Gutiérrez: "There is a Roman saying, 'To the people, bread and circuses.' Whenever you go to Morganton, you see people watching TV. If you've been working all day long, you have soap operas, 7–8, 8–9, 9–10 [P.M.]. You take away the interest of the people to actually learn."

54 Andrés and Juana Pascual interview, October 5, 1997.

55 Ana, Petrona, and Isabel José interview.

56 The Catholic Charismatic Renewal movement (sometimes referred to as

CCR) originated in 1966 at a Duquesne University retreat, where Catholic faculty and students met with Protestant Pentecostals; the early movement was even referred to as Catholic Pentecostalism, although formal connections with Protestants quickly diminished. Anna L. Peterson and Manuel A. Vásquez, "'Upwards, Never Down': The Catholic Charismatic Renewal in Transnational Perspective," in Vásquez, Philip J. Williams, and Peterson, eds., *Christianity, Social Change, and Globalization in the Americas* (New Brunswick, N.J.: Rutgers University Press, 2001), 271–72.

57 See, e.g., Peggy Levitt, "Local-Level Global Religion: The Case of U.S.-Dominican Migration," *Journal for the Scientific Study of Religion* 37 (Winter 1998): 74–89, esp. 82–84. For a nuanced view of the charismatic movement in Latin America, see Peterson and Vásquez, "'Upwards, Never Down,'" 188–209.

58 Ana José interview.

59 Rev. Kenneth J. Whittington interview, December 10, 1998.

60 Gutiérrez interview, July 19, 2001.

61 Paul Hans Kobrak, "Las relaciones interétnicas en Aguacatán, Huehuetenango" (manuscript, 2001, courtesy of P. H. Kobrak), 45–46.

62 The overwhelmingly male Guatemalan profile in Morganton roughly mirrors that which Burns (*Maya in Exile*, 94) found in Indiantown in the early 1990s, a population he estimated at over 70 percent male.

63 Chávez interview.

64 Félix Miguel interview; José Samuel Solís López interview, June 18, 2000.

65 Letitia Paulina Hernández Hernández interview, July 1, 1999.

66 Chávez interview.

67 José Samuel López interview, June 18, 2000.

68 Toribia Gamas interview, May 22, 2000.

69 Letitia Hernández interview, May 22, 2000.

70 Pablo Escobar Méndez interview.

71 Whittington interview, March 13, 2000.

72 Toribia Gamas interviews; Narciso Gamas interview, June 5, 1999.

73 The estimate, in any case, seems low. José Samuel López (interview, April 17, 1999), keeper of the Aguacateco "census" during emergency collection appeals (of which there had not been one for some time), pegged the number of women in Morganton from Aguacatán at 50 to 75.

74 Letitia Hernández interviews, May 21, 1998, July 1, 1999.

75 "Marga" interview.

76 Ibid.; Rincon-Hevlin interview; Francisco Risso interview, March 13, 2000.

77 Katarina López interview.

78 Ibid. On women's changing roles in the larger context of recent migration, see June Nash, "The Transformation of Gender Roles in Migration," *Latino(a) Research Review* (Spring–Winter 1999): 2–15.

79 Marcelino López Castro interview.

80 "Marga" interview.

81 Gutiérrez interview, July 19, 2000.

82 Teofilo Pedro interview. For a nuanced view of second-generation adaptation

based on the concept of "segmented assimilation," see Alejandro Portes and Rubén G. Rumbaut, *Legacies: The Story of the Immigrant Second Generation* (Berkeley: University of California Press, 2001), 44–45, 189–91.

83 Marilyn M. Moors, "Conclusion: The Maya Diaspora Experience," in Loucky and Moors, *The Maya Diaspora*, 227.

84 Kobrak, "Las relaciones interétnicas," 48.

85 Ibid., 49.

86 Edgar R. Ayala, "Guatemalans Voting Abroad," *Report on Guatemala* 20 (Winter 1999): 5.

87 Interviews in Aguacatán at King Express and Intercapitales, May 21, 2000. Francisco Mejía Chávez (interview), e.g., dutifully sent home $1,000 every two months.

88 Nicolas Pérez López interview.

89 Ibid.; Víctor Hernández interview, April 29, 2000; cf. Kobrak, "Las relaciones interétnicas," 44.

90 Neyda López interview.

91 Emiliano Rodríguez interview, June 30, 1999.

92 Felipe López, comment at History 06J class meeting in Morganton, November 7, 1999.

93 Pedro Solís Sales interview. For emigrant influence on the sender community, see also Peggy Levitt, "Social Remittances: Migration-Driven, Local-Level Forms of Cultural Diffusion," *International Migration Review* 32 (Winter 1998): 926–48.

94 Kobrak, "Las relaciones interétnicas," 35.

95 Emiliano Rodríguez interview, June 30, 1999.

96 Moors, "Conclusion: The Maya Diaspora Experience."

97 Acevedo interview.

98 Escobar Méndez interview. Emiliano Rodríguez (interview, June 30, 1999) made a similar point.

99 Osvaldo Saqvich (Industrial Disputes Coordinator, UTQ [Union of Quetzaltenango Workers]) interview.

100 Padre Gabriel Rodríguez interview, May 21, 2000; Whittington interviews, March 13, June 30, 2000. Kobrak ("Las relaciones interétnicas," 39) cited incidences of "vigilante justice" nearly leading to the lynching of suspected delinquents in Aguacatán in 1997 and 1998.

101 Edward F. Fischer and R. McKenna Brown, Introduction to Fischer and Brown, eds., *Maya Cultural Activism in Guatemala* (Austin: University of Texas Press, 1996), 5. On "revitalization," see Kay B. Warren, "Reading History as Resistance," ibid., 102–4.

102 Information courtesy of Rosa Tock.

103 Edward F. Fischer, "Induced Cultural Change as a Strategy for Socioeconomic Development," in Fischer and Brown, *Maya Cultural Activism in Guatemala*, 52–73. On the ALM, see also Nelson, *Finger in the Wound*, 255–63.

104 Kay B. Warren, *Indigenous Movements and Their Critics: Pan-Maya Activism in Guatemala* (Princeton, N.J.: Princeton University Press, 1998), 4–32.

105 Milan Gagnon, "The Maya Are Coming," Pacific News Service, April 1, 2002, <www.pacificnews.org>.

106 Guatemala City, *Guatemala Prensa Libre*, December 29, 1998, <www.prensa libre.com/pls/prensa>.

107 CORN-Maya declaration, quoted in Burns, *Maya in Exile*, 63.

108 Formed in the 1970s to struggle for land and labor rights (and loosely linked to the guerrilla struggle), the CUC, in which Rigoberta Menchú and her family were active, was smashed by the counterinsurgency war and only barely reestablished itself in the late 1980s.

109 Lux interviews, June 19, 1998, June 5, 1999.

110 Lux interview, March 13, 2000.

111 Ibid.

112 Robert M. Carmack, "State and Community in Nineteenth-Century Guatemala: The Momostenango Case," in Carol A. Smith, ed., *Guatemalan Indians and the State, 1540 to 1988* (Austin: University of Texas Press, 1990), 117–18, 125.

113 José Samuel López interview, April 17, 1999.

114 José Samuel López interview, June 18, 2000.

115 Felipe López interview, August 28, 1997.

116 Jacqueline María Hagan, *Deciding to Be Legal: A Maya Community in Houston* (Philadelphia: Temple University Press, 1994), 10. Hagan's study, emphasizing the settlement experiences of Mayan women, offers a valuable counterpart to our focus on a largely male work and political environment.

117 "Mayans in Texas," *All Things Considered*, National Public Radio, November 30, 1998.

118 Edgar Hernández interview.

119 Gaspar Pedro González, *A Mayan Life* (1966; reprint, English ed., Rancho Palos Verdes, Calif.: Yax Te' Press, 1995), 219–23.

120 Maya Declaration in Florida, December 4, 1999, <www.sover.net/~imlusa/congeng.html>. The Pan-Maya movement was also making other connections in the United States. The American Indian Movement of Florida (Florida AIM) dedicated its Seventh Anniversary Conference, August 13–September 1, 2002, in Lake Worth, Fla., to "the Struggles of the Maya Peoples in exile and their struggles here in Florida . . . and for the Maya Nation in its homeland." Seventeenth Florida AIM State Conference Invitation," June 17, 2002.

Chapter Seven

1 Jack Metzgar, *Striking Steel: Solidarity Remembered* (Philadelphia: Temple University Press, 2000), 116.

2 See, e.g., Richard Jules Oestreicher, *Solidarity and Fragmentation: Working People and Class Consciousness in Detroit, 1875–1900* (Urbana: University of Illinois Press, 1986), and David M. Gordon, Richard Edwards, and Michael Reich, *Segmented Work, Divided Workers: The Historical Transformation of*

Labor in the United States (New York: Cambridge University Press, 1982). Indeed, a cottage industry on "American exceptionalism" has spilled much ink dissecting the relative weakness of class feeling in the United States, particularly the inability of American workers to form an effective social bloc at the political level. See, e.g., Seymour Martin Lipset and Gary Wolfe Marks, *It Didn't Happen Here: Why Socialism Failed in the United States* (New York: W. W. Norton, 2000).

3   Efraín Sebastién Martín interview.

4   According to information supplied by the law office, Palmieri and Associates handled about 195 immigration cases, including those of 49 Guatemalans, from the mid-1990s through 2001.

5   Perhaps the greatest emotion on this topic in recent years was stirred up by California governor Pete Wilson's campaign for Proposition 187 (to deny state services to illegal aliens) in 1994 and the presidential primary campaign of Patrick Buchanan in 1996—though both were losing efforts.

6   Perhaps the most famous case was that of eight undocumented Minneapolis Holiday Inn Express workers, fired and targeted for deportation in October 1999 after participating in a winning union organizing campaign. Based on a national union mobilization behind these workers, Holiday Inn Express ultimately settled a $72,000 compensatory damage claim by the U.S. Equal Employment Opportunity Commission, and the INS granted deferrals of deportation to seven of the eight workers. See National Immigration Law Center, <www.nilc.org/immsemplymnt/inswkplce>, and antiracism campaigns, <flag.blackened.net/revolt/arc>.

7   David Bacon, "Immigrant Workers Ask Labor 'Which Side Are You On?,'" *Working USA* 3 (January–February 2000): 7–18.

8   Mike Davis, *Magical Realism: Latinos Reinvent the U.S. City* (New York: Verso, 2000), 143–45 (quotation, p. 145).

9   *LA Weekly*, quoted in James Green, *Taking History to Heart: The Power of the Past in Building Social Movements* (Amherst: University of Massachusetts Press, 2000), 264.

10 Davis, *Magical Realism*, 147.

11 Hector L. Delgado, *New Immigrants, Old Unions: Organizing Undocumented Workers in Los Angeles* (Baltimore: Temple University Press, 1993), 133, 136–38. Other than size, one obvious dissimilarity between the two communities was the added tension in Los Angeles between long-established immigrant Americans and "temporary" resident workers (p. 132).

12 Ibid., 147.

13 In 1998, e.g., the INS reportedly had only eight agents operating in North Carolina, or one agent per 16,000 employers, and not a single employer had been fined (1994–98) for hiring illegals. *Raleigh News and Observer*, November 29–30, 1998; Delgado, *New Immigrants*, 66–67.

14 Delgado, *New Immigrants*, 151. See also Ruth Milkman, ed., *Organizing Immigrants: The Challenge for Unions in Contemporary California* (Ithaca, N.Y.: Cornell University Press, 2000).

15 See Craig Jackson Calhoun, "The Radicalism of Tradition: Community

Strength or Venerable Disguise and Borrowed Language?" *American Journal of Sociology* 88 (March 1983): 886–914.

16   Marx, "The Eighteenth Brumaire of Louis Bonaparte," quoted in ibid., 887.

17   Jefferson to Adams, August 1, 1816, in Paul Wilstach, ed., *Correspondence of John Adams and Thomas Jefferson* (Indianapolis: Bobbs-Merrill, 1925), 136.

18   Talcott Parsons, *The Evolution of Societies* (Englewood Cliffs, N.J.: Prentice-Hall, 1977); David Mitrany, *Marx against the Peasant: A Study in Social Dogmatism* (Chapel Hill: University of North Carolina Press, 1951).

19   Michael Kearney, *Reconceptualizing the Peasantry: Anthropology in Global Perspective* (Boulder, Colo.: Westview Press, 1996), 76.

20   Ibid., 78–90. On the treatment of the "peasant question," see also William Roseberry, "Beyond the Agrarian Question in Latin America," in Frederic Cooper et al., eds., *Confronting Historical Paradigms: Peasants, Labor, and the Capitalist World System in Africa and Latin America* (Madison: University of Wisconsin Press, 1993), 318–68. For recent studies that reflect a nuanced appreciation of peasant society, see Florencia E. Mallon, *Peasant and Nation: The Making of Postcolonial Mexico and Peru* (Berkeley: University of California Press, 1995), and Daniel Nugent, *Spent Cartridges of Revolution: An Anthropological History of Namiquipa, Chihuahua* (Chicago: University of Chicago Press, 1993).

21   Kenneth A. Lockridge, *A New England Town, The First Hundred Years: Dedham, Massachusetts, 1636–1736* (New York: Norton, 1970).

22   Ibid., 165, 169–70, 172, 179.

23   Ibid., 169.

24   E. P. (Edward Palmer) Thompson, *The Making of the English Working Class* (New York: Pantheon Books, 1963); Craig Jackson Calhoun, "The Radicalism of Tradition: Community Strength or Venerable Disguise and Borrowed Language?," *American Journal of Sociology* 88 (March 1983): 886–914 (quotations, pp. 897, 900).

25   See, e.g., Herbert Gutman, *Work, Culture, and Society in Industrializing America: Essays in American Working-Class and Social History* (New York: Knopf, 1976); Lawrence Goodwyn, *Democratic Promise: The Populist Moment in America* (New York: Oxford, 1976); Alan Dawley, *Class and Community: The Industrial Revolution in Lynn* (Cambridge: Harvard University Press, 1976); Leon Fink, *Workingmen's Democracy: The Knights of Labor and American Politics* (Urbana: University of Illinois Press, 1983); and Sean Wilentz, *Chants Democratic: New York City and the Rise of the American Working Class, 1788–1850* (New York: Oxford University Press, 1984).

26   Victor Greene, *The Slavic Community on Strike: Immigrant Labor in Pennsylvania Anthracite* (Notre Dame, Ind.: University of Notre Dame Press, 1968), 109.

27   Gary R. Mormino and George E. Pozzetta, *The Immigrant World of Ybor City: Italians and Their Latin Neighbors in Tampa, 1885–1985* (Urbana: University of Illinois Press, 1990), 24–29, 123, 143.

28   Former LIUNA organizer Panepinto had never heard of the fabled Lorenzo,

but he placed his Italian family in a Sicilian river valley only a few kilometers from Sante Stefano. Marc Panepinto interview.

29 John M. Watanabe, *Maya Saints and Souls in a Changing World* (Austin: University of Texas Press, 1992); Douglas E. Brintnall, *Revolt against the Dead: The Modernization of a Mayan Community in the Highlands of Guatemala* (New York: Gordon and Breach, 1979). As Watanabe notes, "Mesoamericanists have long viewed the cargo system as the core of contemporary Maya social structure. Ideally, all men in the community participate in a system of rotating administrative and religious offices by holding a succession of ranked positions, or cargoes, during lifelong public careers" (p. 106).

30 I am drawing indirectly here on Robert S. Carlsen, *The War for the Heart and Soul of a Highland Maya Town* (Austin: University of Texas Press, 1997), esp. 167, and Watanabe, *Maya Saints*, 5 (quotation, p. 23).

31 Story related to the author by Justo German Castro Lux.

32 Arthur M. Schlesinger Jr., *The Disuniting of America* (1991; reprint, New York: W. W. Norton, 1998), 20, 112, 125–47.

33 Todd Gitlin, *The Twilight of Common Dreams: Why America Is Wracked by Culture Wars* (New York: Metropolitan Books, 1995).

34 Schlesinger, *Disuniting of America*, 13.

35 The comité cívico phenomenon began in the late 1980s in heavily indigenous municipalities as both a search for local control and a symbolic rejection of Ladino-dominated national parties associated with the devastating wars against the Indian countryside. The biggest success of the still-only-loosely coordinated comités (which, thus far, have only run candidates at the municipal level) was in Quetzaltenango, where comité-backed, reelected Mayor Rigoberto Quemé Chay remained the most prominent K'iche' official in the nation.

36 Guillermino Herrero Pallacios interview. A former town official, sixty-five-year-old Guillermino was widely respected for his knowledge and experience of local history.

37 Pablo Escobar Méndez interview. Among subtle differences of the new orthography—a change perceived as favoring Awakateko pronunciation and vocabulary—was the replacement of hard *c* by *k* and the use of "double vowels" such as *aa* and *ii* to emphasize the elongation of sounds.

38 Escobar Méndez interview.

39 Ibid.

40 Ibid.

41 Víctor Hernández interview, April 29, 2000.

42 Felipe López interview, February 13, 2000.

43 José Samuel Solís López interview, June 18, 2000.

44 Ibid.

45 Víctor Hernández interview, October 14, 2000.

46 Emiliano Rodríguez interview, March 24, 2000.

47 Felipe López interview, July 31, 2001.

48 Michael Barrett interview.

49 Yanira Merino interview, October 17, 2001.

50 Francisco Aguirre interview.

51 Felipe López interview, July 31, 2001.

52 *New York Times*, September 7, 2001.

53 Merino interview, October 17, 2001.

54 Phoenix Fund Annual Report, 2000 (courtesy of Anna Fink); Jan Lin, *Reconstructing Chinatown: Ethnic Enclave, Global Change* (Minneapolis: University of Minnesota, 1998), 117–20.

55 Kim Bobo interview, October 31, 2001; Risso interview, July 22, 2002.

56 José Samuel López interview, September 1, 2001.

57 Immigration reform and control issues have so preoccupied certain employment sectors as to move them to the forefront of collective bargaining agreements. Thus, an early 2002 Tyson's chicken contract in the Delmarva Peninsula specified that in the event of a new immigrant amnesty program, the company would honor the seniority of workers who showed documentation of their "real" names and residency. The same contract also specified that the company must call the union representative in the event of an INS raid on the plant. María E. Martínez (UFCW Local 27 organizer) interview. Similarly, Chicago's Hotel and Restaurant Employees, Local 1, secured an agreement from McCormick Place that "no employee . . . shall suffer any loss of seniority, compensation, or benefits due to any changes in the employee's name or social security number, provided that the new . . . number is valid and the employee is authorized to work in the United States." McCormick Place Collective Bargaining Agreement, February 28, 2001 (copy of agreement courtesy of Emily LaBarbera-Twarog).

58 For *Hoffman Plastic Compounds, Inc. v. NLRB*, No. 00-1595 (S. Ct.), see *Chicago Tribune*, April 7, 2002.

59 Joel Rogers and Wade Radke, "A Strategy for Labor," *Dissent* 43 (Fall 1996): 78–84. On moving beyond contract unionism, see also Rogers, "Reforming U.S. Labor Relations," *Chicago Kent Law Review* 69 (1993): 97–129.

Glossary of Spanish Terms

abogado: unlicensed legal advocate

alcalde: mayor, highest elected official in *municipio*

aldea: hamlet, satellite village

cacique: local Indian political boss

campesinos: peasant farmers

cantón: ward or neighborhood, political subdivision within *municipio*

casa agringada: house built with U.S.-earned dollars

castellano: Spanish

caudillo: local political boss

cédulas: government identity cards

cinta: native scarf, especially colorful in Aguacatán

cofradía: religious brotherhood dedicated to the local Catholic saint and once connected to a larger civil-religious hierarchy

comida típica: traditional food

comité: unit of self-government in Mayan communities

comités cívicos: Mayan community committees that took on increasing significance during and after *la violencia*

comunidad: community

Consejo Maya: Maya Council

costumbre: Mayan folk Catholic rituals, often invoking prayers to ancestral or other spirits

costumbrista: one who practices *costumbre*

coyotes: migrant labor smugglers

cuerda: customary (and locally varying) unit of land measure, approximately one-tenth of an acre

curandera: a traditional healer

departamento: any of the twenty-two largest administrative units into which Guatemala is divided; province

directiva: leadership committee

envídia: envy

evangelica: Protestant

familiar: family member, relative

finca: large landholding or plantation

gringo: white foreigner

huelga: strike

huipil(es): traditional blouse(s)

indígena: indigenous, Maya

Ladino: mestizo or nonindigenous Guatemalan; also a person of indigenous origin who has chosen to identify (in dress and outlook) with the Guatemalan national society rather than a specifically Mayan culture

la violencia: the violence, colloquial term for the thirty-year civil war

libro de actas: record book

mano dura: hard hand

marimba: large wooden xylophone, the "national" instrument of Guatemala

mayordomos: foremen, in-plant supervisors

milpa: corn, bean, and squash plot associated with Mayan subsistence agriculture

mixtamal: corn/lime paste for tortillas

municipio: subdivision of a *departamento*; "county" or "township" including a town center (*cabecera*) and outlying hamlets (*aldeas*), which for the Maya also defines an ethnic community

nacionales: military, armed forces

nahual: traditional animal spirit

natural: a native or indigenous person (sometimes used as a pejorative by Ladinos)

paisano: fellow countrymen

paros: quickie strikes

patrón: landlord

pila: stone wash basin

profesores titulados: certified teachers

promotores: language instructors

promotores bilingües: bilingual Mayan teachers

pueblo: village or small town; here also used to denote the central settlement within a *municipio*

ropa típica: traditional dress

sacerdote: priest

shamanes: shamans, native priests presiding over *costumbre*

sindicato: trade union

tienda: shop

traje: traditional indigenous garments

vendido: "corrupted" person or sellout

Index

Note: Italic page numbers refer to illustrations.

Alvarado, Pedro de, 151
American Dream, 76, 200
American Federation of Teachers (AFT), 128
Amish Brand, 119
Amnesty International, 37, 63
André, Jean-Claude, 126
ANN (Alianza Nueva Nación), 170
Appadurai, Arjun, 144
Arbenz Guzmán, Jacobo, 170
Arévalo, Juan José, 66, 170
Arkansas, 12, 18
Assimilation, 143, 155, 170, 174, 228–29 (n. 9)
Association for Community Development (ADESCO), 171
Avondale Shipyards, 137
Awakatekos: as Case Farm workers, 4; compared to Chalchitekos, 57, 58, 74–75, 85, 214–15 (n. 17), 219 (nn. 75, 76); and Guatemalan guerrilla warfare, 62; and education, 69–70; and promotion of Mayan languages, 141; and Mayan traje, 147; and identity politics, 189–94

Barbarough, Edna, 28, 35, 55
Barlowe, Ray, 23–24
Barrett, Michael, 195
Basilio, Andrés, 48
Beck, Richard, 131–32, 136
Beecher, Norman, 17–18, 20, 42, 53, 207 (n. 27)
Benfield, Rosa, 34–35
Bilingual education, 69–70, 170, 218 (n. 62)
Blacks: and Guatemalan Maya, 2, 23; of Morganton, 4, 9; in labor force, 13; and Case Farms work, 17; and Hmong refugees, 25; union attitudes of, 92, 98, 100, 102, 122, 178, 221 (n. 31); reactions of to Hispanics, 102; and ethnic fear argument, 115–16, 117
Bobo, Kimberley, 119–20, 122, 129, 134–35, 198

Bonilla, Orlando, 89, 111
Boone, Daniel, 8
Bosnia-Hercegovina, 115
Bourg-Williams, Gisela, 26–28, 31
Breeden, Tom, 11, 14
Breeden's Poultry and Egg, 8, 11–14, 180. *See also* Case Farms poultry plant
Bridgestone-Firestone tire strike, 106
Brintnall, Douglas, 146
Buchanan, Pat, 25
Burgos-Debray, Elizabeth, 31
Burns, Allan, 153–54
Byrd, Byrd, and Ervin law firm, 21

Calhoun, Craig, 184
Campesino Unity Committee (CUC), 171, 234 (n. 8)
Canada, 137
Capone, Al, 108
Carey, Ron, 105, 130
Cargo system, 186, 237 (n. 29)
Carpio, Jorge, 67
Casas agringadas, 165, 166
Case Farms management: and union contract efforts, 1, 118–19, 124–25, 131–34, 137, 177, 178, 195, 227 (n. 91); and strike of May 1995, 84, 87; and worker demands, 91, 96; reaction of to union election vote, 94; and snow-induced shutdown incident, 94, 221–22 (n. 35); and replacement workers, 97, 125; and vendidos, 97–99; Harbison on, 100–101; Michaelis on, 102–3; and National Labor Relations Board election, 114–17; and ethnic fear argument, 115–17, 224 (n. 30); legal maneuverings of, 129, 199; and accident record, 138; effect of depressed job market on, 196
Case Farms poultry plant, 15; and labor force, 2, 14, 17, 54, 207 (n. 27); and names of immigrant poultry workers, 6, 30; establishment of, 8; and Shelton, 14, 17, 20;

"whole-bird" processing operation, *16*; assembly line work, 16–17; working conditions of, 17, 27–28, 54, 55–56, 67, 70, 80, 87, 91, 96, 102, 112–13, 121–22, 180, 196; and recruitment of Guatemalan war refugees, 17–18, 27, 40, 42, 207 (nn. 27, 28); and company authority, 53, 180; and Fuentes' bus service, 64; and gender division, 206 (n. 15). *See also* Labor conflict at Case Farms poultry plant

Case Farms union: and union building, 30, 54–56, 63–77, 78, 79–80, 81, 130–31; and union contract, 117–25, 131–34, 137, 138–39, 177, 178, 195, 227 (n. 91); illegal workers' support of, 181; and effect of depressed job market, 196; and Workers Center, 197–98. *See also* Labor conflict at Case Farms poultry plant

Case Foods Company, 14–15

Catawba Valley Legal Services, 28, 34–35, 52, 53, 54

Catequistas, 59

Catholic Charismatic Renewal movement, 156, 169, 231–32 (n. 56)

Catholic Church, 17–18, 28, 36–37, 48, 58–59, 123, 156. *See also* St. Charles Borromeo Catholic Church

CEH (Historical Clarification Commission), 37–38

Chalchitekos: as Case Farm workers, 4; compared to Awakatekos, 57, 74–75, 85, 214–15 (n. 17), 219 (nn. 75, 76); and Aguacatán, 61; and identity politics, 189–94; community protest meeting of, *191*

Chavez, Cesar, 97, 179

Chávez, Francisco Mejía, 149, 152, 154, 158–59

Chávez-Thompson, Linda, 105

Che Guevara Front, 38

Christian Democratic (DC) Party, 67

Church of the Word, 48

Citizen Action, 119, 123, 130

Civil rights community, 109, 113, 136

Civil Self-Defense Patrols (PACs), 38, 39, 62

Class issues, 21–22, 177, 181, 184–85, 235 (n. 2)

Clinton, Bill, 108, 123–24, 223 (n. 9)

Coalition of Labor Union Women, 108

Coats, Steve, 120

Coffee cultivation, 36

Coffee plantations, 45, 57, 65, 66, 167

Cofradías, 58, 145, 150, 230 (n. 21)

Cohen, Mel, 10, 22–23

Coia, Arthur A., 90, 108–9, 113–14, 116, 117, 129–30, 223 (n. 9), 224 (n. 25)

Coia, Arthur E., 107, 108

Cojtí, Demetrio, 170

Cold War, 104, 105–6

Colisimo, "Big Jim," 107

Comitán, Mexico, 41, 42

Community: and globalization, 3, 4, 143, 144, 176, 186; effects of immigration on, 3–4, 74, 76, 77, 152; home/migrant community relationship, 5, 74, 140, 149, 152, 174, 186–87, 192; authority/power of, 49; and cooperatives and community self-help, 71, 72–73, 174; and burial societies, 73, 77–78, 174, 220 (n. 84); and directivas, 73–74; and identity, 74, 76, 140, 152, 185; and Aguacatecos, 74, 100; and union building, 76–77, 174; and vendidos, 98; and Laborers International Union of North America, 135, 152; decline of, 144–45, 169, 229 (n. 17); Maya identified with, 145–46; and union movement, 150–52; and inter-Indian disputes, 151; and central plaza, 153; and expectations of women, 161; and materialism, 168, 169; and recuperation of Mayan cul-

Farmworkers, 105
FDNG (Democratic Front for a New Guatemala), 171
Fiestas, 58
First Assembly church, 26
First Maya Congress (1999), 142, 176
Florida, 39, 40, 44, 53, 64, 171. *See also* Indiantown, Florida
FMLN (Martí National Liberation Front), 88
Folk Catholicism, 58–59
Food-processing industry, 2, 109, 112, 198–99
Fosco, Angelo, 108
Fosco, Peter, 107–8
Francisco, Gaspar, 140–41, 143
Fuentes, Francisco: and strike of May 1993, 63, 83; and Aguacateco community, 64, 75, 221 (nn. 15, 17); and Florida recruitment transportation, 64, 83, 85; and guerrilla warfare, 64–65; as Chalchiteko, 65, 75, 85; parents of, *66*; prominence of, 69; and strike of May 1995, 81, 83, 84–85, 87, 220 (n. 9), 220–21 (n. 14); and National Labor Elections Board election, 92; Oscar Fuentes' relationship with, 92, 93; and Panepinto, 93; and lack of support for union, 94, 95; and directiva, 194
Fuentes, Max, 65, 85
Fuentes, Oscar: and Aguacateco community, 64; leadership of, 64–65, 72, 90, 92, 93, 95; prominence of, 69; as Chalchiteko, 75; and union building, 79; and strike of May 1995, 81, 83–84, *83*, 87; and Yanira Merino, 90, 91, 92; Francisco Fuentes' relationship with, 92, 93; and Panepinto, 93; defection of, 93, 94, 95

Gálves, Marta Olivia, 72, 79, 83, 99, 131, 133–34
Gamas, Narciso, 159–60

Gamas, Toribia, 159–60
Gender: and union attitudes, 92; and changes in roles, 158–59, 162–63; and Mayan roots of roles, 172; and poultry industry, 206 (n. 15)
General Inspectorate of Labor, 217 (n. 50)
Georgia, 12, 18
Gitlin, Todd, 188
Global cultural economy, 144
Globalization: and community, 3, 4, 143, 144, 176, 186; and labor movement, 105–6, 182; and cultural issues, 144, 161; and peasant economies, 154
Global labor rights, 182
Global marketplace, 173
Global political economy, 5, 105
Gold, Lawrence, 116–17, 130, 136–37, 224–25 (n. 32)
Gold Kist, 14
Gómez, Rodolfo ("Fofo"), 98, 126, 222 (n. 44)
González, Gaspar Pedro, 175
González, Luís Alberto "Beto," 96–97, 98, *126*, 130, 131, 134, 135–36, 222 (n. 44)
González, Marcos Miguel, 141, 143
Goodrich, Bill, 110
Gould, Jeffrey L., 52
Greene, Victor, 185
Guatemala: peace accords in, 19, 36, 39, 170, 174, 189–90; and patron-client relations, 66, 216–17 (n. 50); labor law in, 66, 217 (n. 50); and remittance income, 165. *See also* Guerrilla warfare in Guatemala
Guatemala City Coca Cola strikes, 65, 118
Guatemalan earthquake of 1976, 72
Guatemalan economic refugees, 3, 39, 63–64, 71
Guatemalan Maya: effects of immigration on, 2–3; map of migration to Morganton, *3*; as immigrants to Morganton, 10; whites' re-

Operation Blessing, 124–25
Ore-Cal shrimp-processing plant, 89
Organized labor. *See* AFL-CIO;
 Laborers International Union of
 North America (LIUNA); Labor
 movement; Unions; United Food
 and Commercial Workers (UFCW)
Ortiz Mendoza, Francisco, Jr., 76

PACs (Civil Self-Defense Patrols), 38,
 39, 62
Padre Gabriel. *See* L'un, Gabriel
 Rodríguez Yol
Palmieri, Phyllis: and immigration-
 related problems, 28, 47, 178; and
 walkout of 1991, 35; and United
 Food and Commercial Workers,
 54, 55; background of, 81–82; and
 strike of May 1995, 83; on Oscar
 and Francisco Fuentes, 84; as local
 union counsel, 94, 127, 130, 178–
 79; and Juan Ignacio Montes, 95;
 and vendidos, 99; and Panepinto,
 112; and union contract, 133, 138
PAN (National Advance Party), 67,
 170
Panepinto, Lorenzo, 185, 236–37
 (n. 28)
Panepinto, Marc: and union organizing strategy, 79–80, 86–87, 99;
 and Oscar Fuentes, 93; and Coia,
 109; and strike of May 1995, 110,
 111; and United Food and Commercial Workers, 112; and union
 contract efforts, 119; and worker
 firing protest, 124; and strike of
 August 1996, 125; and poultry industry, 127; resignation of, 128;
 and community, 135; and Lorenzo
 Panepinto, 185, 236–37 (n. 28)
Pan-Latino identity, 157–58
Pan-Mayan movement, 59, 141–42,
 170, 173, 187. *See also* Consejo Maya
Pascual, Andrés, 42, 50, 53, 82, 155
Pascual, Gaspar, 147
Pascual, Juana, 42, 82, 152, 153

Paternalism, 134, 180
Patriarca, Raymond, 108
Peasantry, 4, 5, 43, 57, 68, 183
Pedro, Teofilo, 164–65
Pentecostal sects, 48, 156
Perdue, Arthur W., 12
Perdue, Frank, 14
Perdue Farms, 14, 110, 116, 127
Perera, Víctor, 43
Pérez Castro, Marcelino, 67, 68–69
Perez López, Nicolas, 167
Pezzula, Neil, 97
Police, 23–24, 54, 56
Poteat, Bill, 20, 21
Poultry industry: meatpacking indus-
 try compared to, 12, 206 (n. 14);
 in South, 12, 206 (n. 15); and labor
 force, 12–13; and organization of
 work in plant, 15–16; and acci-
 dent claims, 17, 206–7 (n. 24); and
 Laborers International Union of
 North America, 86, 109–10, 127–
 30; working conditions of, 112–13,
 120, 123, 226 (n. 64); and religious
 community, 120; Reich's inves-
 tigation of, 123; and gender, 206
 (n. 15). *See also* Case Farms poultry
 plant; Immigrant poultry workers
Pozzetta, George E., 185
Progressives, 32, 81, 105
Project Amigo, 27
Promotores bilingües, 69
Protestant missionaries, 48, 59, 60
Puerto Ricans, 18
Putnam, Robert D., 145

Q'anjob'al-speaking Maya: as Guatemalan war refugees, 4, 40–44;
 and labor conflict at Case Farms
 poultry plant, 4, 44–45, 56; and
 school system, 22; names of, 29,
 35; and walkout of 1991, 35, 53, 54;
 and guerrilla warfare, 37, 38–39,
 46–47, 50, 52, 61; and Indiantown, Florida, 39–40, 41, 42, 211
 (n. 20); Aguacatecos compared to,

Smith, Carol A., 145–46
Smithfield Packing Company, 116, 224–25 (n. 32)
Social capital, 145
Social justice: workers' movement for, 5; and Felix Rodríguez, 70; and union organizing strategy, 87; and Jordan, 118; and Catholic Church, 156; and women, 162; and food-processing industry, 199
Social services: for Guatemalan Mayas, 27–28; and Laborers International Union of North America, 113; and Consejo Maya, 141–42
South Carolina, 1
Spanish conquest, 35, 209 (n. 4)
Spanish language: and communication barriers, 21–24, 155; and Catawba Valley Legal Services, 28; and St. Charles Borromeo Catholic Church, 28; and Guatemalan Mayas, 35, 164; and labor force, 54; and Francisco Fuentes, 64; and bilingual education, 69; and Mayan languages, 69, 79–80; and United Food and Commercial Workers, 86; lack of work guidelines in, 122
Stand, Kurt, 118, 129
Stillwell, Duane, 109, 110–11, 118, 127, 128, 134
Stoll, David, 46, 151, 212 (n. 36)
Stoneman, George, 8–9
Sweeney, John, 105, 106, 109, 110, 123, 128, 130

Tax, Sol, 145
Teamsters, 105, 106, 108
Textile workers, 1, 106, 109, 110, 111
Third World workers, 5, 105
Thompson, E. P., 184
"Tierra Arrasada" (scorched-earth policy), 37, 61
Tinajas, 189
Toller, Father John, 28, 52
Tomás, Matías, 42–44, 47–49, 51, 53
Tomlinson, John, 146

Totonicapán, Guatemala, 174, 187
Trejo, Richard, 55
Trumka, Richard, 119, 130
Turner, Nat, 2
Tyson Foods, 14, 116, 123–24
Tzul, Atanasio, 172

UCN (Unión del Centro Nacional) Party, 67
UFCW. See United Food and Commercial Workers
Union building: and leadership, 5, 72, 80; and Case Farms union, 30, 54–56, 63–77, 78, 79–80, 81, 130–31; and St. Charles Borromeo Catholic Church, 30, 70, 79; and lack of redress in U.S., 66–67; and Víctor Hernández, 71; and community, 76–77, 174; and Palmieri, 82; in Los Angeles, 179–81; and immigrant poultry workers, 208 (n. 45)
Unión del Centro Nacional (UCN) Party, 67
Union of Needletrades, Industrial, and Textile Employees (UNITE), 109
Union organizing strategy: of Laborers International Union of North America, 2, 5, 54, 79–80, 86–87, 99, 109–15, 127–30, 133–38, 177, 178, 195, 197; and Merino, 76, 89–93, 124; ideals of, 87; and Oscar Fuentes, 92; and Salido, 96–97; and Luís González, 97; and vendidos, 97–99; and Francisco Ramírez, 98; and multicultural strength, 99–103; and Stillwell, 110–11; and hotshop organizing, 111, 127, 223 (n. 16); and union contracts, 114–15, 117–25, 131–34, 137, 138, 227 (n. 91); and worker morale, 126–27; local support of, 178
Unions: in North Carolina, 1–2, 10–11; and personnel manager's job,

53; and strike of May 1993, 54; and strike of May 1995, 56; and mutualism, 77, 219 (n. 79); public perception of, 105

UNITE (Union of Needletrades, Industrial, and Textile Employees), 109

United Farmworker Organizing Committee, 198

United Farm Workers, 78, 100

United Food and Commercial Workers (UFCW): and Case Farms union, 54, 55, 82, 86, 119, 136, 197; and Laborers International Union of North America, 90–91, 112, 134, 223–24 (n. 20); and poultry industry, 109

United Postal Service strike of 1997, 105

U.S. Department of Labor, 17, 114, 206–7 (n. 24)

U.S./Guatemala Labor Education Project (US/GLEP), 118

U.S. immigration and refugee policy, 4, 18–19, 47

U.S. State Department, 19

United Steel Workers of America, 106

Vagrancy Laws, 57

Vail, John, 10, 11, 28, 82, 207 (n. 27)

Velásquez, Valentin, 89, 90

Vicente, Francisco, 80

Vicente, Juan Marquín, 85, 86

Volcano Pacaya, 141

Waldensians, 10

Wanless, John, 27–28, 55

Warren, Kay, 50, 52, 150, 151

Watanabe, John M., 186

Waters, Malcolm, 144

Webb, Beatrice, 77

Webb, Sidney, 77

Whites: reactions of to Guatemalan Mayas, 2, 21–26, 30–32; and Case Farms work, 17; reactions of to Hmong refugees, 25; reactions of to Hispanics, 27, 102, 157; union attitudes of, 92, 101–2, 122, 132, 178; and ethnic fear argument, 116

Whittington, Kenneth L., 29; as worker advocate, 28, 70, 113, 118, 122, 125, 177–78, 179, 224 (n. 25); and Spanish language, 28–29; on Guatemalan Mayas, 30, 31; and Palmieri, 82, 99; and Panepinto, 112; and food bank, 124; attitude of towards union, 135; and charismatic movement, 156–57, 169; and Lux, 171–72; and L'un, 194

Wilkinson, Jack, 111, 127, 128

Williams, Robbie, 23, 83

Wilson, Ken, 55–56, 80–81, 83, 120, 124, 125, 131, 134

Wolf, Eric, 183

Women: and alternatives to consumer culture, 31; and education, 69, 217 (n. 60); and labor movement, 105; and Catholic Charismatic Renewal movement, 156, 157; population of, 160; and community expectations of, 161; and cultural continuity, 161; as stabilizing force in Mayan diaspora, 161, 162–63; in labor force, 161–62. *See also* Gender

Workers Center, 197–98